M000307138

WORLD HEALTH AND WORLD POLITICS

JAVED SIDDIQI

World Health and World Politics

The World Health Organization and the UN System

University of South Carolina Press

First published in the United States by
University of South Carolina Press,
Columbus, South Carolina

Printed in Hong Kong

Library of Congress Cataloging-in-Publication Data

Siddiqi, Javed, 1962-
World health and world politics: the World Health Organization and the UN System / Javed Siddiqi
p. cm.
Includes bibliographical references and index.
ISBN 1-57003-038-3
1. World Health Organization 2. Public Health -- International cooperation. 3. World health. 1. Title.
RA8.S53 1995
354.1'77 -- dc20 94-28858

For Ammi, Bhaijan, Appa and Baji

CONTENTS

PREFACE AND ACKNOWLEDGEMENTS

Starting with a discussion of the contemporary crisis of confidence in the UN system, this work examines the influence of political and other factors on the World Health Organization's effectiveness in its efforts to achieve three particular goals: universal membership, a workable decentralized structure and the eradication of malaria.

Using internal documents, records of meetings, personal interviews and secondary sources, the WHO's achievements in these areas are systematically assessed by reference to its own definition of effectiveness. The Organization is found to have been increasingly effective over the period 1948–85 in its efforts to realize its structural aspirations of universal membership and workable decentralization, despite recurrent intrusions of 'negative politics'. But the WHO has been less effective in its massive field effort, the Malaria Eradication Programme (MEP).

The MEP is traced from its enthusiastic inauguration in the 1950s to its demise and substitution by less ambitious control programmes after 1969. Political and other factors accounting for the ineffectiveness of the MEP are assessed. The failure of the MEP led to the abandonment of the 'vertical' approach to dealing with health problems; a 'horizontal' approach (with a multi-pronged attack on all health problems) remains to this day the *modus operandi* of the World Health Organization.

The WHO's limited effectiveness in several of the areas studied is explained: both unavoidable constraints and possible areas of unnecessary ineffectiveness are noted. The WHO is not without significant achievements, however, and this book attempts to illustrate that contemporary Western charges of 'ineffectiveness' and 'politicization' miss much of the complexity disclosed by a more searching evaluation of these concepts. A number of weaknesses in standard functionalist theory are also highlighted.

Acknowledgements

Much of the original work for this book was carried out as part of a doctoral dissertation at Christ Church, Oxford, where my existence and research were supported financially and morally by the Rhodes Trust and my college. Thanks are due to both these institutions. My academic mentors in Oxford, Dr Benedict Kingsbury and Mr Richard Symonds, exhibited superhuman patience and resilience in educating me, and in guiding my research from its haphazard origins to the present product. These gentlemen continue to this day as valued advisors to whom my debt is incalculable.

The unconditional affection, encouragement and moral support of several close friends have been instrumental in the completion of this book. I take this opportunity to express my gratitude to Shipra Das, Suan-Seh Foo, Satish Keshav, Moo-Hyung Lee, Wajahat Mehal and Simon Moore.

I am also indebted to Dr Peter Gellman (Princeton University), Professor Adam Roberts (Balliol College, Oxford) and the late Professor John Vincent (London School of Economics and Political Science) for offering constructive advice on early drafts. Thanks are due to Dr John Bryant (Aga Khan University) and Dr Gowher Rizvi (Nuffield College, Oxford), without whose support no momentum would have gathered for this book.

Numerous primary sources have been referenced in this book. The staff at the Geneva archives of the WHO and the United Nations could not have been more helpful. The insights, knowledge and documentation I received from former and contemporary WHO staff have added tremendously to this work. Special thanks go to Dr Yves Beigbeder, Dr M.A. Farid and the late Dr Alexander Robertson for sustained and unselfish support at every stage of this effort.

Work during the final stages of this book has been financially supported by the following: the Hannah Institute of the History of Medicine and Science (Toronto); the Logan-Clendening Traveling Fellowship of the Department of History and Philosophy of Medicine, University of Kansas; and various sources at the University of Western Ontario, including the Department of History of Medicine, the Faculties of Arts and Medicine, and the Office of the Provost. Thank you all.

A significant portion of this book was written during my neurosurgery training at the University of Western Ontario, where the unwavering support and encouragement of my colleagues and mentors made my second career possible. Their kindness is greatly appreciated.

Finally, as numerous individuals have been associated with this work, I take this opportunity to emphasize that I am solely to blame for any errors of fact or interpretation in these pages.

University of Western Ontario J.S.
London, Ontario
September 1994

EXPLANATORY NOTE

The large number of footnotes in this book has made it necessary that primary sources be cited in as simple and precise a form as possible, using WHO style. In this style, the term 'OR' (Official Record) was used until 1978 to cover all of the following: Technical Preparatory Committee minutes, Proceedings and Final Acts of the International Health Conference, Verbatim Records of the Interim Commission, World Health Assembly (WHA) proceedings, Reports of the Executive Board (EB), Annual or Biannual Reports of the Director-General, Proposed Programme and Budget Estimates (PB), and Reports on the World Health Situation. To check which of the above the 'OR' in the footnote refers to, the reader simply has to look up the OR number of interest in the Bibliography.

After 1978, all the categories that used to be classified by the WHO as Official Records lost that designation and each took on specific designations of its own (WHA, EB, PB and so on). The reader, on finding these in the footnotes, simply has to check the Bibliography to find out to which document it refers.

Any WHO document that has yet to be given an OR number by the Organization is cited in the footnotes with the specific code by which it first appeared. There are very few such documents and they are not listed in the Bibliography.

Some footnotes simply give a Technical Report Series (TRS) number and year. Further details of these are also to be found in the Bibliography.

Most of the WHO personnel interviewed, while willing to discuss the subject of this book, did not want to be formally associated with specific viewpoints. For such interviews, the footnotes simply refer to a 'personal communication with a senior WHO administrator'. Individuals who were not concerned about anonymity have been named. Some individuals were interviewed several times, and thus more than one date appears after their names in the list of interviews in the Bibliography.

ABBREVIATIONS

ACC	Administrative Committee on Coordination
ANC	African National Congress
DG	Director-General
EB	Executive Board
ECOSOC	UN Economic and Social Council
EMed	Eastern Mediterranean
FAO	Food and Agriculture Organization
IAEA	International Atomic Energy Agency
IBRD	International Bank for Reconstruction and Development
ICAO	International Civil Aviation Organization
ICJ	International Court of Justice
IDA	International Development Association
IFC	International Finance Corporation
IFPMA	International Federation of Pharmaceutical Manufacturers' Association
IHC	International Health Conference
ILO	International Labour Organization
IMCO	Inter-Governmental Maritime Consultative Organization
IMF	International Monetary Fund
ITO	International Telecommunication Union
LRCS	League of Red Cross Societies
MEP	Malaria Eradication Programme
OAS	Organization of American States
OIHP	Office International d'Hygiène Publique
OR	Official Record
PAHO	Pan American Health Organization
PASB	Pan American Sanitary Bureau
PASO	Pan American Sanitary Organization
PICAO	Provisional International Civil Aviation Organization
PLO	Palestine Liberation Organization
PRC	People's Republic of China
TPC	Technical Preparatory Committee
TRS	Technical Report Series
UNESCO	United Nations Educational, Scientific and Cultural Organization
UNRRA	United Nations Relief and Rehabilitation Administration
UPU	Universal Postal Union
USAID	United States Agency for International Development
WHA	World Health Assembly
WHO	World Health Organization
WMO	World Meteorological Organization

Part I

EFFECTIVENESS AND POLITICIZATION: THE FRAMEWORK FOR ANALYSIS

1

INTRODUCTION: INTERNATIONAL ORGANIZATIONS IN JEOPARDY

The specialized agencies of the United Nations have experienced severe strains from many directions in recent years, which in the case of UNESCO has culminated in the withdrawal of the United States in 1984, and of Britain and Singapore in 1985. Increasingly, the view has been expressed that the agencies are on a slow, yet relentless, path towards self-destruction. They are perceived to be progressively more ineffective as fora for international cooperation, particularly when the special interests of the superpowers specifically, and developed countries generally, are concerned.[1] A sense of crisis has evolved because of the view of some Western governments that the agencies have strayed from their constitutional mandate by expending excessive time and resources on controversial political and security issues best left to the General Assembly and its committees.[2] Accusations of political bias have been made. Among the major Western backers of the UN system, the United States has been prominent in venting frustrations over what it considers a

1. For recent treatments of this topic, see Adam Roberts and Benedict Kingsbury (eds), *United Nations, Divided World*, Oxford University Press, 1988, pp. 214–20; Yves Beigbeder, *Threats to the International Civil Service*, Pinter, London, 1988, pp. 45–64; and Douglas Williams, *The Specialized Agencies for the United Nations*, Hurst, London, 1987.

2. Not all Western countries have shared this view. For instance, Stephen Lewis, the Canadian Permanent Representative to the UN, has defended the UN system against 'anti-internationalist' sentiments like those of the Heritage Foundation. See Yves Beigbeder, *Management Problems in United Nations Organizations*, Pinter, London, 1987, p. 17. For discussion of extraneous issues in the work of UN agencies, see Victor-Yves Ghebali, *The International Labour Organization: a Case Study on the Evolution of UN Specialized Agencies*, Martinus Nijhoff, Dordrecht, 1989, pp. 44–9; Williams, *op. cit.*, p. xiii.

frank and unremitting attack by the specialized agencies on its economic, social and political philosophies.

Many developed countries consider the attempts by certain agencies to formulate rules of conduct for international business very tiresome and irritating. Attempts by the WHO and UNCTAD to regulate the multinational pharmaceutical industry, and the WHO's promulgation of a code of conduct for the baby-foods industry, are cited as examples of such irritating behaviour. Various agencies are also accused of financial and organizational mismanagement, which in the case of UNESCO was largely attributed to the leadership style of the Director-General, Amadou-Mahtar M'Bow, who was accused of being 'authoritarian, high-handed, and impervious to complaints'.[3]

Shortcomings are also perceived in the specialized agencies by developing countries, which as a group feel that the agencies have yet to devise imaginative and workable means to address the vast disparities that exist between themselves and the developed world. They are not encouraged by their own failed attempts to stimulate the agencies to implement what they have labelled the New International Economic Order (NIEO).

The contemporary sense of crisis in the UN system has evolved over the past two or three decades. For instance, a 1987 report by the United Nations Association of the United States speaks of the situation of the UN system as one of 'deep crisis' in which 'the prevailing skepticism is unsurprising'.[4] Similar views were expressed fourteen years earlier by Mahdi Elmandjra when he pointed out that 'the "image" of the system has, rightly or wrongly, greatly suffered, many aspirations and hopes have been disappointed, and a feeling of uncertainty and doubt has emerged even among the staunchest defenders of its ideals.'[5]

The strains arise for a number of reasons, including disagreements over political issues, philosophical approaches, and more mundane issues such as the proper way to administer, staff, finance and prioritize within the specialized agencies.

These strains have led some member states to question the effectiveness of the agencies in their areas of speciality. The agencies have been repeatedly accused of 'politicization', a process that is said to

3. Leroy Bennett, *International Organizations*, Prentice-Hall, Englewood Cliffs, NJ, 1991, p. 343.

4. See *A Successor Vision: the United Nations of Tomorrow*, UN Association of the USA, New York, 1987, pp. i and ii.

5. M. Elmandjra, *The UN System: an Analysis*, Faber and Faber, London, 1973, p. 17.

lead to ineffectiveness. Accusations of ineffectiveness and 'politicization' have appeared before in the history of the specialized agencies, as when the Soviet Union left the WHO in 1949; yet they were never as vociferously expounded by so many critics of the UN system as they have been since the early 1970s. Moreover, only recently have such accusations been linked with fears about the complete breakdown of multilateral cooperation.

The contemporary charge of politicization seems at times to be a catch-all term for all that is perceived to be going wrong in these specialized agencies. Victor-Yves Ghebali has referred to it as a 'vague and ambiguous notion', though a 'far from meaningless' one.[6] Evan Luard has observed that 'the UN has never been under such a savage and sustained attack as that mounted in some Western countries over recent years.'[7] Perceptions of imminent disruption have produced unfavourable prognoses for the future health of the UN, and seasoned observers have warned of the 'steadily bleaker' outlook for the UN system.[8]

Charges of ineffectiveness and 'politicization' have affected different specialized agencies to varying degrees. Many analysts have suggested that they have weakened the United Nations system as a whole,[9] and that the processes of international cooperation built up after 1945 are now in danger of disruption.[10] While the agencies are not mutually exclusive of the UN, the former have at times attempted to distance themselves from the vicissitudes of the latter.

Not all UN watchers are agreed on the extent of the problem; some do not share the pessimistic view that is generally prevalent. Jeffrey Harrod and Nico Schrijver characterize the crisis in the UN system as existing at its 'fringe'.[11] Douglas Williams refers to the

6. See Ghebali, 'The Politicization of the UN Specialized Agencies: a Preliminary Analysis', *Millennium: Journal of International Studies*, vol. 14, no. 3 (Winter 1985), p. 322.

7. See 'The Contemporary Role of the UN' in Roberts and Kingsbury, *op. cit.*, p. 214.

8. Foreword by Sir Anthony Parsons in Williams, *op. cit.*, p. v.

9. Victor-Yves Ghebali, 'The Politicization of the UN Specialized Agencies: the UNESCO Syndrome', in David Pitt and Thomas G. Weiss (eds), *The Nature of United Nations Bureaucracies*, Croom Helm, London, 1986.

10. Several books have recently appeared either describing the problems or suggesting corrective measures. See M. J. Petersen, *The General Assembly in World Politics*, Allen and Unwin, Boston, Mass., 1986; Thomas Franck, *Nation against Nation*, Oxford University Press, 1985; and David Steele, *The Reform of the United Nations*, Croom Helm, London, 1987.

11. See Jeffrey Harrod and Nico Schrijver (eds), *The United Nations under Attack*, Gower, Aldershot, 1988, p. 5, and Brian Urquhart, 'The United Nations System and the Future', *International Affairs*, vol. 65, no. 2 (Spring 1989) pp. 225–31.

view that international cooperation is in danger of disruption as 'unduly alarmist'.[12]

One cannot fail to be struck by the fact that at least one identical conclusion is reached by optimists and pessimists alike: the UN system (either in parts, or as a whole) is not fulfilling the expectations of many of its member states. Perhaps the greatest indication that something is sorely wrong with the present state of affairs is evident in the calls from opposite quarters, from traditional adversaries of the UN such as the American Heritage Foundation,[13] as well as from traditional supporters such as the UN Association of the United States,[14] for widespread reform.[15] Not all these calls for reform are external – the Joint Inspection Unit of the UN has called for fundamental changes too.[16] The last UN Secretary-General, Perez de Cuellar, may have best described the predicament of the UN system: 'Its harshest critics seem outraged that [it] is imperfect. Its most vocal supporters ask for it to change faster.'[17]

The problems in the UN system provide a useful starting point for a closer scrutiny of the subject of this book, the World Health Organization. The WHO has not been immune from the contemporary charges against the UN system. In fact, even highly placed members of the WHO's Secretariat fear that conflict and controversy have become endemic to the Organization, compromising its effectiveness more than ever before.

The technical roles of United Nations specialized agencies such as the WHO have been extensively studied and written about. There are also numerous academic works on the general role of the agencies in the international political scene. Specifically with regard to the WHO, however, the available English-language literature is fairly sparse on non-medical analyses of programmes and policies.

12. Williams, *op. cit.*, p. xiii.
13. See Burton Yale Pines (ed.), *A World without the UN: What Would Happen if the UN Shuts Down*, Heritage Foundation, Washington, DC, 1984.
14. See *A Successor Vision*, *op. cit.*, for general discussion.
15. Although this work cannot refer in detail to all studies and proposals concerning the reform of the UN system, the following are the most important: Maurice Bertrand, *Some Reflections on Reform of the United Nations*, United Nations, Geneva, 1985; Steele, *op. cit.*; Paul Taylor, 'Prescribing for the Reform of International Organizations: the Logic of Arguments for Change', *Review of International Studies*, vol. 13 (1987), pp. 19–38; and Antonio Donini, 'Resilience and Reform: Some Thoughts on the Process of Change in the United Nations', *International Relations*, vol. IX, no. 4 (Nov. 1988), pp. 289–316.
16. See Maurice Bertrand, 'Can the United Nations be Reformed?' in Roberts and Kingsbury, *op. cit.*, pp. 193–208.
17. See Foreword by J. Perez de Cuellar in Lawrence Finkelstein (ed.), *Politics in the United Nations System*, Duke University Press, Durham, NC, 1988, p. vii.

For instance, as of January 1993, only two scholarly works have been published on decentralization and budgeting: those by Berkov (1957) and Hoole (1976), respectively.[18] While a few popular articles on politics and effectiveness within the workings of the WHO have appeared recently (adding to the general charge of 'politicization' against UN specialized agencies), academic analyses of the same issues within the Organization are virtually non-existent. Thus this work hopes to make a modest contribution to the study of the WHO from a non-medical perspective.

We offer an examination of the effectiveness of certain WHO programmes and policies in the period since 1948, but only incidentally shed light on developments since 1985. The role of politics and other influences on the WHO's effectiveness is examined in an attempt to evaluate the contemporary charges of 'politicization' and ineffectiveness.

After establishing criteria for measuring effectiveness, we evaluate the effectiveness of certain programmes and issues within the World Health Organization, and of the influence of the four types of politics – positive, legitimate, inevitable and negative – on this effectiveness. In doing so, we dissociate lack of consensus from politicization, and the latter from ineffectiveness. In other words, we show that the presence of consensus does not necessarily imply that politicization is excluded, or vice versa; also, that the presence of politicization does not necessarily imply ineffectiveness, or vice versa.

In summary, after analysing certain WHO structural aspirations and assessing the Organization's largest field programme, the malaria eradication programme, we conclude that: (1) effectiveness, as we have defined it, has been at a low level in the WHO ever since the inception of the Organization; (2) politicization has often, but not always, been associated with this low level of effectiveness, and such politicization is not of recent origin (despite the current claims of Western critics of the WHO), but has been evident from the birth of the WHO and indeed from the inception of international health cooperation in the 1850s; (3) the contemporary notion of 'politicization' is merely one of many factors influencing the effectiveness of the WHO's programmes and initiatives; (4) the increasing numbers of developing countries who are members of the WHO, and the associated change in the focus of attention of the

18. Robert Berkov, 'The World Health Organization: a Study in Decentralized International Administration', Ph.D. Thesis, University of Geneva, 1957; Francis W. Hoole, *Politics and Budgeting in the World Health Organization*, Indiana University Press, Bloomington, Ind., 1976.

Organization, have created a highly volatile atmosphere in which the charges of politicization are very common; (5) the major donors' contemporary perception of ineffectiveness is very dangerous for the Organization, because all parties, from both North and South, are unhappy with the *status quo*; (6) perceptions of effectiveness have changed over the years both within the WHO and among its member states; (7) the WHO has made active efforts to limit politicization, and to limit controversy and conflict by various means; and (8) the functionalists' separability-priority hypothesis and the concept of spillover do not reflect the state of affairs in the World Health Organization.

This book spans a long period of the WHO's history; thus it is inevitably also (and secondarily) a chronicle of the growth and evolution of that Organization. Some illustrative contemporary examples of often-quoted instances of politicization in the works of the WHO comprise the next chapter, which is followed by a brief background of world health and world politics from the inception of international health cooperation in the 1850s up to the establishment of the WHO in 1948. Finally, the remainder of Part 1 is devoted to the formulation of working definitions of politicization and effectiveness, as well as to a discussion of factors that influence them.

2

SOME CONTEMPORARY PROBLEMS IN THE W.H.O.

Associated with the recent charges of 'politicization' against the WHO are instances of conflicts and controversies that are often more superficial than substantive, and yet which, in 1985, precipitated an open discussion of the problem in the World Health Assembly. Since many of the contemporary charges concern isolated issues which are not discussed in the rest of the book, for the sake of completeness we outline them in this chapter. This chapter will illustrate the charge as expressed by the Western countries; it is hoped this will give the reader a feeling for some of the expectations and frustrations of some member states, while also providing a resumé of the issues involved.

In May 1985 Dr Suwardjono Surjaningrat, the President of the 38th World Health Assembly, recommended in his opening address that because of 'the unique technical and social mandate of our Organization, we should strive hard to avoid – or at least minimize – the spending of the precious time of the Assembly on extraneous political issues which perhaps are best discussed elsewhere'.[1] The same plea was echoed by the then Director-General of the WHO, Dr Halfdan Mahler.[2]

The pleas of the Director-General and the President of the WHA apparently went unheard. Among the 'political' issues discussed at that gathering were resolutions on 'Health conditions of the Arab population in the occupied Arab territories, including Palestine' (WHA38.15), 'Repercussions on health of economic and political sanctions between States' (WHA38.17), and 'Liberation struggle in southern Africa: Assistance to the front-line States, Lesotho and Swaziland' (WHA38.28).[3]

Resolution WHA38.15 'condemned' Israel on various grounds, among them the continued occupation of Arab territories, hindering the development of Arab public health-care in those territories, and the continual raising of obstacles to the establishment of

1. See Document WHA38/1985/REC/2, p. 11.
2. See WHO Press Release WHA/15, 20 May 1985. The use of the same phrase by the Director-General and the President of the World Health Assembly is not coincidental – the latter was asked by the former to express concerns about excessive politicization. Personal communication from a senior WHO administrator.
3. Resolution WHA38.17 was addressed at the US trade embargo against Nicaragua.

health centres in the territories under the direct supervision of the WHO.[4]

The delegate for Israel, Mr Dowek, commented that the wording and spirit of the draft resolution were 'totally and exclusively political in nature'. He said that, 'in a less politicized body', the draft resolution would have been 'deemed inconceivable for being in blatant breach of the Constitution of WHO and its noble goals'.[5] The delegate from Jordan, Dr Oweis, responded by pointing out that the objective of the WHO's mandate is not restricted merely to physical well-being – it also includes mental and social well-being. He claimed that 'mistreatment' of Arabs in the occupied territories was denying them their right to health, and that the passing of the resolution would place international law squarely on the side of the oppressed.

It was frustration over the introduction of what he considered politically sensitive issues in the WHO, and more specifically a discussion of the health-care of Arabs in the Israeli-occupied territories, that led US Ambassador William Scranton in 1976 to accuse the WHO of 'politicization'. The Ambassador insisted that

> the absence of balance, the lack of perspective and the introduction by the WHO of political issues irrelevant to the responsibilities of the WHO do no credit to the United Nations. Indeed, this is precisely the sort of politicized action which decreases respect for the United Nations system.[6]

A resolution on trade embargoes was introduced by Nicaragua, which felt wronged by the US naval blockade of its shipping lanes. Although any specific references to the United States were deleted, the resolution that was eventually passed by the Assembly condemned developed countries which 'apply economic measures that have the purpose of exerting political coercion on the sovereign decisions of developing nations'. The language of the resolution was adopted directly from UN General Assembly Resolution 39/210.[7]

The US State Department delegate to the Health Assembly, Neil Boyer, condemned what he called the 'politicization' of the WHO

4. In 1976, the WHO had passed a similar resolution condemning Israel for its 'illegal exploitation of the natural wealth and resources of the Arab inhabitants'. The Palestine Liberation Organization had held observer status in the WHO since 1974.
5. WHA38/1985/REC/2, p. 242.
6. 'Statement by Governor Scranton on Action Taken by the World Health Assembly', Press Release USUS-58, 21 May 1976. Cited in G. Lyons, D. Baldwin and D. McNemar, 'The "Politicization" Issues in the UN Specialized Agencies', in David Kay (ed.), *The Changing United Nations: Options for the United States*, Academy of Political Science, New York, 1977, p. 89.
7. WHA38/1985/REC/2, p. 171.

and warned that 'direct and insulting political attacks by one country against another country . . . serve only to destroy the reputation of this technical agency and its capacity to fulfil the purposes for which it was created.'[8] He cautioned that 'if the Assembly can adopt [resolutions] with no concern for the divisive political attacks made in the debate then we see little hope for the future of WHO.'[9]

Mr Boyer also suggested that if the resolution were adopted,

> the Assembly will be taking one more step down the road towards transforming this technical organization into another United Nations Security Council, another United Nations General Assembly, another forum for debate on any political issue whether or not it relates to WHO.[10]

Thus, he said, a vote in favour of the trade embargo resolution would be another vote 'towards damaging the reputation of WHO . . . A vote against this resolution is a vote to preserve WHO.'[11] In passing, Mr Boyer did add that the US embargo did not affect health supplies to Nicaragua.

The delegate from Nicaragua, Mr Miranda, responded to both the suggestion that the discussion was extraneous to the concerns of the WHO, and to Mr Boyer's statement that health was not affected by the US embargo: 'It is a puerile subterfuge to attempt to claim that a total trade embargo has no consequences for health.'[12] He was supported in this by the delegate from Cuba, Professor Menchaca, who said:

> Health, of all sectors, is one of the most sensitive to actions of this nature [ie. the embargo], although attempts are being made to obscure the scope of a trade embargo, which inevitably impinges in the first place on the very concept of health and the health status of the people . . . what [is a] better forum [for the discussion of the embargo] than this?[13]

The first two resolutions (WHA38.15 and WHA38.17) were passed by the Assembly, with the United States, Israel and most Western countries voting against, and the Soviet Union, Nicaragua and many developing countries voting in favour. Resolution WHA38.28 was passed with 102 votes for, 1 against (the United States) and 10 abstentions.

Within weeks of the 38th WHA, at the subsequent session of the Executive Board of the WHO, the question of the 'politicization' of

8. *Ibid.*, p. 246.
9. *Ibid.*
10. *Ibid.*
11. *Ibid.*
12. *Ibid.*, p. 247.
13. *Ibid.*

the Organization was considered.[14] It was decided that at its session in January 1986 the Board would consider how to deal with political matters in ways conducive to the fulfilment of WHO health policies, and would make suggestions to the 1986 Health Assembly to that end.

The document 'Global Strategy for Health for All by the Year 2000: Political Dimensions' was produced by the WHO Secretariat as a response to the Board's concern. This was the first document of its type to be produced by the WHO, although the kind of issues which it addressed had been prevalent in the Organization for some time.

The discussion, and passing, of controversial resolutions at the 38th WHA presents a recent example of the sort of contemporary difficulties the Organization is facing. An issue which did not arise at the 38th WHA, but which has been discussed in WHO fora, is that of disarmament, both conventional and nuclear. This is another example of the kind of issue that many of the major contributors to the WHO feel should not even be introduced, much less discussed, and it is among the factors which led to the critical introspection that culminated in the 'Political Dimensions' report.

The evolution of the disarmament debate in the WHO is in some ways representative of the whole genre of issues which many countries have found undesirable in that Organization, but which many others consider of significant symbolic value to reintroduce repeatedly.

In 1973 the WHO discussed the danger to health from the fall-out produced by nuclear weapons tests and decided that it presented a major danger to future generations, as well as to the environment. It deplored 'all nuclear weapons testing'.[15]

The latest round of discussions on nuclear weapons in the WHO comes under the heading of 'The Role of Physicians and Other Health Workers in the Preservation and Promotion of Peace'. The first resolution that these discussions produced was in 1979, asking the Director-General to prepare a report on the further steps which the WHO, as a UN specialized agency, would be able to take in the interests of international socio-economic development, with the further aim of assisting in the implementation of the United Nations resolutions 'on the strengthening of peace, detente and disarmament'.[16]

14. See WHO Document EB76/1985/REC/1, pp. 32–44.
15. See WHO, *Handbook of Resolutions and Decisions, 1973–1984*, vol. II, Geneva, 1985, p. 121.
16. *Ibid.*, p. 397.

In 1981 the 34th WHA established (Resolution 34.38) an international committee composed of eminent experts to write a report on the ways of 'facilitat[ing] the strengthening of peace, detente and disarmament and preventing thermonuclear conflict'.[17] In 1984 the WHO Expert Committee established in 1981 (under a resolution sponsored by the Soviet Union and seventeen other countries) completed a controversial report entitled 'Effects of Nuclear War on Health and Health Services'.[18] This report discussed, among other matters, the likely effect of nuclear attacks on New York City and Moscow.[19]

There was no question that Resolution WHA34.38 of 1981, and the report that was produced as a result of it, essentially dealt with disarmament. While discussing Resolution 34.38 – that is, the creation of the Expert Committee – the American delegate, Dr John H. Bryant, suggested that the issue of disarmament was marginal, at best, to the concerns of the Organization and should be referred to other fora competent to discuss such matters.[20] Professor Lisicyn, the Soviet delegate, disagreed, claiming that 'it was easier for physicians than anyone else to imagine the horrors of a nuclear holocaust.' He pointed to the Regional Committee for Africa, which in its 27th session (Resolution AFR/RC2/R9) had stated that atmospheric or underground tests of nuclear weapons were a direct health hazard to the entire continent and the world as a whole and had recommended the introduction of a ban on such tests.[21]

The discussion of disarmament within the WHO included various member states making allegations about others. Dr Ferreira of Mozambique said that his country

> stood for peace, but she was beset by colonialism. The States bordering on the Indian Ocean desired that the area should be demilitarized, but imperialist powers continued to increase their military potential there and the Southern African racist regime threatened Mozambique, more

17. *Ibid.*, p. 398.
18. See *Effects of Nuclear War on Health and Health Services*, WHO, Geneva, 1984.
19. According to the US-based Heritage Foundation, this report is 'seriously flawed and biased against Western defense'. The Foundation goes on to say that the report 'in effect bans any kind of missile defense system by stating that the only approach to the treatment of the health effects of nuclear explosions is primary prevention.' See J. Pilon, 'For the WHO, the Moment of Truth', *Backgrounder*, Heritage Foundation, Washington, DC, 1986, p. 4.
20. See WHA34/1981/REC/3, p. 425.
21. The Soviet delegation had circulated a memorandum before the start of the session, stressing the role of doctors in preventing nuclear war and encouraging disarmament.

particularly since it had developed a nuclear weapon through close links with its imperialist allies.[22]

The delegate from the Netherlands, Mr Fein, retaliated on behalf of the ten members of the EEC and the delegation from Canada, which wished to associate itself with his statement. He stressed that the WHA was not the proper forum for the discussion of disarmament questions,[23] which were political in nature and diverted the Organization's attention, time and resources away from its primary goal of improving world health. He also said that he was 'surprised to find among the co-sponsors certain States which had only recently aggravated international tensions considerably by their military intervention and occupation of neighboring countries'. Pointing to the fact that in the EEC countries the per capita expenditure for health was equal to or even considerably larger than that for defence, he urged these aggressive states to 'set a good example by rearranging their national budgets' in favour of health.[24]

The draft resolution was approved by 46 votes to 43, with 11 abstentions.[25] Every developing and Eastern bloc country delegate who made his or her views known on the issue spoke in favour of the resolution, emphasizing a clear connection between health and peace, and thus between health and disarmament. Every Western delegate spoke against the resolution. Sweden, a developed country which often votes with the non-aligned bloc and is thus considered 'enlightened' by many developing countries, also voted against the motion on the grounds that disarmament issues should be referred to the appropriate bodies established by the UN Secretary-General.

Among other controversial issues discussed in the WHO are questions as diverse as chemical warfare,[26] national liberation movements such as the ANC and the PLO, Zionism and apartheid. In sum, most of the major political controversies of the day have found their way into the WHO, either ostensibly as corollaries of some health issue, or independently.

The disarmament debate, as well as the other controversial issues listed above, point to several recurrent features of the contemporary

22. WHA34/1981/REC/3, p. 422.
23. He pointed to the Committee on Disarmament in Geneva, the UN General Assembly and the UN Disarmament Conference as examples of appropriate fora for the debate.
24. WHA34/1981/REC/3, pp. 424–5.
25. This was transmitted to the Health Assembly in sub-committee B's seventh report and adopted as Resolution WHA34.38.
26. See *Health Aspects of Chemical and Biological Weapons*, WHO, Geneva, 1970. This report was used as justification by Iran in the 1985 Health Assembly to propose a resolution against member states using chemical weapons on each other.

discussion of controversial, or what are called 'political', matters in the World Health Organization. First, the alignment of the developed and developing countries (with the socialist countries supporting the latter) in what are more or less voting blocs, though not always predictable, seems to be the rule rather than the exception. How the role of the former socialist countries will change in the post-Cold War era with the dissolution of the Soviet Union is yet to be seen. Secondly, many controversial resolutions are supported because health is juxtaposed with peace, or with some other broad aim listed in the Organization's constitution. Thirdly, one group of countries – usually referred to as Western – often seems to consider the introduction of controversial resolutions into the debate as extraneous, or at least marginal, to the interests or mandate of the Organization. Fourthly, the major contributors to the WHO's budget are frequently rendered impotent on resolutions which they consider inappropriate, extraneous or irrelevant.

3
ORIGINS OF INTERNATIONAL HEALTH COOPERATION

The International Sanitary Conferences, 1851–1903

The Industrial Revolution in Europe, and the subsequent rapid development of trade and travel with the advent of the steamship (*circa* 1810) and the railway (*circa* 1830) and the construction of the Suez Canal (1869), laid the foundation for an exponential rise in international commerce. The new ease of travel and trade also transformed hitherto foreign epidemic diseases such as cholera into European scourges. One early response of European states to limit the spread of cholera involved the quarantining of shipping at different ports for months at a time.

Arbitrary and unequal quarantine regulations at various ports inevitably created great burdens on the international trade of chiefly maritime nations such as Britain and France, whose fear of economic collapse overwhelmed their dread of imported disease and led them to support some sort of international action to relieve shipping from the burdensome shackles of quarantine regulations. Other countries with smaller maritime interests, for example the Italian states, Russia, Greece, Spain and Portugal, were more exposed to the spread of disease from Asia and Africa and so were reluctant to change their practice of quarantine.

The final momentum for international health cooperation was generated by the two pandemics of cholera that overran Europe between 1830 and 1847. Public opinion led to increasingly strict quarantine regulations, but all efforts were impotent to stop the disease. With one eye on the common peril and the other on the worsening outlook for their maritime trade, European governments found themselves without any other option than to attempt international collaboration against cholera and other epidemic diseases, including plague and yellow fever.

The International Sanitary Conference that was convoked in Paris on 23 July 1851 was the first of eleven meetings over the next half century which represented the earliest examples of international health cooperation, culminating in the establishment of a permanent international health organization.

Little was accomplished in the first six International Sanitary Conferences (1851, 1859, 1868, 1874, 1881 and 1885), due partly to lack of understanding of the etiology of cholera, but to a significant extent to the inability of European powers to define their political interests as coterminous with those of their neighbours. At the first Conference, the interconnection between world health and world politics was self-evident: each state had sent one physician and one diplomat, each of whom had one vote in the proceedings. At least officially, each delegate was to vote as an individual and not as a government representative. This system of voting created tensions between medical men and diplomats, who frequently voted on opposite sides, thus rendering the vote of limited value and painfully slow.[1]

While the official objective of the first Conference was stated as the desire to 'regulate in a uniform way the quarantine and lazarettos in the Mediterranean', the national motives for participation were primarily political and commercial, with public health being merely an incidental issue. The primacy of concerns about shipping over those about public health was no secret, as this had been explicitly laid out at the start of the Conference by its President.[2] Moreover, it was agreed at the outset of the Conference that scientific theories of disease would not be discussed. If this was not sufficiently peculiar for a health conference, the Austrian medical delegate, G.M. Menis, insisted that the subject of cholera be struck from the agenda since he was only authorized by his government to discuss plague and yellow fever.[3]

Cholera was discussed, but in most cases the positions of physicians and diplomats alike reflected the positions of their national governments. The British argued that the disease was not contagious, and thus quarantine measures would not be effective against it. Of course, it was in the British interest to play down the significance of quarantine. Whether or not cholera was indeed a contagious disease was a contentious enough subject to be removed from the plenary session and to warrant the establishment of a committee (comprising four physicians and three diplomats) to examine the issue. When the report was presented, it was stressed that it excluded all political questions and discussion of disease etiology. As Norman Howard-Jones has observed, 'one can only wonder what was left!'[4] By a vote of four to three, the committee declared its finding: it was humanly impossible to fight cholera, for

1. John Taylor, 'First Steps', *World Health*, WHO, Geneva, March 1968, p. 5.
2. *The First Ten Years of the World Health Organization*, WHO, Geneva, 1958, p. 6.
3. *Ibid.*, p. 10; and Norman Howard-Jones, *The Scientific Background of the International Sanitary Conferences*, WHO, Geneva, 1975, p. 12.
4. Howard-Jones, *op. cit.*, p. 13.

quarantine measures were ineffective and 'contrary to the end for which they were intended'.[5]

Rival national points of view on quarantine can be summarized as follows: Austria, Britain, France and Sardinia were united in declaring quarantine useless; Russia, Spain, Greece and three of the four Italian powers favoured quarantine; Portugal was non-committal. A draft International Sanitary Convention and annexed draft International Sanitary Regulations were agreed upon, but it was recognized that these were of no significance in view of the fact that they would not be ratified by the national governments.

The only common ground between the physicians and diplomats was their total ignorance of the etiology and mode of propagation of the three diseases under consideration: cholera, plague and yellow fever. But even if a uniform medical opinion had been forthcoming, which it was not, the diplomats had strict instructions from their governments on how to vote on quarantine.[6]

A second International Sanitary Conference was called in 1859. France again played host. During the eight years since the first Conference, John Snow had shown that there was a strong correlation between cholera incidence and the water supply in London;[7] while Fillipo Pacini of Florence had demonstrated that cholera was caused by a microscopic organism of a parasitic nature.[8] The findings of both Snow and Pacini had no impact whatsoever on the second Conference. In fact, because of the disagreements among physicians, and between physicians and diplomats, at the first International Sanitary Conference, the various governments had concluded that medical experts did not fully grasp the political significance of international health regulations. All physicians were subsequently excluded from the second, third, fourth and fifth International Sanitary Conferences, at which only diplomats discussed disease and its consequences.[9] The convention produced at the second Conference was never ratified by any of the states which signed it.

5. *Procès-verbaux de la Conférence Sanitaire International ouverte à Paris le 27 Juillet 1851*, Paris, Imprimerie National, 1852.

6. Neville Goodman, *International Health Organizations and their Work*, Churchill Livingstone, London, 1971, p. 40; F. Quimby, *Science Technology and the American Government*, Congressional Record Service, Washington, DC, 1971, p. 8.

7. See John Snow's pamphlet *On the Mode of Communication of Cholera*, 2nd edn., (unknown publisher) London, 1855.

8. See Howard-Jones, *op. cit.*, p. 17.

9. Quimby, *op. cit.*, p. 7, has stated that the pattern of one diplomat and one physician from each country continued unchanged in all ten International Sanitary Conferences. This is refuted by several authors: see Goodman, *op. cit.*, p. 53; Norman Howard-Jones, *op. cit.*, p. 20; and *First Ten Years*, *op. cit.*, p. 11.

Even though the number of participating states increased with each subsequent Conference, the next four Conferences made insignificant progress. Robert Koch had concluded, one year prior to the sixth Conference, that the cholera vibrio was the etiologic agent in the disease. But outside Germany there was almost universal resistance to his finding. One Italian government memorandum described the situation on quarantine matters as 'the most complete anarchy'.[10]

The sixth Conference was most remarkable for its unmasking of the traditional Anglo-French political and commercial rivalries. The British strongly resented the French claim that cholera was always introduced from British India. Indeed, the British were sufficiently animated by these claims to threaten to divert their shipping away from the French-run Suez Canal.[11] Problems also occurred when Persian and Turkish sensitivities were offended by the claim that cholera was endemic within their borders. They considered any call for tougher quarantines of ships leaving Persian and Turkish ports to be an infringement of their sovereignty.

In 1885 the editor of a German medical journal formally noted the obvious, namely that there was a 'surprising concordance between England's commercial interests and its scientific convictions'.[12] The last decade of the century was more fruitful in the fight against cholera, and limited agreement was reached among states because of the severe epidemics of that disease in 1893 and 1897. National sensitivities were still pandered to, as for instance in the assurance to the British Prime Minister by Austria-Hungary (the host state for the seventh Conference) that it 'would endeavour to exclude from discussions at the Conference everything that might seem unacceptable to English interests'.[13]

The seventh Conference did manage to produce sufficient agreement to result in the first International Sanitary Convention, which was approved without reservation by five Powers at the Conference, while all other participating states ratified it within four months. This Convention governed sanitary measures regarding westbound shipping through the Suez Canal.

By the end of the eighth Conference, another Convention was produced and ultimately ratified by all participating states, who

10. Quoted in Goodman, *op. cit.*, p. 65.

11. This threat was sent in a note to the President of the Conference and was annexed to its proceedings. It is reproduced in Goodman, *op. cit.*, p. 66.

12. *Deutsche Medizinische Wochenschrift*, vol. 11 (1885) p. 347.

13. Papers of the Secretary of State for Foreign Affairs, Great Britain, 'Correspondence Relating to the Conference Held in Venice in January 1882 Respecting the Sanitary Regulations of Egypt', London, 1892.

agreed among other things to notify each other immediately of any cholera outbreaks within their borders. The ninth Conference was devoted exclusively to the subject of Muslim pilgrims to Mecca, who were dying in large numbers from cholera. A third International Sanitary Convention was produced and recommended hygiene measures for pilgrim ships, a quarantine at the northern tip of the Persian Gulf at the Shatt-al-Arab waterway, and a means test for pilgrims.[14] Thirteen of the sixteen participant states ratified the third Convention; the other three (Sweden, Turkey and the United States) abstained.

The tenth Conference was devoted exclusively to plague. Unlike the resistance faced by Koch earlier, the 1894 finding by Alexandre Yersin that a bacillus was the etiologic agent for the disease did indeed diminish medical and political controversy with regard to plague. The fourth International Sanitary Convention was signed by all but three participating states. Obligatory notification of the first case of plague was unanimously included in the Convention. There was also unanimous agreement that an international committee should be constituted to codify the four Sanitary Conventions produced in the past four Conferences. By the end of the tenth Conference, the establishment of a permanent international health office was imminent.

Codification and consolidation of the four Sanitary Conventions was carried out at the eleventh International Sanitary Conference in 1903.[15] At this time, agreement was reached on the establishment of a permanent international health office to centralize epidemiological information and to oversee international quarantine arrangements. Appropriately, Paris, the location of the eleventh Conference (and also of the first), was chosen as the location for this new organization, the Office International d'Hygiène Publique (OIHP). The OIHP did not come into existence till 1907, five years after the Pan American Sanitary Bureau (PASB) was established by the American states as the first permanent international health organization. Both organizations played important epidemiological roles in their respective regions, establishing grounds for the WHO's present decentralized structure.

The establishment of the OIHP and the PASB concluded the era of the International Sanitary Conferences, launching the age of the

14. The Turkish delegate stated that the pilgrimage was one of five basic commandments for Muslims, and thus ability to pay for the return journey from Mecca should not be a condition for the pilgrimage. See *Procès-verbaux de la Conférence Sanitaire Internationale*, *op. cit.*, p. 380.

15. The Ottoman Empire did not ratify any of the four Conventions. Goodman, *op. cit.*, p. 68.

permanent international health organization which continues to this day in the form of the World Health Organization. However, as will be evident throughout this book, despite the advance of scientific understanding of many diseases by the turn of the century, the political rivalries that were so prominent in the Conferences played an equally significant role in the OIHP, the PASB and indeed the WHO. World health and world politics seemed inseparable.

International Health Organizations in the Inter-war Years

Within weeks of the Treaty of Versailles coming into force in 1920, the League of Nations Council was considering establishing a permanent international health organization. The OIHP was extant at this time and represented the culmination of seventy years of international health cooperation; however, its role was restricted to epidemiological intelligence and the reporting of cholera, plague and yellow fever. By this time also, the League of Red Cross Societies (LRCS) had established itself as an international health organization.

Instead of expanding the role of the OIHP or the LRCS, the desire to centralize political, economic and social endeavours within the League of Nations won the day. The International Health Conference of 1920 recommended that the Council of the League should establish its own permanent health organization to deal with the resurgence of diseases such as typhus and influenza in war-ravaged countries. In 1919 over 2 million cases of typhus were reported in Russia and Poland alone; the influenza pandemic of 1918–19 was estimated to have extinguished 15 million lives. The small staff and limited budget of the OIHP were patently inadequate to fight the scourges of the day.

The functions of the proposed health organization were to advise the League on health matters; to encourage international health cooperation; to simplify and accelerate the exchange of epidemiological information between states; to secure and revise international health agreements; to cooperate with the LRCS and the International Labour Office (ILO); and to provide health missions to League member states upon request. These functions were much broader than those of the OIHP and the LRCS individually at the time, and set the precedent for the broad role of the subsequent World Health Organization.

The founders envisaged that the League Health Organization would consist of an Executive Committee, an International Health Bureau (the Secretariat) and a General Committee that would incorporate the OIHP. This implied the end of any independent existence for the OIHP. However, as the American government refused to join the League of Nations it also vetoed any amalgamation of the OIHP with the League Health Organization. This veto reinforced the chauvinisms of those OIHP officials who did not wish to be subordinated to the League. The issue of American membership provided the OIHP with the perfect excuse to avoid being swallowed up by the League Health Organization. Indeed, the OIHP refused to participate in the Temporary Health Committee of the League convened in Paris in May 1920, and subsequently it was only an independent collaborator with the League in name.

Between 1920 and 1936, the OIHP rejected four proposals from the League of Nations to rationalize international health activities, to eradicate any overlap in functions and to establish a single international health organization. The reasons for the OIHP's intransigence is unclear to scholars such as Howard-Jones who have studied the matter in great detail. Indeed, as he has pointed out, there was a remarkable overlap in the membership of the OIHP and the League Health Organization, while a majority of member states in each organization were making proposals in Geneva that they themselves would reject in Paris.[16]

During its lifetime, the League Health Organization built a reputation for doing excellent work in war-torn areas. Indeed, the former Deputy Secretary-General of the League of Nations, F.P. Walters, acknowledged that the Health Organization 'was by general consent the most successful of the auxiliary organizations, although it was the only one whose creation had met with serious difficulty'.[17] Unfortunately, the demise of the League was also the death blow to its health organization. Ultimately the OIHP managed to outlive the League Health Organization, only later to be amalgamated with the World Health Organization.

Despite the relative success of the League Health Organization, one cannot fail to notice that the difficulties it faced with regard to the amalgamation of the OIHP were anything but political.

16. See Howard-Jones, *International Public Health between the Two World Wars – the Organizational Problems*, WHO, Geneva, 1978, p. 73.
17. As quoted in *ibid*.

4

EFFECTIVENESS: ITS MEANING AND MEASUREMENT

The Meaning of Effectiveness

When one enumerates the difficulties that international cooperation on health has faced from different quarters, certain questions arise. How have these difficulties, whatever their nature or origin, influenced the successful implementation of the Organization's programmes and policies? Have these difficulties been necessarily detrimental to the WHO, or has the Organization utilized them as focal points for improvements? Could the problems have been avoided? Finally, how have the difficulties influenced the overall ideology and/or approach of the Organization towards health issues? An evaluation of effectiveness should shed light on some of these questions.

The term 'effectiveness' means different things to different people. In a profit-making venture, for instance, the effectiveness of a strategy often refers to the monetary return, or output, following a given input. Measuring output is difficult in many health ventures. The benefit from the eradication of a disease and its associated misery is not easily calculated in dollar terms. Some measurements of 'effectiveness' (or the lack of it – that is, 'ineffectiveness') within the WHO and other specialized agencies have utilized very subjective criteria. For instance, one group of American authors gauge the degree of 'politicization' (read: 'ineffectiveness') of the specialized agencies according to how often they have been accused of this by the US government. Such an approach emphasizes not only the subjectivity of the measure, but also the presumption that the various agencies can actually be compared, despite their differing mandates.[1] For other authors, a further explanation of the extent of an agency's ineffectiveness is seen to lie in the habitual scale of media attention devoted to it, for it is assumed that the effectiveness will be more compromised where the normal degree of media concern is higher.[2]

1. For this approach, see G. Lyons, D. Baldwin and D. McNemar, 'The "Politicization" Issue in the UN Specialized Agencies', in David Kay (ed.), *The Changing United Nations: Options for the United States*, Academy of Political Science, New York, 1977, p. 88.
2. See H. Jacobson, 'ITU: . . .'; and L. Scheinman, 'IAEA: Atomic Condominium', in R. Cox and H. Jacobson (eds), *The Anatomy of Influence*, Yale University Press, New Haven, Conn., 1973, pp. 76 and 234.

Much of the criticism of the UN system is unsophisticated. For instance, many critics of the system have not defined effectiveness before drawing conclusions about it;[3] many others have not distinguished between the effectiveness of the system and that of its specific agencies or programmes. Similarly, perceptions about certain health programmes are routinely extrapolated to judgements about the entire World Health Organization.

For our purposes, the evaluation of 'effectiveness' is limited to specific programmes, policies and debates, and is not seen as a comprehensive measure of the Organization's (or the UN system's) performance as a whole. Within these limitations, effectiveness is conceived as the extent or degree to which the WHO has fulfilled its own explicitly stated mission, goal or objective in a specific area of interest. This area of interest can refer to a clearly defined initiative such as the Malaria Eradication Programme (MEP), or to certain administrative aspirations such as universality in membership.

When analysing an area of interest of the WHO, we also pay some attention to member states' hopes and expectations of the Organization; our view of these hopes and expectations, however, is restricted to those programmes and initiatives that the member states have themselves seen fit, or have attempted, to establish as WHO policy. As will be evident in the case study, this has at times resulted in the WHO setting health goals with an eye towards the political requirements and interests of member states.

Our conception of effectiveness is similar to that of the WHO itself as

> an expression of the desired effect of a programme, service, institution or support activity in reducing a health problem or improving an unsatisfactory health situation. Thus, effectiveness measures the *degree of attainment* of the pre-determined objectives and targets of the programme, service or institution. [Emphasis in the original][4]

For the WHO, the assessment of effectiveness is aimed at improving programme formulation or the functions and structure of health services and institutions through analysis of the extent to which the Organization's objectives are attained.

Since effectiveness is measured against the background of certain expectations which are themselves subject to change with time and circumstance, it is crucial to outline these expectations clearly in the light of the evolution of the WHO itself. Not all signatories of the

3. See, for instance, David Kay, *The Functioning and Effectiveness of Selected United Nations System Programs*, American Society of International Law, Washington, DC, 1980.
4. See *Health Programme Evaluation*, WHO, Geneva, 1981, p. 17.

WHO's constitution, for example, have similar conceptions of its contents; moreover, as will be evident later, not all their ambitions are contained in that document. The latter is particularly true of several states which are not founding members of the Organization.

Thus it would seem that if the expectations of each member state were used as a standard for gauging effectiveness, an exhaustive study of each country's perceptions of the WHO's 'mission' or *raison d'être* would have to be undertaken. Such external standards or expectations (that is, external to the Organization itself) could not be limited to the member states – they would have to include the expectations of non-governmental organizations, citizens' groups, multinational businesses and so on; all these groups may have their own ideas regarding the WHO's *raison d'être*. Such analytical confusion has been avoided here by focusing on criteria that relate to the WHO's own hopes and aspirations – that is, internal criteria. The fact that internal criteria are themselves subject to the vicissitudes of member states will become evident in the case study.

The WHO's assessment of effectiveness involves a very broad set of variables, or 'indicators', that represent an analysis of the outcomes of specific national health programmes. These indicators include variables such as 'high-level political commitment to health for all', 'allocation of adequate resources to health-care', child mortality and life expectancy.[5] These indicators are not easy to compare or measure, making the evaluation of the success of individual programmes rather difficult.

Historically, the WHO's standards and expectations have changed as a programme progresses. However, these standards and expectations, referred to here as internal criteria, have been promulgated by the Organization in two different ways: (1) they are established by the WHO's constitution, as interpreted in the practice of the Organization; and (2) they are expressed by the Organization at the start of a given health programme in terms of what it considers feasible over a given amount of time, taking into consideration whatever resources are at its disposal. Understandably, the establishment of internal criteria is subject to varying perceptions among member states as to the desirability and feasibility of a given initiative. For our purposes, we define the WHO's standards and expectations by the wishes of the majority of member states. At the same time, the interaction of majority and minority views to produce the internal criteria are not overlooked.

5. For a list of the indicators, see *ibid.*, pp. 19–22; for further explanations, see *Development of Indicators for Monitoring Progress towards Health for All by the Year 2000*, WHO, Geneva, 1981.

Once the criteria are established, the degree of in/effectiveness of an international organization can theoretically be assessed either by selecting a set of 'typical' case studies or by trying to survey the overall functioning of the organization on as comprehensive a basis as possible. From our experience, it is virtually impossible to produce a single measure of the overall effectiveness of the World Health Organization because of the vastness of its mandate. On the other hand, if the concept of effectiveness is defined in narrow terms that are only relevant to specific facets of the Organization's work, we are left with an unrealistically limited view of the WHO.

Thus, instead of surveying the Organization as a whole or scrutinizing a single specific aspect of it, we limit our scrutiny to certain aspects of the WHO's structural and administrative aspirations, as well as to one case study on the largest field programme in the WHO's history, the MEP. We will evaluate effectiveness using criteria established later in this section.

Reasons for Selecting Specific Areas of the WHO for Study and Limitations of this Approach

The two specific areas of the WHO selected for our study trace the evolution of some of the most serious challenges - structural, operational and political - that the Organization has faced in its history. Since the areas of investigation encompass the major approaches of the WHO towards health-care, they provide a good basis for investigating and highlighting the main concerns of this work.

The WHO's approach to international health-care has evolved over time as a result of its experience. To begin with, the emphasis was on tackling 'one disease at a time' (the vertical approach). A prominent example of the vertical approach is the Malaria Eradication Programme of the 1950s and 1960s. The unfavourable outcome of the MEP prompted the WHO to change its dominant philosophy, and currently it focuses on 'all health concerns as a whole' (the horizontal approach). The contemporary primary health-care strategy is an example of the latter approach.

The effective implementation of both these approaches has depended to a great extent on the international legitimacy commanded by the Organization. Such legitimacy is crucial in view of the recognition that diseases do not recognize borders and that if they are to be combated by an international authority like the WHO, universal cooperation is essential. Understandably then, the existence, value and credibility of the WHO are based to a large extent on the principle of universality of membership.

In light of the failure of the (non-universal) health organization of the League of Nations, the importance of the establishment of the WHO's universal membership and decentralization cannot be underestimated. Practically all the world's states are members of the WHO,[6] rendering it the first truly universal organization in the history of international health cooperation. The WHO's effectiveness has partly depended on its ability to achieve its essential administrative goals of universal membership and the organization of that membership into a rational regional structure.

An analysis of the structural aspirations of the WHO is essential for evaluating the effectiveness of the Organization as a whole as well as that of its individual programmes. Accordingly, the next section is devoted to the WHO's structural and administrative aspirations. Some of the issues discussed include the withdrawal of the socialist bloc countries within a year of the formation of the WHO, the exclusion of the People's Republic of China from the Organization, and the exclusion of Israel from participation in the Regional Committee of the Eastern Mediterranean Region of the WHO. In addition, the integration of the Pan American Health Bureau into the WHO is traced.

The discussion on the WHO's structural aspirations provides a useful launching ground to evaluate the operation of the field effort involved in the MEP. In the case study on the Malaria Eradication Programme, we outline the organizational and national motives that made malaria eradication (as opposed to malaria control) such an appealing venture to almost all parties concerned, and how a programme that started with international consensus ended in disharmony and failure, ultimately reverting to a policy of malaria control.

For reasons of practicality, and by the nature of the subject itself, the scope of this book is limited: none of the issues discussed here is studied in the broader context of all other issues of the same genre. Indeed, it would be virtually impossible to examine the effectiveness of all aspects of WHO structure, or all mass campaigns for disease eradication, in a work of this length. For our purposes, the evaluation of effectiveness has had to be fairly selective, without being arbitrary. For instance, the structural issues examined were chosen because they were considered most pressing and most crucial for the creation of an international infrastructure for health. Similarly, malaria eradication has not been evaluated in the broader context of WHO mass campaigns in general – it has been discussed because

6. As of January 1993, the WHO had 183 full members and two associate members (Puerto Rico and Tokelau).

it appeared to be the most obvious and dramatic example of such campaigns.

Thus the correlation between the structure/administration section and the case study is one of an evolving outlook in the WHO, from the initial establishment of an international infrastructure for health (discussed in the chapters on WHO's structure); to the use of the legitimacy and influence accorded that infrastructure to implement a mass campaign in a vertical fashion (discussed in the malaria case study); to an abandonment of the vertical approach for a more comprehensive and horizontal view (as present in the post-MEP WHO). A study of effectiveness of this sort is necessarily dependent on using the empirical and case study approach, as the task of measuring effectiveness - even limited to a small aspect of the Organization - would be too large and unmanageable otherwise.

Another acknowledged limitation of this study is its strong, and almost exclusive, emphasis on the WHO - there is only marginal discussion of, or comparison with, the role of other specialized agencies in international health programmes. This limitation has been largely dictated by the overwhelming amounts of WHO primary sources utilized in this study. An equally thorough study of other international organizations, and a comparison with the WHO, was not practically possible. A further reason why the scope of this work is limited to the WHO is that most of the issues and programmes discussed (with the exception of some structural issues) are specific to that Organization.

Finally, we recognize the considerable limitation of this work regarding the degree to which our conclusions on effectiveness can be extrapolated to the Organization in part or as a whole. This is not intended as a comprehensive examination of effectiveness in the WHO. Thus findings in specific programmes cannot be extrapolated to arrive at broad generalizations.

The membership, philosophy, approach and priorities of the WHO have changed dramatically over the past four and a half decades. Any meaningful evaluation of the Organization's activities must take these factors into account. Additionally, we show that effectiveness may not always be influenced in the same manner by a given factor; the influence depends on the conditions under which the programmes operate, and we demonstrate that under two different circumstances a given factor may have the *opposite* influence on effectiveness. For this reason, it is difficult to extrapolate the success of any individual programme to another, or even to itself when the operating conditions are not identical. It is worth stressing that because of this, the findings from specific areas cannot be extrapolated to the Organization as a whole.

There is, too, another reason for not directly linking, and thus interpreting, the effectiveness of an organization on the basis of the sum of the effectiveness of the different programmes it implements. The overall effectiveness of an Organization can, and often does, extend beyond that given by the sum of the effectiveness of the different individual programmes.

The Measurement of Effectiveness

Since the Organization's broad-ranging activities make measurement of effectiveness on a purely quantitative basis virtually impossible, our evaluation of effectiveness by internal criteria is largely qualitative. Qualitative assessments of effectiveness in relation to internal criteria have also been used by other authors. For instance, Robert Cassen and Associates have measured 'developmental effectiveness' of aid to developing countries by this method in their book *Does Aid Work*?[7] These authors have defined certain objectives and criteria by which to judge whether aid to certain developing countries is producing the hoped-for results. These criteria and objectives deal with development variables such as the contribution of the aid to social and economic development of the country as seen in health education, village committee participation in developmental efforts, and the presence of an operational strategy.

We evaluate the effectiveness of particular programmes and administrative initiatives under three main sets of criteria: the general aims, or 'mission', of the Organization; the targets aimed for and results achieved; and the totality of measures and resources employed in pursuing the aims and targets.

General Aims, or 'Mission', of the Organization. The 'mission' of an organization consists in the general aims, taken as a whole, assigned to it by the founders. The main points considered with regard to it are: (1) the precise aims adopted by the Organization when it was constituted and the role(s) which the founders envisaged for it; (2) changes in aims that may have taken place over time and the reasons why such transformations have taken place (changes imposed by circumstances; modifications due to the practical impossibility, for internal or external reasons, of realizing the original aims; consequences involved in the evolution of the concept of international organization; changes in membership; changes in values and norms; and so on).

7. Robert Cassen and Associates, *Does Aid Work?*, Clarendon Press, Oxford, 1986.

Targets Aimed for and Results Achieved. The targets or goals for specific programmes and initiatives are examined by analysis of: (1) the exact targets fixed by the Organization during the period under analysis; (2) the method of fixing targets, especially the degree of planning - implying a long-term programme - achieved by the association; and possibly the reasons which have rendered such planning difficult or impossible; (3) the procedures used by the Organization to study the degree to which results obtained correspond to targets aimed at; characteristics and mode of operating schemes adopted where there is delay or inadequate fulfilment of the programme; (4) the nature and strength of the principal obstacles - both internal and external - which have impeded, delayed or prevented the achievement of the targets; and (5) a list of some of the activities regarding the programme which could only be carried out successfully by the WHO.

Totality of Measures and Results Employed in Pursuing Aims and Targets. The totality of the measures employed in pursuing certain aims and targets is examined on various levels: (1) is a constant (or even increasing) part of the budget devoted to the endeavour over several years? (2) is there collaboration with other international organizations whose mandate overlaps that of the WHO in the given area? (3) is there a fund-raising effort from sources outside the Organization? (4) is the Organization committed to the effort financially, and in terms of manpower in relation to the pre-specified requirements? and (5) is the programme flexible enough to accommodate set-backs and successes at short notice?

There is little agreement about any one definition of effectiveness that is acceptable to all students and critics of the UN system. Although we have settled on our own working definition and established our own criteria, we have only uncovered the tip of the iceberg. Effectiveness depends on numerous other factors which influence each of the three sets of criteria listed above. Among these factors are included phenomena such as 'politicization', 'consensus', 'national interest' and 'international interest'. Expectations and perceptions of effectiveness have also been influenced by the theory of functionalism. All these influences are defined and described in the next two chapters.

5

SOME FACTORS INFLUENCING EFFECTIVENESS

Many contemporary detractors of the WHO and other specialized agencies have argued that 'politics' has detrimentally affected the work, and thus the effectiveness, of the Organization. Those more sympathetic to the WHO suggest that the detractors (overwhelmingly Western) are displeased merely because they have lost control of these organizations following the influx of an increasing number of developing countries into the UN system. These sympathizers suggest that for some time the West used the agencies as platforms for their own 'politics' and propaganda; now that the Third World is in a position to do the same (owing to its voting majority in these fora), the West accuses the agencies of 'politicization' and ineffectiveness. This opinion suggests that the West is equating the decline of its influence within the specialized agencies with an ineffectiveness on the part of the agencies, and that the West sees the national interests of Western countries as the only proper determinants of what is in the best interests of the world community. Given the absence in the WHO of a veto power for the large members, and the accession of developing countries into the UN system over the past three decades, the majority position of the West has been transformed into an uneasy minority position.

One of the phenomena that the Western countries point to as an indicator of 'politicization' in the WHO is the breakdown of consensus after the entry of the developing countries. They suggest that making decisions by majority vote is an obvious indication of the controversy which is engendered in issues being voted on – that these issues are extraneous to considerations of health.

Associated with the breakdown of such consensus is the impression that the taking of certain decisions within the WHO on the basis of pure national (or statist) interests has sacrificed the internationalist aspirations of the Organization to the 'political' machinations of some member states.

Finally, it is evident that many of the criticisms of the WHO and other specialized agencies have been made with the implicit or explicit assumption that 'politics', together with its associated lack of consensus and 'international interest', is destructive to the work of the WHO; moreover, it is also assumed that such destructive 'politics' can and should be removed from the Organization's considerations. These assumptions are based intuitively, if not also theoretically, on similar ideas present in functionalism, a theory of international organization.

Thus the three factors – 'politics', 'national interest' and functionalism – offer explanations for what is viewed by many observers as the WHO's contemporary loss of effectiveness. Politics and consensus, as well as national and international interest, are discussed in this chapter. The next chapter is devoted wholly to the influence of functionalism on contemporary concepts of effectiveness.

Politics and Consensus

The terms 'politics' and 'politicization' have been used interchangeably during the present crisis in the UN system to denote both a process and an outcome. Thus, for example, the discussion of disarmament within the WHO is considered to be an instance of 'politicization', as is the passage of the resolution resulting from the discussion. Despite the changing focus of 'politicization', one thing is clear: it is a charge against the UN system which has been used often in a sweepingly pejorative manner. For many detractors of the system, the recent infusion of certain issues that are 'political' in the 'technical' works of a functional organization such as the WHO denotes 'politicization', which is in turn thought to be the major compromiser of the Organization's effectiveness. Such a charge of 'politicization' was first aired in the mid-1970s by Henry Kissinger, who referred to 'the trend in the Specialized Agencies to focus on political issues'.[1] To understand such 'politicization', we must first understand the meaning of 'politics'.

Numerous conceptions of 'politics' are available. Aristotle referred to politics as the 'art or science of producing a good community'. Max Weber described it as 'the leadership by a political body called the state, or any influence exerted in that direction'. Hans Morgenthau has defined politics simply as 'the struggle for power'.[2] The WHO's own definition of 'politics' represents a synthesis of classic conceptions of the term: the art or science of government involving a 'competition for power between interest groups,

1. Kissinger has been quoted in M. Nerfin, 'Is a Democratic United Nations Possible?', *Development Dialogue*, vol. 2 (1976), p. 86.
2. See Ernest Baker, *The Politics of Aristotle*, Oxford University Press, Oxford, 1948, p. 360; Jacques Ellul, 'Politicization and Political Solutions', in Kenneth S. Templeton Jr. (ed.), *The Politicization of Society*, Liberty Press, Indianapolis, 1979, p. 220; and Hans Morgenthau, *Politics among Nations*, Alfred Knopf, New York, 1978, p. 29.

pressure groups or individuals, and the use of such power'.[3] A problem with this definition is that it attempts to circumscribe all activities that come under the rubric of 'politics'; as such it is too general for our purposes – it is not specific enough to take account of the special circumstances of the Organization itself.

If we accept the classic definitions of politics, it would appear that, in as much as the specialized agencies constitute a channel of communication between the political units (member states), interacting in both cooperative and conflictual situations, they are exposed to politics. As one author has said of the specialized agencies: 'They were created as a result of political agreements, and their resolutions and work inevitably reflect, in one way or another, the prevailing political climate.'[4] Moreover, many of the matters within the competence of any particular specialized agency call for decisions which affect national interests; some indeed involve a conflict of interests either within countries, or between countries; many involve genuine conflicts of political philosophy between, for example, liberals and conservatives. All such decisions are, by their very nature and to varying degrees, political, even though they may relate to responsibilities which are clearly functional. When seen in this light, 'politics' within the WHO is hardly anything new.

From these general formulations of politics, it is clear that not all politics is necessarily detrimental. If 'competition for power' and 'use of power' are used as sole indicators of politics, almost every activity within an international organization would be political. However, this is not considered to be the case: both the WHO and its detractors distinguish between that kind of politics which is detrimental to the work of the Organization, and that kind which is inevitable and even necessary. An example of the latter would include the election of the Director-General, a situation in which there is an obvious 'competition for power'. One document, prepared by the WHO's Secretariat, recognizes two distinct forms of politics, seen as positive and negative, which are separated by a fine line. Difficulties arise when different actors draw the line in different places, thus creating a grey area. Thus a common perception of the limits of the two forms of politics is crucial if controversy within the Organization is to be limited.

From the WHO Secretariat's perspective, the meaning of both forms of politics hinges on the assumption that the Organization is

3. See WHO document EB77/17, p. 2.

4. See Victor-Yves Ghebali, 'The Politicization of the UN Specialized Agencies: a Preliminary Analysis', *Milennium: Journal of International Studies*, vol. 14, no. 3 (winter 1985), p. 321.

not a supranational body; rather, it is an international organization and so has no jurisdiction whatsoever over the political ideology, economic and administrative systems, or social, cultural or religious preferences of its member states.

The political action (that is, 'use of power') that the WHO can take, and discuss, is limited to that which is required to support national political action in the field of health, and which the country has itself asked for. When asked, the WHO can use its constitutional role as coordinating authority on international health work to lead to the definition by member states of collective policy which can then act as a frame of reference for corresponding national policy. In doing this, the Organization has a 'sacred' obligation to promote the health of *people* in all countries as demanded by its constitution, which underlines cooperation among member states and with others 'to promote and protect the health of all peoples', and which states that 'the enjoyment of the highest attainable standard of health is one of the fundamental rights of every human being without distinction of race, religion, political belief, economic or social condition'.[5] In this context, then, the politics of health refers to how the WHO can, when asked, assist national governments to use their power to improve the health of their nationals. This is one aspect of the positive form of politics. Also, while it is possible for the WHO to support governments and people in taking political action in support of policies for health that have been agreed collectively at the World Health Assembly, it cannot enforce compliance with this or any other policy or with ethical or commercial codes of any kind. Even if the World Health Assembly were to adopt regulations in accordance with its constitutional powers, these would only come into force for those members that accepted them;[6] others have the right to reject them or express their reservations simply by notifying the Director-General.[7]

The second meaning ascribed to politics in the WHO refers to that which it is impossible for the Organization to do within the constraints of its constitution. So, for example, it is not possible for it to interfere in the foreign policy of any of its member states, in ideological differences or political controversies between them, in economic battles or sanctions between member states, or in military conflicts. In other words, the Organization must not be seen to be

5. See Preface to the WHO's constitution in *Basic Documents*, 36th edn, WHO, Geneva, 1986, p. 1.
6. The World Health Assembly (WHA) is the policy-making body of the WHO in which all member states are represented.
7. See Article 22 of the WHO's constitution in *Basic Documents*, *op. cit.*, p. 8.

taking sides in issues which are potentially divisive. Although there is no clause in the WHO's constitution specifically inhibiting the Organization from taking part in such issues, it is perfectly clear from the discussion at the Technical Preparatory Committee and the International Health Conference that such was the intention of the founders. Perhaps the absolute lack of guidance in the constitution with regard to fissiparous issues was one means of clearly indicating the irrelevance of these issues to the work of the Organization. If such issues arise in the debates and priorities of the Organization, this opens its fora to open controversy and conflict over issues in which it has little influence – this is the negative form of politics, which is considered disruptive and undesirable to the constitutionally mandated activities of the WHO. The infusion of such negative politics into the work of specialized agencies has been referred to by various observers of the UN system as 'politicization'.

An important caveat in the discussion of negative politics is that the presence of controversy in itself does not denote such politics, since many issues that are considered germane to the work of the WHO, such as the exact method of eradication of a disease, may involve controversy among the medical experts. Only that controversy which accompanies political matters extraneous to the work of the Organization is seen to result in politicization.

The detractors of the UN system appear to conceptualize politics in purely pejorative terms, while only recognizing the positive contribution of politics implicitly. The WHO has made more of an explicit acknowledgement of two types of politics, positive and negative. For our purposes, the two forms of politics discussed above represent the two extremes in a spectrum of types of politics within the WHO. We subdivide this spectrum into four categories of politics: (1) positive politics, as evident in the use of power to establish the infrastructure for cooperation, that is the World Health Organization itself; (2) inevitable politics, as evident in the competition for power that is unavoidable in any organization where power has to be carved up for personnel posts, regional offices and the like; (3) legitimate politics, as evident in attempts by different medical experts to secure (through 'competition for power' and 'use of such power') victory on legitimate disputes, such as those involving disagreements on public health methodologies; and (4) negative politics, or the use of power to introduce extraneous issues.

We are largely, though not exclusively, concerned with the fourth type of politics: for our purposes, 'politics' means negative or extraneous politics.[8] Since the inclusion of the other forms of politics under the rubric of politicization would only lead to terminological confusion, we are limiting our usage of 'politicization' to refer to the inclusion of negative politics in the activities of a specialized agency. Although not directly stated by the critics of the UN system, this is also the usage of politicization that they favour. The fact that accusations of politicization are pejorative in nature would imply that the positive form of politics has been considered so obviously a proper part of the workings of functional specialized agencies that it has not merited much attention by the detractors of the UN system. For instance, this meaning is obvious in Richard Hoggart's definition of politicization as 'the distortion of debate by the *irrelevant* introduction of political issues' (Hoggart's emphasis).[9]

In the above delineation of politicization, one common presumption is evident both within and outside the UN system: that fora such as the Security Council and the General Assembly should be the places for dealing with political matters extraneous to the work of the specialized agencies; that the agencies should concentrate on their functional mandates with the aid of positive, inevitable and legitimate politics, and that they should eschew politicization.[10] In a recent public statement the Secretary-General of the UN made this very clear:

> The Security Council and the General Assembly were both established to promote the resolution of political problems . . . The functional agencies, on the other hand, were not created for the pursuit of political objectives. A principal reason why the United Nations system was established on a highly decentralized basis was so that the operational agencies and offices would be separated from the political controversies to be dealt with in the political organs.[11]

Such comments by the Secretary-General, together with suggestions from UN bodies such as the Group of Eighteen (formed to study

8. The term 'politics' will denote 'negative politics' for the rest of this book, and the two terms will thus be used interchangeably. The three other forms of politics will be referred to as 'inevitable', 'legitimate' and 'positive'.
9. See Richard Hoggart, *An Idea and Its Servants: UNESCO from Within*, Chatto and Windus, London, 1978, p. 58.
10. The USA gave this advice to the ILO as it withdrew from that Organization in 1977. The USA rejoined the ILO in 1980. See Yves Beigbeder, *Management Problems in United Nations Organizations*, Pinter, London, 1987, p. 28; and Victor-Yves Ghebali, *The International Labour Organization: a Case Study on the Evolution of UN Specialized Agencies*, Martinus Nijhoff, Dordrecht, 1989, pp. 113–15.
11. In this statement, it is obvious that the Secretary-General uses the term 'political' to refer to that which we have earlier described as negative politics. As quoted in WHO document EB77/17, Oct. 1985.

reform of the UN system), illustrate the concern of the UN regarding the politicization of its specialized agencies.

The absence of any clear, and universally acceptable, definition of which specific instances of politics within the agencies constitute negative politics is at the crux of the contemporary crisis in the UN specialized agencies.[12] There is consensus in most quarters that politicization is detrimental to the work of the Organization; however, with the increasing polarization of the UN system along North–South lines, there is seldom agreement on which issues are negatively political and thus should be excluded from the Organization's agenda. East–West polarization of the specialized agencies during the Cold War era produced similar disagreements.

In these North–South or East–West disagreements, when politicization has been evident to part of the membership and not to the rest, conflict over the issue has been inevitable, with the opposing sides arguing about whether or not the issue in question is within the realm of negative politics and thus extraneous to the constitutional mandate of the WHO. The issue of politicization is often reduced to a problem of interpretation of the constitution. In such situations, there is a danger of the conflict itself becoming the centre of debate, while genuine health issues fade into the background.

At other times, politicization has been present without being evident to any substantial part of the membership - at least, any perception of politicization was not voiced as loudly and clearly as the charge is today. At these times, politicization was not a cause of major schisms and controversies among the membership of the WHO. For instance, before the entry of the developing countries into the WHO and during the absence of the socialist bloc countries from that Organization between 1950 and 1955, the United States and its allies had a determining influence over the Organization's programmes and priorities. As we will show later, some of these priorities can, in retrospect, be referred to as politicized. Other examples of politicization at a time when the present form of the charge was not evident have been documented by Clare Wells and others; these include 'American practices during the McCarthy era, notably FBI vetting of the security credentials of American members of the UNESCO staff, and American interest in

12. As mentioned earlier, there is a tendency among some critics of the UN system to subsume all that they consider undesirable in the agencies under the rubric of politicization. For instance, see Daniel Patrick Moynihan, *A Dangerous Place*, Atlantic-Little, Brown, Boston, Mass., 1978.

UNESCO as an instrument of US foreign policy during the Korean War'.[13]

There is no question that the Organization will have to display a high degree of maturity in handling negative political matters in such a way that it will not only continue to survive but it will do so with the degree of tolerance and tranquillity required to permit it to devote its efforts to the main focus of its activities - which, as decided by the World Health Assembly, is presently the attainment of 'health for all by the year 2000'.

Within the confines of the WHO's activities, negative politics within, and between, states is something over which the Organization has little influence and which it thus wants to exclude from its work and considerations. The notion of negative politics being extraneous to health considerations within the Organization is strongly entrenched.

The pejorative connotation many attribute to negative politics is due partly to such politics being considered the opposite of 'consensus'. 'Consensus' is widely considered extremely important for the smooth operation of the Organization. These same people suggest that negative politics within the WHO is responsible for the breakdown of 'consensus' within the Organization.

'Consensus' has been defined as 'the converging of opinion upon a common judgement'.[14] Ideally, a consensus will come into being automatically where there are common interests, a common understanding of those interests and of the fact that they are shared, and a common agreement on the means to advance them. However, within the UN system consensus has not been automatic, and when achieved it has often existed alongside other conflicting interests.[15]

Within the WHO, consensus has meant the taking of decisions 'without vote', 'by agreement', by 'consultation of the members', 'by acclamation', on the basis of 'non-objection', or 'without proceeding

13. See Clare Wells, 'The UN, UNESCO, and the Politics of Knowledge', unpubl. D. Phil. thesis, Oxford University, 1984, pp. 14 and 88–90; Hoggart, *op. cit.*, pp. 66 and 138; and J. Sewell, 'UNESCO: Pluralism Rampant', in R. Cox and H. Jacobson (eds), *The Anatomy of Influence*, Yale University Press, New Haven, 1973, pp. 162–8.

14. See Roger Scruton, *A Dictionary of Political Thought*, Macmillan, London, 1982, p. 88.

15. An important example of the use of consensus in the UN itself occurred in 1964, following the Congo and Suez Canal peacekeeping operations, the expenses of which France and the Soviet Union refused to share in. In an attempt to stop those two countries from losing their voting rights through application of Article 19 of the UN Charter, which provides for this sanction in cases of two-year tardiness in paying annual contributions to the Organization's budget, the only matters dealt with in the General Assembly were those where a vote did not need to be taken.

to a vote'. It is suggested that any (positive) political influence that the WHO might have on health policy depends on consensus among its member states, since such collective policy decisions bind member states together.

On the other hand, policy decisions taken by majority vote are seen as fissiparous, destroying the consensus that might make it possible to use the WHO as the world's collective health conscience whose policy inspires national health policies. Most decisions taken in the WHO are morally rather than legally binding on member states;[16] they represent the desire of member states to collaborate in order to improve people's health. As a corollary of such national sovereignty, without consensus only those member states in favour of decisions taken by majority vote will consider themselves bound by them and therefore committed to carry them out domestically and in their international relationships. Member states which are in the minority will not feel committed to these decisions. For instance, the approval by the great majority of the WHO's membership of a code of practice for the infant formula industry, against the negative vote of the United States, imposed no legal obligation on the latter to impose the code on American companies.[17]

Consensus can theoretically exist where there is no real agreement. This is possible, for instance, by including in an agreement key words which different groups are free to interpret differently. It is feared that such fragmentation of efforts may spell the doom of health efforts.

The United States at present pays 25 per cent of WHO's budget. While complaining about the decline of consensus and the rise of majority-vote decisions in the WHO, it has at the same time insisted on weighted voting (according to the size of the contribution paid) on issues involving budgetary growth and allocations. The Kassebaum Amendment in the United States limited the American contribution to UN specialized agencies to 20 per cent of the budget, beginning in the 1987 UN fiscal year, until such time as voting on 'matters of budgetary consequence' is proportional to each state's contribution. The Kassebaum Amendment has not come into effect in regard to the WHO because of the Organization's record of approving its annual budgets by consensus (that is, without a vote), involving major donor nations in key budgetary committees, setting budgetary ceilings, and developing techniques for item-by-item

16. Some decisions of the World Health Assembly are legally binding on all member states. The election of the Director-General is one example of such a decision.
17. In this instance, the presence of a moral obligation is hard to evaluate, especially in the absence of the American refusal to accept any legal obligation.

review rather than dealing with the entire budget as a package.[18] Most developing countries have favoured majority vote when consensus is not possible, and are openly hostile to ideas of weighted voting.

The official WHO stand on voting is fairly clear. The last Director-General, Halfdan Mahler, made it clear that any kind of voting by majority is undesirable, as is voting weighted by such criteria as population size, scale of assessments with respect to the regular budget, or size of voluntary extra-budgetary contributions to the WHO or directly to developing countries to carry out agreed WHO policy. Approval by consensus, that is without a vote, is considered preferable in all issues that the Organization deals with, irrespective of whether they concern health policy, budgetary or administrative policy – the fact that the Organization depends on a collective moral responsibility on the part of its member states in order to implement approved policies makes decisions by majority vote a contradiction in terms to its ideal.

The issue of negative politics and consensus may be summarized as follows: politicization of the WHO has led to a breakdown of consensus, resulting in decisions being taken by majority vote which, due to the divergence of national interests, produces tensions that hinder the ideal application of the Organization's constitutional mandate. According to this viewpoint, it is presumed that legitimate differences on health matters produce decisions not by majority vote, but by consensus.

Since the formation of the developing country majority within the WHO, the flexible, and at times ambiguous, nature of the WHO's constitution has allowed a shift in the Organization's emphasis towards problems considered more urgent by the new member states. As long as these countries interpret the constitution differently from the Western countries which pay most of the WHO's budget, and as long as their perception of what constitutes politicization is different, it seems inevitable that more and more issues will be decided by majority vote and not by consensus.

18. However, as of July 1989, the United States owed the WHO US$98.3 million, of which 72 per cent was the assessment for 1989 and the rest was due from 1988: 'Status of Contribution, 1988–1989', WHO unpublished document, Geneva, May 1989. Also confirmed by personal communication with T.H. Mirza, Head of Treasury of the WHO, Geneva, 26 July 1989. See Yves Beigbeder, 'Administrative and Structural Reform in the Organizations of the United Nations Family', in Chris de Cooker (ed.), *International Administration – Law and Management Practices in International Organizations*, UNITAR/Martinus Nijhoff, London, 1990.

National and International Interest

An organization such as the WHO, which aspires to universal participation, at least theoretically reflects the perspectives of global, or international, interests. Global interest can be defined as the promotion of peace, the entrenchment of economic or ecologic well-being, and the reinforcement of principles of social justice.[19]

Statist doctrines argue that national interest is the final arbiter of national policy, and that general principles of the more widespread international welfare are secondary even to the individual state members of a functional (welfare-oriented) organization such as the WHO.

While international interest may be too idealistic a concept to influence international relations in general, it is the guiding principle of the employees of the UN system, otherwise known as international civil servants. According to staff regulations, for the duration of their appointments the staffs of UN agencies owe their allegiance not to the states of which they are nationals, but to the UN alone.[20] Even though international interest is theoretically committed to eroding the authority of states, it was national decision-makers who established the international civil service.[21] This situation appears to be more of a paradox to some observers of the UN system than to others, who suggest that the establishment of international organizations is merely another means of furthering the national interest with the help of an international civil service whose members retain their national allegiances. Moreover, international organizations provide their members with the opportunity to air their own viewpoints and interests in a more open and public forum than that provided by bilateral diplomacy. In this sense, the WHO can be thought of as an arena for the voicing of national interests, rather than a victory for international interest.[22]

The two scenarios painted above represent what Maurice Bertrand has referred to as the 'crisis of multilateralism' – that is, the lack of political will for or national commitment to international

19. See Thomas Weiss, *International Bureaucracy*, Lexington Books, Lexington, Mass., 1975, p. xvi.

20. See Yves Beigbeder, *Threats to the International Civil Service*, Pinter, London, 1988, p. 21.

21. See Weiss, *op. cit.*, p. xix.; and for a general discussion see Robert Jordan (ed.), *International Administration*, Oxford University Press, New York, 1971.

22. See Clive Archer, *International Organizations*, Geo. Allen and Unwin, London, 1983, p. 136.

welfare.[23] Many countries frequently do not consider international interest to be in their national interest.

If health is considered a 'sacred' undertaking of the WHO (as indeed all its Directors-General have claimed it is), to which all member states are pledged, there can ideally be no place for the exercise of diplomacy in the classic sense – the conduct of business between states strictly on a basis of national interest. The conception behind an international organization is that its members, far from using it as a place to further their national interests, should subordinate those interests to the international interest. As David Kay points out, practice has fallen short of the theory and it is in fact true to say that diplomacy in the classic sense is still commonly practised at the WHO.[24]

Like the UN itself, the specialized agencies are fora for multilateral diplomacy. They are a diplomatic contrivance to facilitate collective action and are limited in their freedom to doing only that which their member states are prepared to approve. It is thus not surprising that most states emphasize those organizational initiatives which are in line with their own particular national objectives, and avoid or actively oppose the rest. The prospects for collective action usually turn, therefore, far more on the majority's recognition of a coincidence of national interests than on a genuine deference to the Organization's various programmes and policies.[25] Such majoritarian ideas of the international interest may be perceived by those that oppose the majority initiative as politicization, and thus detrimental to effectiveness.

23. See Maurice Bertrand, 'Can the UN be Reformed?' in Adam Roberts and Benedict Kingsbury (eds), *United Nations: Divided World*, Oxford University Press, 1988, p. 199.
24. David Kay, *The UN Political System*, Wiley, New York, 1967, p. 81.
25. *Ibid.*, p. 4.

6
FUNCTIONALISM AND EFFECTIVENESS

Virtually every contemporary statement connecting politics with ineffectiveness in the WHO and other specialized agencies, whether made by a detractor or a defender of the agencies, seems to be based on the assumptions that politics is not an inevitable evil and that the Organization's failure to limit or exclude it is the main cause of ineffectiveness. The belief that politics can be segregated from the technical or 'apolitical' work of an organization like the WHO is at the heart of much of the criticism levelled against it. This conception of effectiveness is based on assumptions elaborated in the theory of functionalism.

While we hope to illustrate that politics is responsible for detrimentally influencing the criteria of effectiveness, we also propose to show that it is not possible to exclude such politics from the works of the WHO. This latter observation will help us in our analysis of effectiveness, because it will set realistic limits on our expectations from the outset. Functionalism is an approach that offers a method of removing politics from certain interactions between sovereign states; as such, it is relevant to our study because politics may be a detractor of effectiveness, and, if so, it is important for us to determine if this is avoidable. An explanation of functionalism is also important for an understanding of a theory of international organization that exercises overt influence on the WHO Secretariat, its member states and many observers of the Organization.

Functionalism in Theory

The first important theoretical formulation of functionalism in international organizations was that of David Mitrany,[1] who started with the postulation that the root of international problems,

1. See, for instance, the following works by Mitrany: *A Working Peace System*, Oxford University Press, 1943, *The Progress of International Government*, Yale University Press, New Haven, 1933 and *The Road to Security*, National Peace Council, Pamphlet 29, London, 1944. Also, for a remarkable parallel to Mitrany's views, see Herman Finer, *The United Nations Economic and Social Council*, World Peace Foundation, Boston, Mass., 1946, and Finer, *The T.V.A.: Lessons for International Application*, Da Capo Press, New York, 1972; L.S. Woolf, *International Government*, Brentano's, New York, 1916; and *The Development of International Cooperation in Economic and Social Affairs* (Bruce Report), League of Nations, Geneva, 1939.

and the real obstacle to international cooperation and peace, is the division of the world into sovereign states. Mitrany has observed that while sovereign states are the basic units of the contemporary international political system, they comprise a far from ideal framework for the provision of the economic and social services needed by their populations. Indeed, states frequently exercise their sovereignty in a manner detrimental to the best interests of their populations. Mitrany and other functionalists suggest a way around the problem of sovereignty: they offer hope for slow, steady and cumulative international integration via international cooperation on pressing economic and social issues, where it is self-evident that national action alone is of limited utility. The significance of international 'functional' cooperation is paramount to functionalists, who view the prevalence of economic and social inequity as a major precipitant of war.

Functionalist thinking is clearly reflected in the policy of both the United Nations and the WHO with regard to the role of health in international relations. The UN Charter, in Article 55, considers inadequate provision for health as one of the indirect causes of war: 'With a view to the creation of conditions of stability and well-being which are necessary for peaceful and friendly relations among nations . . ., the United Nations shall promote . . . solutions of international economic, social, health and related problems.'[2] Moreover, the preamble to the WHO's constitution starts with the statement that 'the health of all peoples is fundamental to the attainment of peace and security and is dependent upon the fullest cooperation of individuals and states.'[3]

Mitrany believes that past attempts to create or sustain peace by convening disarmament conferences, and by establishing essentially political organizations such as the League of Nations, were doomed from their inception because they attempted to tackle directly problems of security and power politics. For Mitrany, this approach was imprudent because it cut straight to the heart of sovereignty, where the greatest chance of conflict and controversy lay. Mitrany does not expect functionalism, if successful, to make war between states obsolete. Rather, he envisages that as the benefits of cooperation become self-evident and the costs of war become prohibitively high, states will increasingly choose the option of cooperation over belligerence.[4]

2. See UN Charter, Article 55.

3. See preamble to the WHO's constitution in *Basic Documents*, 36th edn, WHO, Geneva, 1986, p. 1.

4. See Mark F. Imber, 'Re-reading Mitrany: a Pragmatic Assessment of Sovereignty', *Review of International Studies*, vol. 10 (1984), p. 112; and Mitrany, *A Working Peace System*, *op. cit.*, p. 21.

Finding that 'the political way is too ambitious',[5] the functionalists have proposed a more flexible and circuitous approach to peace. They expect that a world society is more likely to develop as the result of 'doing things together in workshop and market place rather than by signing pacts in chancelleries'.[6] By marrying power to function (for instance, health, education), functionalists attempt to bypass the traditional association of authority with a given territory, or state. In this formulation, 'one world' is rendered a functional, not a political, concept. Accordingly, functionalists believe that functional bodies such as the specialized agencies of the United Nations should be 'executive agencies with autonomous tasks and powers'.[7]

The tenets of functionalism are based upon a complex set of assumptions about the nature of war and about the role of international functional agencies in bringing about a 'working peace system'.[8] An examination of the basic assumptions and prescriptions of functionalism follows:

Assumption 1. Socially inequitous conditions, including hunger, poverty, homelessness, illness, illiteracy and certain forms of oppression and exploitation such as slavery, breed fear, anger, desperation and hatred among those affected and act as precipitants of war.[9] Functionalists propose to extirpate the root causes of war by raising the standard of living of the poor, promoting public health measures, fighting illiteracy and ensuring social justice.

Assumption 2. Functionalists lay the blame for war at the door of the nation-state, which institution they consider obsolete and increasingly irrelevant for the proper fulfilment of the needs of the world's disenfranchised. While economic and social problems are often international, the nation-state system (which is not conducive

5. Mitrany, *A Working Peace System*, *op. cit.*, p. 62.
6. *Ibid.*, p. 5.
7. *Ibid.*, p. 7.
8. For a brief summary of the assumptions of functionalism, see A. A. Fatouros, 'On the Hegemonic Role of International Functional Organizations', *German Yearbook of International Law*, vol. 23 (1980), p. 15. Functionalist assumptions are also well discussed in Samuel Shih-tsai Chen, *The Theory and Practice of International Organization*, Kendal/Hunt Publishing Co., Dubuque, Iowa, 1979, pp. 133–7.
9. See Mitrany's 'The End of Morality in War', *International Relations*, vol. 14, no. 4 (Nov. 1973), pp. 231–8. Mitrany's analysis of the etiology of war closely parallels the writings of Leonard Woolf and Norman Angell. For the former see *International Government*, *op. cit.*; for the latter, see *The Great Illusion*, Heinemann, London, 1911. (The illusion to which Angell referred was the perception that war between states could possibly serve the national interest.)

to a universal outlook) is limited in its ability to offer any viable solutions. To overcome the limitations of the nation-state, functionalists recommend the establishment of international organizations based around specific functions, whose importance is perceived worldwide.[10] Such international organizations are considered 'functional organizations', whose activities relate 'directly to economic, social, technical, and humanitarian matters . . . [and] are immediately and explicitly concerned with such values as prosperity, welfare, social justice, and the "good life", rather than the prevention of war and elimination of national insecurity'.[11] Moreover, functionalists believe that, even though they may be under the general supervision of an overall world organization, functional organizations must be allowed a great deal of autonomy – that is, the system must be a decentralized one. Finer has put this proposition quite strongly with regard to the United Nations:

> First, in no way ought the Economic and Social Council encroach upon the responsibility accorded to the governing bodies, the Conferences and Secretariats established by the conventions establishing the special organizations. The authority of these bodies must be commensurate with their responsibilities if they are to carry through their work with vigour and zeal.[12]

Assumption 3. Functionalists assume that human affairs can be divided into two spheres – political and non-political – and that these spheres can be segregated. Economic and social issues are included in the latter, and are also sometimes referred to as 'technical'. The 'political' sphere is seen as being rife with controversies; the 'technical' sphere offers promise for international consensus. Under this assumption, functionalists suggest dealing with the economic and social problems first and foremost not only because they are more significant, but also because they are exactly the kind of issues on which international agreement is possible. Inis Claude has called this the 'separability-priority' thesis.[13]

Assumption 4. Convinced of the validity of the 'separability-priority' thesis, functionalists believe that once international co-operation on economic and social problems has become habitual,

10. This 'function determines form' attitude is meant to limit the encroachment of the political sphere into the technical sphere. David Mitrany was of the opinion that 'Sovereignty cannot in fact be transferred effectively through a formula, only through a function.' See *A Working Peace System*, *op. cit.*, p. 9.
11. See Inis L. Claude Jr, *Swords into Plowshares*, 4th edn, Random House, New York, 1971, p. 378.
12. Finer, *United Nations Economic and Social Council*, *op. cit.*, p. .
13. Claude, *op. cit.*, p. 350.

the political sphere will become more approachable and tractable as the mentality and habit of cooperation overflow from the technical sphere. Paul S. Reinsch has compared this phenomenon to a pebble dropped into a pond, giving rise to a series of concentric circles of international cooperation, 'which will ramify from the limited area of technical agencies to the vast circumference of a global political organization'.[14] This phenomenon has been labelled the doctrine of spillover, transferability, expansibility, ramification, or accumulation. In reference to such spillover, Karl Deutsch has spoken of functionalism as a theory that 'avoids the perils of premature overall amalgamation, and . . . gives the participating governments, elites, and peoples more time gradually to learn the habits and skills of more far-reaching, stable, and rewarding integration'.[15]

Mitranian functionalism may be summarized as follows: an international welfare community represents the ideal of human organization because it actively undermines those social and economic inequities which are the basic causes of war; this ideal may be realized by establishing international functional organizations, which deal with 'non-political' issues such as public health, illiteracy and hunger more adequately than individual states can possibly do. The cooperation built up in the functional or 'non-political' sphere is ultimately expected to 'spillover' into the frankly 'political' sphere of human interactions, eventually rendering peaceful relations between nation-states the only viable and inevitable outcome.

The intuitive appeal of functionalist ideas has been effaced on closer, more scientific examination. Indeed, functionalist ideas were tested practically in 1950 with the establishment of the European Coal and Steel Community, a collaborative venture between six countries with a common supranational authority. From this experience emerged 'neo-functionalism', a reformation of functionalism in theory and practice.[16]

Neo-functionalists such as Ernst Haas have avoided abstract analysis in an attempt to address some of the perceived shortcomings of functionalism. They emphasize empirical evidence which suggests that international functional organizations do indeed promote the learning of cooperative habits and that the creation of such

14. Paul S. Reinsh, *Public International Unions*, Ginn and Co., Boston, Mass., 1911. As referenced in Chen, *op. cit.*, p. 134.

15. See Karl W. Deutsch, *The Analysis of International Relations*, Prentice-Hall, Englewood Cliffs, NJ, 1968, p. 198.

16. See for example, Ernst Haas, *Beyond the Nation State*, Oxford University Press, 1964.

organizations may produce some integrative effects. Concentrating on the issue of European integration, the neo-functionalists have modified some of the sweeping generalizations of functionalism in the light of practical experience. For instance, while functionalism avoids supranantionalism, neo-functionalism explicitly establishes supranationalism as a goal of integration.[17]

Neo-functionalism contains elements of both federalism and functionalism: elements of the former are evident in the assumed goal of supranationalism; those of the latter in the explanation of the integrative process itself. Interdependence between various sectors of the international economy is seen by Haas and others as an asset, and in fact an overwhelming incentive, for supranational integration: integrating one or more sectors under a supranational authority is expected to generate a momentum for economic stimuli, psychological willingness and political will that will lock the process in an ever-expanding loop until a single economy has emerged governed by a single authority. This spillover is envisaged in much the same way as functionalists predict. However, neo-functionalists add the important proviso that such needs and pressures from the environment can only be said to cause integration to the degree that they lead to and 'constrain the international bargaining process among interest groups, parties, government officials and international organizations – all of whom are attempting to exploit these pressures in their own interests'.[18]

While the functionalists view spillover as inevitable or automatic, neo-functionalists suggest that spillover (or 'forward linkage') is only one of several outcomes. Its likelihood is said to depend on the issue at hand, the degree of initial consensus and the previous success and contemporary ability of the supranational authority to bring about settlements which 'upgrade the common interest'.[19]

The greatest criticism of neo-functionalism is generated by its frank aspirations for political integration. Of this aspiration, Mitrany has said that it is obvious:

17. Functionalism does not accept this as a preconceived end, and may be considered a compromise between universalism and nationalism. See David Mitrany, 'The Functional Approach in Historical Perspective', *International Affairs*, vol. 47, no. 3, 1971, p. 539; and A. J. R. Groom and P. Taylor (eds), *Functionalism*, University of London Press, London, 1975, p. 17.

18. Ernst Haas, who first developed the theory, describes integration as the product of 'an institutional pattern of interest politics, played out within existing international organizations'. See his *Beyond the Nation State*, *op. cit.*, p. 35.

19. Ernst Haas, 'International Integration: the European and the Universal Process', *International Political Communities*, New York, 1966, pp. 95–7.

that political integration can come about only within a limited dimension; that the greater the number of units to be integrated, the more dubious the prospect; that the greater their number and variety, the more intense would have to be the pressures for giving them a new cohesion.[20]

The factual evidence against neo-functionalism of course has come most poignantly from the lack of European political integration, which was to be the logical conclusion of the processes that the neo-functionalists first studied.[21] Whether the Treaty of Maastricht and the European Union will provide new vitality to neo-functionalism is yet to be seen; however, political integration still does not seem inevitable in Europe.

Functionalism in Practice

With the declining political influence of the League of Nations, its leadership attempted to accentuate those rare efforts of the organization which received acclaim from the world community: international social and economic work. Understandably then, the last year of the League saw a movement to develop and expand these 'non-political' or functionalist activities. As Northedge has observed, the 'idea was to snatch this one surviving section of the League's work from the tides engulfing it and strengthen it against the gathering storm'.[22]

Functionalist ideas within the League reached a culmination in May 1939 with the League Council's acceptance of the Secretary-General's proposal for the establishment of a committee to study the development and expansion of the League's technical activities. Stanley Bruce of Australia was named chairman of the committee which presented its report on 22 August 1939.[23] Ironically, on this day when functionalist ideas achieved their most eloquent expression within the League in the form of the Bruce Report, the organization's primary political mandate to maintain peace suffered a death blow as the Nazi-Russian Non-Aggression Pact was signed in Moscow, enabling Hitler to invade Poland ten days later and unleash the Second World War.

The Bruce Report presented the need for increased international cooperation in economic and social affairs. The report recommended

20. See Mitrany, 'The Functional Approach in Historical Perspective', *op. cit.*, p. 535.
21. *Ibid.*, p. 535; and see also Imber, *op. cit.*, p. 103.
22. See F.S. Northedge, *The League of Nations: its Life and Times, 1920–1946*, Leicester University Press, 1986, p. 190.
23. *The Development of International Cooperation* (Bruce Report), *op. cit.*

that the economic and social activities already carried on by the League should be expanded and that a special organ, the Central Committee for Economic and Social Questions, should be created to supervise this work.

The influence of functionalist thinking is evident in the 1940 remarks of Arthur Sweetser, an American member of the League Secretariat, who thought that increased functional cooperation of the kind suggested in the Bruce Report marked 'a phase in [the] slow transition of mankind from international anarchy to the world community'.[24] Such enthusiasm for functionalist cooperation, although not unanimously acceptable to those involved in the League,[25] did not die with the League. It was commonly held that the political activities of the League were responsible for the demise of the organization's technical activities. Thus the functionalist notion of a separation of political and non-political activities was received with favour in both 'political' and 'technical' circles.

The recommendations of the Bruce Report were buried in the chaos of the Second World War, but resurfaced after the demise of the League of Nations and the end of the war. Indeed, the United Nations Economic and Social Council (ECOSOC) later took the form of the special organ recommended by the Bruce Committee. Although the founders of the UN system did not formally endorse all aspects of the functionalist theory, the attention they paid to economic and social issues (and the array of agencies created to deal with them) constituted a significant functionalist experiment.[26]

Many specialized agencies of the United Nations have distinctly functionalist goals and ambitions.[27] For example, B.F. Jenks

24. See Arthur Sweetser, 'The Non-political Achievements of the League', *Foreign Affairs*, vol. 19, no. 1 (Oct. 1940), p. 192.

25. For instance, the USSR felt that the League's activities should concentrate on peace and security and it opposed the movement to give increased emphasis to economic and social programmes. See Charles Prince, 'The USSR and International Organization', *American Journal of International Law*, vol. 36, no. 3 (July 1942), p. 425; and Harold Jacobson, *The USSR and the UN's Economic and Social Activities*, University of Notre Dame Press, Notre Dame, Ind., 1963, p. 8.

26. For discussion, see Lawrence Finkelstein (ed.), *Politics in the United Nations System*, Duke University Press, Durham, NC, 1988, p. 120.

27. Many of these organizations have explicitly embodied functionalist aims and thus have provided opportunities to test functionalist hypotheses. The most comprehensive tests have been undertaken by Ernst Haas in *Beyond the Nation State*, *op. cit.*, which deals with the ILO, and J.P. Sewell, in *Functionalism in World Politics*, Princeton University Press, 1966, which is a study of economic development programmes in the UN.

has spoken of the 'impressive body of literature in favour of a functionalist interpretation of UNESCO's role'.[28] The functionalist separation of political and non-political realms is explicitly stated in the Articles of Agreement of the World Bank under the heading 'Political Activity Prohibited'. Within the WHO, although the theory itself is not well known or understood, functionalist ideas retain a certain intellectual legitimacy. The assumptions of functionalism listed earlier are echoed in many statements and policies of the WHO. For instance, the WHO is a decentralized organization constitutionally mandated for one function – public health; the fulfilment of this function is related to the promotion of peace in its constitution; finally, all the Directors-General of the WHO have expressed the view that politics can, and should, be separated from their technical work within their Organization.[29] The tenets of functionalism are equally explicitly stated in the constitutions of several other UN specialized agencies.

Functionalism has been severely criticized on several grounds,[30] starting with its assumption that war is the product of unsatisfactory economic and social conditions. Samuel Shih-tsai Chen suggests that this assumption is based on Karl Marx's materialistic interpretation of history and is thus 'subject to the same criticism as Marxism'. On the same issue, Hans Kelsen has said: 'It is not true that war is the consequence of unsatisfactory economic conditions; on the contrary, the unsatisfactory situation of the world economy is the consequence of war.' In the same vein, Inis Claude has declared: 'It was advanced Germans, not primitive Africans, who shattered world peace in 1939.'[31]

With regard to the present crisis facing the specialized agencies, perhaps the most criticized tenet of functionalism is its separability-priority thesis – the belief in the separability of the 'technical' sphere from the 'political' one. Most contemporary academic writings on

28. See B.F.E. Jenks, 'The Concept of International Organization: the Case of UNESCO', unpubl. D.Phil. thesis, Oxford University, 1982, p. 59.

29. A recent Director-General of the WHO, Dr Halfdan Mahler, has made the observation that 'Health improvement is a goal desired by all and therefore less subject to political controversy than other social goal. Let us use it then as a lever for social development.' See Halfdan Mahler, 'Health for All by the Year 2000', *WHO Chronicle*, vol. 29 (1975), p. 458.

30. Perhaps the most thorough critiques of functionalism have been produced by Ernest Haas, James P. Sewell and Charles Pentland; these works have been referenced in other footnotes, above or below.

31. See Chen, *op. cit.*, p. 136; H. Kelsen, *Peace through Law*, University of North Carolina Press, Chapel Hill, NC, 1944; Claude, *op. cit.*, p. x.

'politicization' of the specialized agencies, for instance, suggest that the separation of political and technical is a myth.[32]

Apart from arguing that it is not possible to separate the political from the non-political in an increasingly politicized world, Samuel Shih-tsai Chen has questioned the value of putting non-political problems before political ones: 'As evidenced in the United Nations, it is rather difficult, if not impossible, to talk about any non-political questions without a good political atmosphere. Why should we put the non-political cart before the political horse?'[33]

Oddly enough, the separability-priority thesis is also the tenet of functionalism which is most widely accepted by some detractors of the UN.[34] Despite the criticism of that thesis of functionalism in academic circles, the notion of politics as an alien and undesirable factor that can be removed from the day-to-day functioning of the Organization is quite prevalent among the critics of the UN system; and also within the WHO's Secretariat itself, where it has more of an intuitive appeal.[35]

Theoretically, the UN system offers a rich source of material for the study of functionalist tenets. Certainly, the WHO would be an ideal specimen for study. For our purposes, however, what is more interesting is the influence of functionalist or pseudo-functionalist thinking on conceptions of politicization of the Organization, and thus on ideas about its effectiveness.

The notion of politics as alien has not only created expectations of 'non-politicized' action by the WHO, but has also resulted in accusations of ineffectiveness when that ideal has not been realized. Indeed, when critics accuse the specialized agencies of politicization,

32. See G.M. Lyons, D.A. Baldwin and D.W. McNemar, 'The "Politicization" Issue in the UN Specialized Agencies' in David Kay (ed.), *The Changing United Nations: Options for the United States*, Academy of Political Science, New York, p. 83. Also see D. Pitt and T. Weiss (eds), *The Nature of United Nations Bureaucracies*, Croom Helm, London, 1986; Douglas Williams, *The Specialized Agencies of the United Nations*, Hurst, London, 1987; David Steele, *The Reform of the United Nations*, Croom Helm, London, 1987; and Houshang Ameri, *Politics and Process in the Specialized Agencies of the United Nations*, Gower, Aldershot, 1982, p. 105.

33. See Chen, *op. cit.*, p. 136.

34. A look through many publications of the American Heritage Foundation regarding the specialized agencies will clearly demonstrate the acceptance of the separability hypothesis as the basis of charges of politicization. For instance, see John M. Starrels, *The World Health Organization: Resisting Third World Ideological Pressures*, Heritage Foundation, Washington, DC, 1985.

35. Most high-level WHO Secretariat staff I interviewed were dismayed by the presence of negative politics within the Organization and felt that it was theoretically possible to keep it out. Most of the people interviewed had never heard of David Mitrany, or of functionalism. See the list of people interviewed in the Bibliography.

they suggest that it is possible for these bodies to be 'non-politicized'. This charge of politicization is different from the politicization charge discussed earlier in that it is based on the presumption that it is possible to separate negative politics from the workings of specialized agencies; the earlier formulation recognized the presence of negative politics and its detrimental influence on the Organization, but made no judgement about its eradicability. Thus, while the other expectations of functionalism are considered unrealistic by many of its critics, expectations of non-political functional agencies still persist in some quarters.

The functionalist antipathy to the 'political' or the 'non- technical' is obvious in their disparaging comments about this aspect of international relations. Such antipathy is also betrayed in their attenuated discussion of politics and in their highly ambiguous use of these terms. As James Sewell has remarked:

> In the functionalist literature 'political' is generally used to denote that portion of the universe of human relations which lies beyond the functional pale. As such the functional is by definition the non-political, and this is synonymous with 'non-controversial', or 'technical' in terms of procedure, and 'economic' or 'social' in its substantive aspect. Politics is a residue.[36]

Without entering the definitional debate, we propose to use the concept of negative politics as interchangeable with the 'politics' to which the functionalists refer. Certainly, our own idea of negative politics (as that category of politics which results in the consideration of extraneous issues such as those concerning security and power-politics within the confines of a specialized agency like the WHO) is not incongruent with the functionalist idea.

In conclusion, it is obvious that in spite of all its weaknesses, functionalism has left a mark on both the critics and the supporters of the UN system. It is clearly evident in the philosophy and *raison d'être* of the World Health Organization. More important, functionalist expectations generated by assumptions such as the separability-priority thesis have contributed to the accusations of politicization faced by the specialized agencies of the UN today. Within the limits of our own investigations, we will assess the validity of some functionalist assumptions of Mitrany and others in relation to the WHO, and gauge the influence of these on the effectiveness of the structural aspirations of the Organization and on the Malaria Eradication Programme.

36. See Sewell, *op. cit.*, p. 43.

Part II
ATTEMPTS TO BUILD A DECENTRALIZED, UNIVERSAL HEALTH ORGANIZATION

7
DECENTRALIZATION AND UNIVERSALITY IN THE W.H.O.

The earliest, most persistent and highly controversial difficulties faced by the WHO have been directly or indirectly related to the Organization's structural aspirations. The primacy given to such aspirations indicated the Organization's attempts to establish a solid structural (and administrative) base with which to confront future operational and technical public health challenges. In their deliberations about the WHO's structure, the founders had to take into account the reality of already existing regional organizations and the various regional differences in health concerns and priorities.

In view of the importance of a universally acceptable structure and administration to the programmatic and operational legitimacy of a truly *world* health organization, effectiveness in realizing the WHO's structural aspirations (and the difficulties faced in pursuing them) are assessed here. We limit our analysis of structural effectiveness to two broad areas of interest: the desire for universal membership, and the establishment of a decentralized organization with regional offices, including the assignment of member states to those regions.

These two aspirations of the WHO are emphasized for several reasons. First, they were accorded a primary position among the considerations of the founders of the WHO with regard to structure. Thus by evaluating the effectiveness of the WHO in realizing these aspirations, we also examine the Organization's ability to achieve its declared first priority.

Secondly, the WHO's attempts to foster a universality of outlook and approach (as evidenced in the malaria eradication programme discussed later in this book) could not have been wholly possible without the initial organizational legitimacy acquired from attempts to achieve universality in membership, and from providing that membership with an acceptable (decentralized) administrative structure. The presence (or absence) of consensus is arguably more meaningful in the light of an appreciation of a changing membership and the influence of that membership on the Organization's priorities.

Thirdly, the lack of universality in former international health organizations attaches an added significance to universality in the WHO. Universal membership appeared crucial to the founders of the WHO in view of the absence, withdrawal or expulsion of certain countries from the Health Organization of the League of Nations, effectively limiting the freedom of action of that organization.[1]

Financial considerations were not unimportant. The fact that the United States was not a member of the League of Nations meant the League Health Organization could not obtain the financial support that was later available to the WHO.[2] As demonstrated later in the malaria eradication case study, such financial support, or lack of it, can be crucial in terms of the resources an organization can devote to its efforts for public health.

Finally, for practical reasons, we chose to concentrate only on membership and decentralization in the WHO. It would be impossible to examine the structure and administration of the WHO as a whole in a work of this length. Thus we examine those WHO priorities which are considered the most important for the establishment of an international infrastructure for health.

The present WHO is a decentralized organization with its headquarters in Geneva, Switzerland, and six regional offices. The significance of the decentralized regional structure can be understood in the light of the *status quo* with regard to international public health organizations just prior to the establishment of the WHO. The presence of the Pan American Sanitary Bureau in itself meant that some regional arrangement would have to be arrived at,[3] especially if the United States was to participate in, and contribute to, the

1. The United States was not a member of the League's Health Organization; Germany and Japan withdrew from it, and the Soviet Union was expelled from the League (and thus also from its Health Organization).
2. When the WHO was founded, the United States paid approximately 30% of its budget. The present US contribution in 25%.
3. Doubts were expressed at the Technical Preparatory Committee regarding the financial feasibility of too sudden a decentralization of the WHO. These doubts were set aside following a statement by the Director of the Pan American Sanitary Bureau that the Bureau had started work in 1902 with a budget of only US$5,000. See *The First Ten Years of the World Health Organization*, WHO, Geneva, 1958, p. 76.

new WHO. The practical problem that the WHO's founders faced was how to bring about a smooth integration of extant regional organizations into the WHO and establish them as regional offices.

Decentralization of the WHO has rendered the regional offices very important.[4] For instance, in 1967 the WHO's staff included 3,178 individuals, of which 2,090 were based in the six regions and 1,088 at headquarters. Moreover, the majority of the Organization's budget was devoted to regional and inter-regional activities. As of 1985, the WHO had 4,449 employees, who were distributed in a similar way.[5] By 1993, the WHO's staff comprised 4,458 individuals, of whom 1,666 were located at headquarters in Geneva, 2,690 were in the six regions, 11 were seconded to other organizations and 91 were unassigned.[6]

Each regional office has a Regional Committee, in which each member state of the region is represented. The major functions of the Regional Committees involve the formulation of policies on matters of an exclusively regional character, and the supervision of the activities of the regional office. As the malaria eradication case study will show, much of the operational decision-making for worldwide programmes is coordinated at the regional level.

Of the many conflicts and controversies faced by the WHO with regard to membership and regionalization, we find that most can be placed within one of two broad categories: those that have been effectively dealt with by the Organization, or have faded away; and those that persist to this day. The latter problems are significant with regard to the contemporary charges of politicization and shed light on the relevance of such charges in a historical context.

Starting with a very brief chronology of the establishment of the WHO, this section is devoted to problems associated with regionalization and membership of the Organization. The final chapter of the section provides an evaluation of effectiveness.

4. See Appendix A for breakdown of member states by regions.

5. See *The Second Ten Years of the World Health Organization*, WHO, Geneva, 1968, pp. 398–9; and Douglas Williams, *The Specialized Agencies of the United Nations*, Hurst, London, 1987, p. 254.

6. See Appendix B for breakdown of WHO staff by location and employment category.

8

FORMATION OF THE WORLD HEALTH ORGANIZATION

Scientific progress made during the Second World War was one of the most important influences favouring the establishment of a truly international health organization after the war ended.[1] Together with the desire to build peace on firm foundations came the expectation that, perhaps for the first time, science – which had already given the world two outstanding wartime discoveries in DDT and penicillin – would play a major role in precipitating such a peace. Many believed that the necessary resources would be available for the continued progress of science without interruption because finally there would be no more war. Subsequent difficulties with the new technologies, and the onset of the Cold War, led to this early optimism being reappraised.[2]

Functionalists considered scientific progress and peace as inextricably linked: they felt that a 'working peace system' could be established and that 'science would provide them with the means to do so'.[3]

That functionalist ideas influenced the delegates attending the United Nations Conference on International Organization at San Francisco in 1945 is evident in a memorandum submitted by the Brazilian delegation. This quoted a statement by Cardinal (then Archbishop) Spellman that 'Medicine is one of the pillars of peace'.[4] According to one WHO publication, this memorandum led to the insertion of health in the UN Charter as one of the subjects to be considered by the UN, and later to the joint declaration by Brazil and China recommending that 'a General Conference be convened within the next few months for the purpose of establishing

1. Other factors included: impetus from past international health organizations, perceptions of the relative success of the health organization of the League of Nations as compared to the parent body, and the dismal public health situation in the wake of the Second World War.

2. See 'Science, Technology and American Diplomacy: the Politics of Global Health', Committee on Foreign Affairs, US House of Representatives, Washington, DC, 1971, p. 14.

3. See WHO, *The First Ten Years of the World Health Organization*, Geneva, 1958, p. 38.

4. As quoted in *ibid.*, p. 38. Interestingly enough, Brazil had also initiated the establishment of the health organization of the League of Nations in 1920.

an international health organization [that can be] brought into relationship with the Economic and Social Council'.[5]

The San Francisco Conference unanimously approved the joint declaration.[6] In subsequent deliberations leading up to the formation of the World Health Organization, the notion of health was to be amplified and the health of all peoples was considered 'fundamental to the attainment of peace and security'.[7]

Among the first acts of the newly established (January 1946) Economic and Social Council was its resolution 'to call an international conference to consider the scope of, and the appropriate machinery for, international action in the field of public health and proposals for the establishment of a single international health organization of the United Nations'. The resolution also established a Technical Preparatory Committee (consisting not of states, but of individual health experts) to draft the agenda and proposals for the consideration of an International Health Conference (IHC) that was to follow.[8]

The IHC which convened at New York on 19 June 1946 was the first international conference held under the auspices of the United Nations.[9] All fifty-one members of the United Nations were represented, as were thirteen non-members, the Allied Control Authorities for Germany, Japan and Korea, and ten organizations interested in international public health: the Pan American Sanitary Bureau, the United Nations Relief and Rehabilitation Administration (UNRRA), International Public Health Office, League of Red Cross Societies, International Labour Office, the Food and Agriculture Organization (FAO), UNESCO, the Provisional International Civil Aviation Administration (PICAO), the World Federation of Trade Unions and the Rockefeller Foundation.

Although the IHC was an international gathering, its leadership was provided largely by the developed countries. For example, only two of the six most senior positions at the Conference – President and five Vice-Presidents – were held by developing countries, Brazil and China. The United States, the Soviet Union, Britain and France held the other four. This is not coincidental, as these countries were also to be the major financial contributors to the WHO.

The President of the IHC, Dr Thomas Parran, summarized its

5. OR 1, 1946, p. 39.
6. See WHO, *The First Ten Years*, *op. cit.*, p. 38.
7. See the constitution preamble in *Basic Documents*, 36th edn., Geneva, 1986, p. 1.
8. For the full text of the resolution of the ECOSOC of 5 Feb. 1946, see UN Document E/9 Res. 1, 1946.
9. See Ruth Masters, 'International Organizations in the Field of Public Health', Carnegie Endowment for International Peace, Washington, DC, 1947, p. 24.

task as being 'to prepare a constitution or charter providing for the establishment of a World Health Organization, and to outline its purposes, functions, structure and administrative arrangements and relationships'; the IHC was not expected 'to draft a daily programme of work, or to set up in all detail the methods of operation of the Health Organization'.[10]

Three major developments emerged from the IHC: (1) the constitution of the WHO (which had been drafted by the Technical Preparatory Committee) was signed by all states present, with the exception of Hungary, Iceland and Sweden. Of the forty-eight signing states, all but two (China and the United Kingdom) did so subject to approval or ratification by their own governments;[11] (2) the Office International d'Hygiène Publique (OIHP), an earlier international health organization, was terminated and its functions transferred to the WHO; and (3) pending the coming into force of the constitution of the WHO, an Interim Commission was set up by the IHC to prepare for the permanent organization, to carry out the statutory functions of the previous health organizations and to perform emergency international health work.

The structure of the WHO decided on by the IHC, and outlined in the Organization's constitution, was similar to that of the League of Nations Health Organization. The work of the Organization was to be carried out by: (1) the World Health Assembly (WHA), in which all member states are represented and which determines the policy of the Organization; (2) the Executive Board, which acts as the executive organ of the Assembly; and (3) the Secretariat functioning under the supervision of the Director-General, who is the chief technical and administrative officer of the Organization and is elected by the WHA after nomination by the Executive Board. The Director-General and the staff of the Secretariat are 'international officers' and are forbidden to 'seek or receive instructions from any government or from any authority external to the Organization'.[12]

Although the Interim Commission was established as a temporary measure, it remained in existence for two years, owing to the slow accumulation of the required twenty-six ratifications of the WHO's constitution from member states. While awaiting ratification of the permanent organization, the Interim Commission took health initiatives that could not be postponed. During its lifetime, the Interim Commission produced the first ever international classifica-

10. See UN Document E/H/PV/2, p. 10.
11. See OR 2, 1948, p. 115.
12. Article 37 of the WHO's constitution in *Basic Documents*, *op.cit.*, p. 10.

tion of diseases and injuries, as well as the first single classification permitting internationally comparable morbidity and mortality statistics.[13] The Commission also prepared the agenda for the first World Health Assembly of 1948. Among other items on this agenda was the issue of dividing the world into geographical regions with a view to the eventual establishment of a decentralized WHO. Regional organizations were envisaged in conformity with Chapter XI of the Organization's constitution,[14] which also required the integration of existing and future inter-governmental regional health organizations into the WHO.[15] The decentralization issue was controversial from the beginning, and it became more so the more it was scrutinized.

13. See complete discussion of these and other activities of the Interim Commission in WHO, *The First Ten Years*, *op. cit.*, Chapter 6.

14. For discussion of the WHO's constitution adopted at the International Health Conference, see H. van Zile Hyde, 'The International Health Conference', US Department of State *Bulletin*, 8 Sept. 1946, pp. 453–4, 459; Thomas Parran, 'Chapter for World Health', *Public Health Reports*, vol. 61 (1946), pp. 1265–8; Thomas Parran and Frank G. Boudreau, 'The World Health Organization: Cornerstone of Peace', *American Journal of Public Health*, vol. 36 (1946), pp. 1267–72; and WHO, *The First Ten Years*, *op. cit.*

15. The WHO's constitution speaks of the need for each regional organization to be 'an integral part' of the WHO, while all other inter-governmental regional health organizations in existence prior to the date of signing the constitution are to be 'integrated with the Organization'. See Chapter XI of the WHO's constitution in *Basic Documents*, *op. cit.*, pp. 11–13.

9
THE DECENTRALIZATION DEBATE IN THE WHO

Although it was relatively easy to achieve consensus at the International Health Conference with regard to the WHO's objectives and functions, obtaining agreement about the Organization's structure proved to be more difficult. At present, the WHO is a decentralized organization with six regional organizations, each with its own Regional Director and Regional Committee: Eastern Mediterranean Region, Western Pacific Region, European Region, Americas Region, Africa Region and Southeast Asia Region. The establishment of the decentralized organizational structure, the delineation of areas and the subsequent assignment of countries to those regions were much easier said than done.

Arguments for Regionalization in the WHO

Elements of regionalization in international health work are not restricted to the WHO, but can be discerned in earlier health organizations. The OIHP, which was founded in 1907, did not have its own branch offices or subsidiaries; it was aided in the collection and dissemination of information by three regional bureaus of other organizations: the Alexandria Bureau (of the former Egyptian Sanitary Council), the Pan American Sanitary Bureau (of the Pan American Sanitary Organization) and the Eastern Bureau of the League of Nations Health Organization, at Singapore.[1]

After its foundation in 1920, the League of Nations went further towards regionalization in its health concerns than the OIHP had done. It had an Eastern Bureau at Singapore, whose work was complemented by a sub-bureau at Melbourne. The latter maintained a Secretariat and convened international conferences for public health leaders of South Pacific countries. According to Berkov,

1. See OR 9, 1948, p. 20; Robert Berkov, 'The World Health Organization: a Study in Decentralized International Administration', unpubl. Ph.D. thesis, University of Geneva, 1957, p. 43; A.A. Moll, *The Pan American Sanitary Bureau: 1902–1944*, PASB Publication no. 240, Washington DC, 1948, p. 37. For thorough discussion of the work of the Paris Office see Norman Howard-Jones, *International Public Health between the Two World Wars – the Organizational Problems*, WHO, Geneva, 1978, pp. 13–17; and Ruth Masters, 'International Organizations in the Field of Public Health', Carnegie Endowment for International Peace, Washington, DC, 1947, p. 14.

'These arrangements were strikingly similar to those for regional committees and regional offices which the WHO was later to institute.'[2]

The United Nations Relief and Rehabilitation Administration (UNRRA), established in 1943, went still further towards decentralization: in its two main areas of action, Europe and the Far East, it established regional organizations with decentralized administration and policy-making organs to attend to the differing health needs of the two areas. The policy-making organs, the Committee for Europe and the Committee for the Far East, were made up of representatives of member states in the area and, in addition, of representatives of other governments (such as the USA) with interests in the region.[3] The experience of UNRRA influenced, if not inspired, the system of regional organizations which the WHO later adopted.[4]

Thus the functionalist notion of a decentralized administrative structure, close to the people it serves, has not only persisted with remarkable regularity, but has also been strengthened with each new international health organization.

It was at a session of the TPC, from 18 March to 5 April 1946, that the first significant discussion of the need for regional organizations took place.[5] Some provision for regionalization seemed inevitable since the Pan American Sanitary Bureau (PASB) and the OIHP were already functioning before the WHO was established, while the Health Bureau of the Pan Arab League was just being established.[6] Whether the PASB would be incorporated into the WHO, or merely 'utilized' (as it had been by the OIHP, the League

2. See Berkov, *op. cit.*, p. 46. Also consult Neville Goodman, *International Health Organizations and Their Work*, Churchill Livingstone, London, 1971, p. 257; Masters, *op. cit.*, p. 17; and F.P. Walters, *A History of the League of Nations*, Oxford University Press, 1952, pp. 180-3.

3. Goodman, *op. cit.*, pp. 138–50; Berkov, *op. cit.*, p. 47. For further details on UNRRA, see Larry Leonard, 'UNRRA and the Concept of Regional International Organization', *Iowa Law Review*, vol. 30, no. 4 (1945), pp. 489–514.

4. See Larry Leonard, *International Organization*, McGraw Hill, New York, 1951, p. 461; Berkov, *op. cit.*, p. 49. For a comprehensive treatment of UNRRA's work, see George Woodbridge (ed.) *UNRRA, the History of the United Nations Relief and Rehabilitation Administration*, Columbia University Press, New York, 1950 (3 vols).

5. For a complete discussion, see 'Minutes of the TPC for the IHC' (held in Paris from 18 March to 5 April 1946), United Nations, Oct. 1947.

6. The Pan American Sanitary Organization is now referred to as the Pan American Health Organization, the regional health organization for the Americas. It was founded in 1902 and now constitutes one of the six regional organizations of the WHO. The PASO was made up of the Pan American Sanitary Bureau and the Pan American Sanitary Conference. The former was essentially the Secretariat of the PASO; the latter its governing body. See Moll, *op. cit.*, as a general reference.

of Nations Health Organization and UNRRA), was the main question for the TPC and the ensuing International Health Conference.[7] As Berkov has noted: 'It was generally recognized that the resolution of the problem of the PASB would set a precedent for other regional organizations, existent or contemplated, in relation to the WHO.'[8] Arguments in favour of the decentralization of the WHO included suggestions that the objectives of the Organization might be achieved more effectively by decentralizing its operating arrangements; decentralized administration was more able to remain in touch with reality and with the people it served; decentralization allowed greater ease of coordination of services rendered and enhanced control within a given region; and that it would facilitate cooperative relations with subordinate governmental units.[9]

As evident in the previous discussion, and in what follows, very few arguments were made against the proposed decentralized structure of the WHO. The only vaguely controversial parts of the issue were the timing and extent of such decentralization. There was no discussion of the danger of the regional organization coming under the influence, if not the control, of political or regional blocs. Also ignored by the TPC and the IHC were the considerations that the tasks to be dealt with might not follow compact geographic boundaries, and that administrative separation introduced by geographic division might complicate, rather than simplify, the work. The latter consideration is especially important with regard to the WHO, in view of the peculiar delineations of areas where its regional organizations were later established.

The Process of Decentralization

The representatives at the TPC and the IHC were almost unanimous in the opinion that the existing international health organizations should be replaced by a single organization.[10] It was also agreed, however, that the disparity of health conditions in different parts of the world was one of the several reasons requiring a decentralized organization. Agreement ended there. It was not generally accepted that the regional offices would be established immediately in all parts of the world, or what the exact relationship of these regional offices with the WHO would be.

There were influential individuals who harboured strong suspicions about centralizing power at the expense of regional organiza-

7. See Berkov, *op. cit.*, p. 51.
8. *Ibid.*, p. 52.
9. OR 2, 1948, p. 15.
10. See Howard-Jones, *op. cit.*, p. 81.

tions. Hugh Cumming, an Observer of the PASB at the IHC, was one such individual. At a working dinner for the representatives of PASO member states during the IHC, he cautioned against communist takeover of the new world health organization because of the participation of Eastern European delegates in the deliberations. Some time earlier, in a memorandum to the US Department of State, he had also argued that the desire for a single international health organization was the product of 'an insane desire to destroy existing institutions'. Howard-Jones recounts how Thomas Parran, the US Surgeon-General, 'hastened to assure delegates that Cumming's ill-considered remarks in no way reflected the attitude of the US Government'.[11]

Although the representatives at the TPC were there as individual experts, their opinions concerning the time-frame and extent of regionalization largely reflected the views of their national Health Ministries, in which most of them held office. Indeed, thirteen of the sixteen TPC members were present or past employees of their own Health Ministries.[12] Four of the delegates had submitted proposals for the future constitution of the WHO, including ideas for the regionalization of the Organization. All these proposals were formulated in the respective national Health Ministries, further diluting the idea of experts independent of government influence. The proposals came from Sir William Jameson of Britain,[13] Surgeon-General Thomas Parran of the United States,[14] Dr A. Cavaillon and X. LeClainche of France,[15] and Dr Andrija Stampar of Yugoslavia.[16] The main gist of the four proposals is summarized here.

The British plan suggested the creation of a strong central organization, with regional organizations only responsible for epidemiological intelligence. This plan effectively proposed the removal of most of the mandate of the Pan American Sanitary Bureau.[17] The American plan showed more concern for the future of the PASB than of the WHO, and Dr Parran suggested that the WHO 'enter into arrangements' with regional organizations for the use of their facilities.[18] The establishment of new regional offices was not seriously considered. The French proposal also favoured the technique of contracting with regional agencies for specific services;

11. See List of Members of the Technical Preparatory Committee, Minutes of the TPC, 18 Mar. to 5 Apr. 1946, published 1947, p. 5.
12. See UN document E/H/PC/9.
13. See UN document E/H/PC/6.
14. See UN document E/H/PC/5.
15. See UN document E/H/PC/10.
16. See OR 1, 1946, p. 44.
17. *Ibid.*, p. 48.
18. *Ibid.*, p. 52.

however, it suggested that further regional organizations might be established by the WHO, if needed. No doubt with their own OIHP in mind, the French suggested that the future of existing international health organizations be decided entirely by their own governing bodies, and not by the new WHO. The Yugoslav plan proposed a central organization with regional bureaus, each with a directing committee and small Secretariat.[19]

Regarding the role of the regional organizations, the four plans can basically be reduced to two sets of suggestions. Dr Thomas Parran thought it wise not to delegate functions to regional offices, 'at least until the central machinery was well established'.[20] At the same time, however, he advised that 'The Charter of the World Health Organization should be kept flexible enough to allow all regional organizations to be absorbed into a single administrative structure, or, on the other hand, to encourage regional agencies with a high degree of autonomy.'[21] He added that the WHO should experiment with both choices, with the Pan American Sanitary Bureau falling in the second category: 'the term "single international health organization" does not necessarily contemplate the abolition or absorption of the PASB.' He even suggested that 'friendly competition' between autonomous or semi-autonomous regional organizations might be constructive.[22]

Dr Stampar of Yugoslavia and Dr Cavaillon of France also spoke in favour of regionalization, but without any obvious preference for a time-frame. They disagreed with Dr Parran's autonomy option, advocating the establishment of regional organizations either by decree of the IHC, or 'by [the] transformation of already existing regional organizations'.[23]

Unable to reach a consensus on either plan, the TPC decided to submit both suggestions to the IHC. The Interim Commission had also been unable to define clear-cut criteria for regions after reviewing the four proposals submitted by interested governments. The various proposals were transmitted to the First World Health Assembly without recommendations.[24]

By far the most controversial questions that came before the IHC

19. *Ibid.*, p. 56.
20. Minutes, 2nd meeting of the TPC, 19 Mar. 1946.
21. UN document E/H/PC/21, 28 Mar. 1946.
22. See E/H/PC/21.
23. See E/H/PC/W/II.Add.3, 2 Apr. 1946.
24. For further information respecting the transition, see D.P. Myers, 'Liquidation of the League of Nations', *American Journal of International Law*, vol. 42 (1948), pp. 339–41; and Walter Sharp, 'The New WHO', *American Journal of International Law*, vol. 41, no. 3 (1947), p. 514.

concerned the arrangements to be made for the establishment and functions of new regional offices or branches of the WHO, and the relationship of existing regional health agencies to the WHO. The form that decentralization in the WHO finally took was the establishment of regional organizations rather than administrative decentralization. As mentioned earlier, this form was dictated by circumstances at the time, particularly by the existence of the PASB.[25] The US delegation submitted a resolution advocating the principle of 'dual allegiance',[26] proposing that the PASB should not only promote regional health programmes and undertakings among the American republics 'in harmony with the general policies of the WHO', it should also serve when necessary as the WHO's regional committee in the western hemisphere.[27]

The United States proposal received unqualified support from most of the Latin American states, which wanted to maintain a separate identity for the PASB.[28] This prompted the Egyptian delegate to demand the same consideration for the recently created Health Bureau of the Pan Arab League. However, the delegations from Canada, China, Norway and Britain emphasized the need to integrate the PASB into the WHO. Another group of delegates – from India, Liberia, Poland, South Africa, the Soviet Union, the two Soviet republics (Ukraine and Byelorussia) and Yugoslavia – urged with varying degrees of insistence that all existing regional health agencies should be transformed as quickly as possible into 'regional committees subordinated to the World Health Organization'.[29] The Soviet delegate suggested that the World Health Assembly should unilaterally transform all regional health organizations into regional committees, subordinate to the WHO.[30]

With a view to minimizing the controversy, the IHC appointed a special 'harmonizing sub-committee' of sixteen members to devise a formula acceptable to all parties. After prolonged deliberations, the sub-committee arrived at the following text, which was later approved unanimously by the Conference:

The Pan American Sanitary Organization, represented by the Pan American Sanitary Bureau and the Pan American Sanitary Conference, and all other inter-governmental regional health organizations in existence prior

25. The Pan American Sanitary Bureau is now part of the Pan American Health Organization (PAHO), the regional organization of the WHO in the Americas. The term PASB is today used for the headquarters and Secretariat of the PAHO.
26. OR 2, 1946, p. 23.
27. OR 1, 1946, p. 23.
28. See OR 1, 1946, p. 23.
29. *Ibid.*
30. OR 2, 1946, pp. 23–4. Also see Sharp, *op. cit.*, pp. 509–30.

to the date of signature of this Constitution, shall in due course be integrated with the Organization. This integration shall be effected as soon as practicable through common action based on mutual consent of the competent authorities expressed through the organizations concerned.[31]

The phrases 'in due course' and 'through common action based on mutual consent' left enough room for interpretation to allow an extant regional organization such as the Pan American Health Organization to make integration difficult.

The IHC also gave the Health Assembly authority to define geographical areas for the establishment of regional organizations,[32] and the WHO's constitution accordingly requires that:

(a) The Health Assembly shall from time to time define the geographical areas in which it is desirable to establish a regional organization. (b) The Health Assembly may, with the consent of a majority of the Members situated within each area so defined, establish a regional organization to meet the specific needs of such area. There shall not be more than one regional organization in each area.[33]

Interestingly, the WHO's constitution makes no mention of any criteria to be applied in defining the geographical areas; moreover, it sets no limit as to the total number of such areas.

Administrative power was not fully decentralized by the IHC, which made the regional offices subject to the authority of the Director-General. The regional organizations were given responsibility for carrying out, within the regions, relevant decisions of the Health Assembly and the Executive Board, in agreement with the Regional Committee.

Regional organization was among the earliest issues addressed by the first WHA. The varying opinions regarding the timing and extent of regionalization that had already been aired in the IHC were replayed in the first WHA. Again, there were differences of opinion as to the desirability of defining geographical areas and of establishing regional organizations before the central organization was firmly entrenched. The Irish delegate opined that the WHO could establish services in given regions of the world without necessarily setting up regional offices. He considered only the former an immediate necessity:

The WHO is only a new-born child and in addressing an assembly of eminent medical men, I need not labour the point that one does not expect a child to produce a family until it has reached the age of maturity.[34]

31. OR 1, 1946, p. 24.
32. OR 2, 1946, pp. 23–4.
33. See the WHO constitution, Article 44, in WHO, *Basic Documents*, 36th edn., Geneva, 1986, p. 11.
34. OR 13, 1948, p. 69.

An opposite view, favouring regionalization as soon as it was practicable, was zealously advanced by other delegations. For instance, Dr Hugh Cumming, at the time of writing Director of the PASB, suggested that countries would be more inclined to finance regional health initiatives in which they had a direct interest than international ventures centred at WHO headquarters, run with limited funds.[35] The delegates from China, Egypt and India, Drs Y. Sze, A. Shousha and C. Mani, were also strong advocates of an early delineation of geographical areas and the quick establishment of regional organizations. Unsurprisingly, Drs Mani and Shousha went on to be the first Regional Directors of the Southeast Asia and Eastern Mediterranean Regions of WHO.

Despite pressures to delay the decision, sufficient support was mobilized in the Assembly for the immediate definition of six geographical areas. Three of them – Southeast Asia, Eastern Mediterranean and Western Pacific – were defined by the listing of member states; two were defined by continental boundaries – Europe and the Americas; and only one, Africa, was defined in terms of natural and political boundaries. Regional offices could now be established whenever the member states of a particular region so desired. Neville Goodman, the first of the two Assistant Directors-General of the WHO, later admitted:

> It was perhaps a little premature to establish the regional organizations before the WHO had time to get its central establishment working smoothly, but it certainly stimulated regional interest from the beginning, and ensured that centralization did not become too firmly established.[36]

As will be evident later, 'regional interest' was not always to take a positive form, making many health experts despair over the regional structure of the WHO.[37]

The first Assembly responded to calls for immediate action not only by delineating geographical areas but also by establishing regional organizations. The Executive Board was instructed to accomplish three tasks with all speed: (1) establish a temporary administrative office in Europe to deal with the health needs of war-devastated countries; (2) integrate the Alexandria Regional Bureau into the WHO, pursuant to Article 54 of the constitution; and (3) establish regional organizations in the geographical areas delineated upon receipt of the consent of a majority of the members situated

35. *Ibid.*, p. 68.
36. Goodman, *op. cit.*, pp. 253–4.
37. In our conversations with senior WHO administrators, we found virtually unanimous dissatisfaction with the regional arrangement in the Organization. Personal communications with senior WHO administrators. See list of interviews in Bibliography.

in these areas. By the end of 1951, regional organizations were established and operational in all six geographical areas.

As far as the composition of the regional organizations was concerned, Article 46 of the constitution required that each should consist of a regional committee and a regional office. The Regional Committee, according to Article 47, was to be composed of representatives of member states, with associate members also having right to representation,[38] and possibly to a vote.[39] The nature and extent of the rights to participation of associate members were to be determined by the Assembly in consultation with the members responsible for the international relations of the territories and with the member states in the region.[40]

As of January 1993, there have been twenty-two associate members in the WHO's history; all but two of these (Puerto Rico and Tokelau) have since become independent states and acquired full membership of the WHO. Unless the two remaining non-self-governing territories are denied statehood or full membership in international organizations on becoming independent, the provision in the WHO's constitution concerning associate members will eventually fade into insignificance. Territories such as the Cook Islands, which are defined by the United Nations as associate states, are full members of the WHO. Territories that are essentially colonies, such as Hong Kong and New Caledonia, have never been members of the WHO; their interests are represented by the sovereign powers concerned.

38. Article 8 of the WHO's constitution provides that territories not responsible for the conduct of their international relations may be admitted as associate members upon application by the member or other authority having responsibility for their international relations.

39. Unsuccessful efforts have been made to obtain voting rights for associate members, largely due to fears by member states in the region that the colonial power would gain additional votes. However, the World Health Assembly had previously decided that the former, which were responsible for the international relations of the territories situated in the region, are entitled to participate in Regional Committees on behalf of non-self-governing territories on the same basis as member states, but with only one vote, regardless of the number of such territories under their jurisdiction. Several African states gained independence in 1960, up till which time the majority of their Regional Committee comprised metropolitan states representing their dependent territories in the region. See Howard B. Calderwood, 'The World Health Organization and its Regional Organizations', in *Temple Law Quarterly*, vol. 37, no. 1 (Fall 1963), p. 19.

40. 'Member state' was defined by the second WHA as a state whose seat of government is situated within the region.

10

DIFFICULTIES WITH INTEGRATING THE P.A.H.O.

In view of the goal of producing a single international health organization, the WHO's constitution (under Article 54), approved by the International Health Conference, provided that the Pan American Health Organization (PAHO) be 'integrated' with the WHO as soon as practicable. At the same time the Article recognized the autonomy of the PAHO.[1] There was stiff resistance to integration from some member states which were also members of the PAHO.

The Interim Commission inherited the controversy surrounding the integration of the PAHO. It appointed a committee to negotiate with the Director of the PASB its earliest possible integration into the WHO. However, the PASB was in no hurry to be integrated and, a few months after the IHC, the Directing Council of the PAHO adopted a resolution that was an obvious attempt to present obstacles towards the integration and, by implication, the dissolution of the PASB. It recommended the rejection of any action that might result in: 'affecting the identity of the Bureau, lessening its administrative autonomy, limiting its economic independence, disturbing its essential development and detracting from its character as a continental, coordinated health organization of the people of the Americas'.[2] The Directing Council also advised the American states to add a specific reservation to their ratifications of the WHO constitution, recognizing the supremacy of the PAHO constitution over that of the WHO.

The Pan American Sanitary Conference which met the following January (1947) decided against an obstructionist approach and approved the principle of integration. Formal agreement between the two organizations regarding integration was not to come into force, however, until fourteen of the twenty-one members of the PAHO ratified the WHO's constitution. In effect, the Pan American Sanitary Conference, through the Directing Council and the PASB, agreed to serve as the Regional Committee and the regional office

1. The name 'PAHO' did not come into being till 1958; hitherto the Organization was referred to as the Pan American Sanitary Organization, or the PASO. We use the names interchangeably.

2. As quoted in Howard B. Calderwood, 'The World Health Organization and its Regional Organizations', in *Temple Law Quarterly*, vol. 37, no. 1 (Fall 1963), p. 23.

of the WHO, respectively.[3] It was also agreed that this arrangement could be supplemented with the consent of both parties on the initiative of either of them. This was a first step towards integration.

Full integration still appeared difficult because of the relationship of the PAHO with the Organization of American States (OAS), established when the OAS Charter was adopted in June 1948. The PAHO is the largest specialized organization of the OAS.[4] Article 100 of the OAS Charter states that:

> specialized organizations shall establish cooperative relations with world agencies of the same character in order to coordinate their activities. In concluding agreements with international agencies of a worldwide character, the Inter-American specialized organizations shall preserve their identity and their status as integral parts of the OAS, even when they perform regional functions of international agencies.[5]

Whether the PAHO could continue as an integral part of the WHO and still retain its identity as an inter-American organization was unclear.

Part of the issue was resolved when the PAHO and the OAS reached agreement in 1950 such that the former was recognized as an inter-American specialized organization as well as a regional office of the WHO in the western hemisphere.[6] Calderwood points out that, as a specialized agency of the OAS, the PAHO 'could legally continue to enjoy the fullest autonomy within the limits of the instruments that governed it, including a role as a regional office of WHO'.[7] Yet, at the same time, it was bound to 'take into account' the recommendations made by the Council of the OAS. Thus the PAHO found itself legally bound to two different organizations. In the PAHO–OAS agreement, there is a provision concerning the revision of the agreement by mutual consent and (unlike the WHO–PAHO agreement) it may be denounced on three months' notice by either of the contracting parties.

The paradox of the PAHO being governed not only by its own constitution but also by those of two different organizations was

3. The Pan American Sanitary Conference meets every four years in place of the Directing Council.

4. *Health in the Americas and the Pan American Health Organization*, Committee on Government Operations of the United States Senate, Washington, DC, 1960, p. ix. Also see Neville Goodman, *International Health Organizations and their Work*, Churchill Livingstone, London, 1971, pp. 318–43.

5. Organization of American States Charter, Article 100. Also see Miguel Bustamante, *The PASB: Half a Century of Health Activities, 1902–1954*, PASB, Washington, DC, 1955, p. 45.

6. Calderwood, *op. cit.*, p. 24.

7. *Ibid.*

ultimately reduced to an issue of semantics.[8] The PAHO has been able to continue its relations with both the WHO and the OAS without much difficulty. It has fulfilled its obligations to both organizations remarkably well and, as Berkov notes, the PAHO enjoys 'the same status as the other regional offices' of the WHO.[9]

A solution was also found for the problem of the representation of WHO member states which had interests in the Americas, but which were not members of the OAS. France, the Netherlands and Britain came into this group because of their political interests in French, Dutch and British Guianas, respectively. According to a WHA resolution, the three European countries were entitled to participate in the Regional Committee for the Americas because they were responsible for the international relations of the Guianas.[10] However, the provisions of the OAS Charter did not allow these states any privileges in an organization of inter-American states.

The Directing Council of the PAHO eliminated this dilemma in 1951 by adopting a resolution which was later also incorporated into the rules of procedure of the World Health Organization. Henceforth, all the meetings of the Directing Council of the Pan American Sanitary Conference were also to be considered meetings of the Regional Committee of the WHO, except when constitutional matters were being considered. Furthermore, issues involving juridical relations between the PAHO and the WHO, or other questions relating to the PAHO as an inter-American specialized organization, were to be open to participation by member states in the Americas only. Accordingly, after 1951 the European states were able to attend the meetings of the Pan American Sanitary Conference, and participated with voting rights, except when the exceptions listed above were under consideration.

No further efforts have been made to advance the integration of the PAHO beyond the stage discussed above. While the PASB continues to function as the regional office of the WHO in the Americas, the PAHO is nonetheless a separate and distinct organization in its own right, with its own budget and personnel. The problem of semantics mentioned earlier still exists. However, it is effectively ignored and, in this sense, the integration of the PAHO is one instance of potential conflict within the WHO that has been

8. The PAHO's own constitution had been modified in 1947 generally to complement that of the WHO. See 'Report of the Director of the PASB to the Member Governments of the Pan American Sanitary Organization', Jan. 1947, pp. 9–10.
9. Robert Berkov, 'The World Health Organization: a Study in Decentralized International Administration', unpubl. Ph.D. thesis, University of Geneva, 1957, p. 139.
10. Resolution WHA2.103 is discussed in OR 21, 1949, p. 55.

handled very pragmatically. As Norman Howard-Jones points out: 'Today the PAHO is an international health organization second in scope, usefulness, influence, and prestige, only to WHO, of which it is functionally, if not legally, an integral part.'[11]

The attempts on the part of the WHO to limit politics in the establishment of its regional structure, while remarkable, did not herald the elimination of politicization in other issues involving the regional structure. Such issues have in turn influenced the effectiveness of the administrative apparatus of the Organization. This is discussed below.

11. Norman Howard-Jones, *The Pan American Health Organization: Origins and Evolution*, WHO, Geneva, 1981, p. 20.

11

THE DELINEATION OF REGIONAL BOUNDARIES

When the first Health Assembly delineated the six geographical areas in which regional offices were to be established, it was evident that factors other than geography influenced the boundaries. For example, Pakistan chose to be included in the Eastern Mediterranean area rather than in the Southeast Asia area with its close neighbours, India and Afghanistan. The Pakistani decision was presumably made because the regional office for Southeast Asia was located in New Delhi. Other such anomalies of membership in regions included that of Indonesia and Thailand in the Southeast Asia Region while neighbouring Vietnam was in the Western Pacific; Ethiopia in the Eastern Mediterranean Region rather than in the African region; Morocco in the European Region rather than in the Eastern Mediterranean Region. Greece was originally included in the Eastern Mediterranean Region, but later chose to join the European Region.[1]

Partly with a view to remedying such anomalies, and partly with the hope of minimizing political controversy, the fifth WHA requested the Executive Board and the Director-General to undertake a study of rules and criteria that might be applied to determine the assignment of any territory to a geographical area.[2] Pending the findings of the report, the World Health Assembly decided that countries which were awaiting assignment to regions would provisionally be included in regions of their choice. Territories not yet assigned, and with no obvious preference, were to be provided services through headquarters and assigned to 'Region Undesignated'.[3] This approach suggests that the Assembly felt it easier and more practical to incorporate non-designated territories into the existing regional system rather than to start again with a clean slate, exercising its constitutional authority to define geographical areas 'from

1. See OR 13, 1949, p. 80. Morocco has been in the Eastern Mediterranean Region since 1986.

2. See OR 42, 1952, p. 31. Another reason for this review was the controversy in the Eastern Mediterranean Region, when Israel wanted to continue its membership although this was opposed by a majority of states in the region. This is discussed more fully later in this section.

3. *Ibid*.

time to time'.[4] A conscious attempt was being made to minimize politicization.

The EB drew up two alternative proposals which were submitted to the Assembly. In both proposals geographical proximity, similarity of health problems, economic aspects and administrative considerations were among the possible criteria listed.[5] The only difference in the two plans lay in the weight to be attached to the wishes of the appropriate sovereign authority.

Unable to agree on the criteria, the sixth WHA's decision was indecision, with territories to be temporarily assigned 'on the same lines as hitherto adopted'.[6] In other words, the wish of the sovereign authority in each case was to be the determining factor. The same Assembly assigned thirty-eight territories not responsible for their own international relations to regions on that basis: 9 were assigned to the African area, 2 to the Americas, 1 to Southeast Asia, 6 to Europe, 5 to the Eastern Mediterranean and 15 to the Western Pacific.

Several political questions arose in the assignment of some of the thirty-eight territories. There were, for instance, disputes between Argentina and Britain over sovereignty of the Falkland Islands, and between Britain and Iraq over Bahrain Island. The Assembly chose to avoid the issue of sovereignty by provisionally assigning the territories to certain geographical areas, 'without prejudice to any question regarding sovereignty'.[7]

Another striking example of politics is evident in the case of French Morocco, which became an associate member of the WHO at the same time as Tunisia.[8] Following a proposal by France, Morocco, like Tunisia, was assigned to the European Region.[9] The next (sixth) Assembly, upon a request from Spain, assigned that part of Morocco known as the Spanish Protectorate Zone to the African Region.[10] Not only did this create the obvious administrative problem of Morocco belonging to two different regions, but further difficulties arose from the Arab effort to have French Morocco and Tunisia assigned to the Eastern Mediterranean Region despite the

4. Article 44 of the WHO's constitution, in WHO, *Basic Documents*, 36th edn., Geneva, 1986, p. 11. Those countries which showed a preference were allowed to join the region of their choice. See OR 42, 1952, pp. 117–19.
5. See Resolution EB11.R51 in WHO, *Handbook of Resolutions and Decision, 1948–72*, vol. I, Geneva, pp. 315–16.
6. OR 48, 1953, p. 34.
7. *Ibid.*, pp. 34–5 and 302–3.
8. Both French Morocco and Tunisia were French protectorates at the time.
9. OR 71, 1956, p. 18.
10. OR 48, 1953, p. 34.

fact that the health authorities of both states had asked to be assigned to the European Region. The French insisted that French Morocco and Tunisia were more closely related to Southern Europe in matters of health and economics than to the Eastern Mediterranean, where the Arab delegates felt the two territories belonged because of their close cultural ties.[11] The Arab efforts were unsuccessful.

After independence, both Morocco and Tunisia were admitted to full membership of the WHO in 1956 and were allowed to join the region of their choice. Tunisia joined the Eastern Mediterranean Region and Morocco provisionally joined the European Region. The Moroccan membership of the European Region entrenched the idea that assignment of a country to a region need not necessarily be permanent. The significance of provisional membership was evident in 1986, when Morocco joined the Eastern Mediterranean Region, following the transfer of Israel in 1985 from the Eastern Mediterranean to the European Region.[12]

Another challenge to the WHO's regional system came in 1959 when the twelfth World Health Assembly considered the Soviet request to be permitted to participate in the Southeast Asia Region, in addition to the European Region to which it already belonged. The Soviet delegate emphasized that there were five Soviet republics in Asia which bordered countries of the Southeast Asia Region. In health problems, he said, they constituted a single whole.

The point at issue was whether the metropolitan territory of a member state of the WHO could be represented in two regions simultaneously. Since the five republics concerned were not separate from the mainland politically or geographically, and since they did not qualify either as territories not responsible for their own international relations or as sovereign states, the Assembly decided that they did not fulfil the requirements for membership under the resolution of the second Assembly.[13] The claim for membership was, in the Assembly's opinion, exclusively based on contiguity and therefore not valid. The USSR eventually withdrew its request.

After this incident the Assembly, not wanting to reopen a debate on criteria for regional membership, decided to approve a resolution which merely called for 'a study of the situation of the regional structure'. This issue was essentially dead for the time being.

A poignant remark about the problems originating from the decentralized system in the WHO was made by Sir Arcot Mudaliar of India at a meeting of the Assembly of 1955:

11. OR 42, 1952, pp. 117–19.
12. See OR 71, 1956, pp. 18 and 33.
13. OR 21, 1949, p. 17.

If unfortunately certain trends of a not too happy nature have created difficulties, let us realize that they are not due to any defects of regionalization but to a tendency to push political phobias into what should be a matter of simple professional advice on matters of health.[14]

Sir Arcot's frustration stemmed from belief in the functionalist separation of politics and health.

The regional organization of the WHO nurtured, if not promoted, a milieu in which undesirable national and regional interests could be aired with an annoying frequency. Not only did states raise issues regarding their own status or membership, but the legitimacy of other states' membership of their region or of the WHO proper was also challenged.

14. OR 88, 1955, p. 88.

12

THE DEVELOPMENT OF BLOCS IN THE W.H.O.

Two main types of blocs have developed within the WHO over the years: regional blocs and political blocs. The former are perhaps an inevitable manifestation of organizations which are decentralized or which have large regional programmes and are not unique to the WHO. The latter emerged partly due to a perceived desire on the part of certain states to present a unified front not only in the United Nations but also in the WHO, and partly as a response to the disparity between the financial contributions of states and their voting power.[1]

There is some overlap between the two kinds of blocs, but this is generally limited to issues pertaining to the budget. Although neither need necessarily hinder the technical performance of the WHO, they are both perceived by neutral observers as obstacles to effectiveness in the WHO.

Problems with Regional Blocs

The regional structure of the WHO, while offering the palpable advantage of bringing the Organization close to the people it is meant to serve, has also bred several problems, the most significant of which has to do with the basic structure of the Organization. As Berkov has noted: 'The existence of formally constituted regional organizations, each with its own regional committee and regional office, has made it appear, from time to time, as if the region were the basic unit of all WHO activity.'[2] This seven-organizations-in-one (six regions and headquarters) phenomenon has manifested itself in searching questions regarding the basis of allocation of WHO resources among and within various regions.[3]

1. For instance, the United States contributes 25 per cent of the WHO's budget but at least nominally has only one vote in the WHA: the same as a small country like Kiribati, which contributes a negligible sum.
2. See Robert Berkov, 'The World Health Organization: a Study in Decentralized International Administration', unpubl. Ph.D. thesis, University of Geneva, 1957, p. 145.
3. Since the WHO's headquarters has very little control of influence over the budgets proposed by the regional offices, not much has been done traditionally by headquarters to monitor the expenditures. It was only in the 1980s that the Organization began to encourage programme audits, as opposed to financial audits.

A purely regional approach is evident in various WHO issues, of which perhaps the most obvious is the composition of the WHO's Executive Board. At the Organization's inception, the World Health Assembly was given the responsibility to designate eighteen member states, which would in turn nominate an equal number of delegates to comprise the Executive Board.[4] Although such members have always been under oath to serve in an absolutely personal capacity and not as representatives of their governments,[5] on several occasions various regions have expressed dissatisfaction about what they perceive as an unfair geographic distribution of Executive Board memberships. Composition of the Board has reflected, at different times, two controlling coalitions: during the early 1950s, the Western group of countries formed a majority in the Executive Board; after decolonization, developing countries were in the majority.[6] Table 12.1 quantifies Executive Board membership over the past few decades by bloc of origin. Because of the end of the

Table 12.1. COMPOSITION OF W.H.O. EXECUTIVE BOARD BY NATIONAL ORIGIN (%)

	1950	*1958*	*1967*	*1985*	*1993*
Western	47	39	21	13	26
Socialist	11	6	12	3	6
Developing	42	55	67	84	68

Cold War and the overthrow of the socialist philosophy in the former 'Iron Curtain' states, the 1993 figures in this Table include the former Soviet republics and the Eastern European states allied to them in the 'developing' category. The People's Republic of China and Mongolia are still included in the socialist group.

As early as 1948, an Italian delegate to the Executive Board suggested that 'the Constitution be amended so that the number of members of the EB should be one third of all the members of the

4. According to Article 24 of the WHO's constitution, Executive Board members are to be designated by the World Health Assembly, 'taking into account an equitable geographical distribution'. See WHO, *Basic Documents*, 36th edn., Geneva, 1986, p. 8.

5. In 1968, a constitutional amendment was proposed to change the status of members of the EB from that of individuals to that of government representatives. The proposal gained little support.

6. The size of the Executive Board has increased from eighteen members in 1950 to thirty-two in 1992.

7. See World Health Assembly document WHA1.68, 1948. Also see OR 13, 1948, p. 345.

Organization'.[7] This discontent was also evident at the Health Assembly of 1949, when a memorandum signed by all the member states of the Eastern Mediterranean Region questioned the adequacy of their representation on the Executive Board, in the light of the number of states in the region.[8] The President left the issue for the third World Health Assembly, which was to 'take into careful consideration the arguments and the points of view expressed'.[9]

The next year, the Regional Committee for the Southeast Asia Region also expressed dissatisfaction regarding its representation on the Executive Board. The Committee requested the WHA to increase its representation 'not on the basis of numerical strength, but because of the general importance of the region'.[10] It suggested that the Assembly be guided by such factors as geographic importance, population, magnitude and variety of health problems, and the need of WHO assistance in solving such problems.[11]

By the third WHA, four more countries - Indonesia, Vietnam, Laos and Cambodia - had joined the Southeast Asia Region. The Ceylonese delegate observed that this increased membership in his region rendered its representation on the Board increasingly inadequate. The Lebanese delegate, on the other hand, urged the World Health Assembly to reconsider the representation of the Eastern Mediterranean Region on the Board, along the lines suggested in the 1949 memorandum to the second WHA.[12]

The demands of the regions were not met by the third Assembly, and the issue became more pressing at the fourth WHA. The Syrian delegate claimed that, with two members, the Eastern Mediterranean Region was the 'least adequately represented' on the Executive Board.[13] Strong language was also heard from the Saudi Arabian delegate, who demanded the World Health Assembly take action 'to remedy a deficiency which is no longer admissible and put an end to a situation which can in no way be justified'.[14]

The *status quo* remained unaltered. The Deputy Director-General of the WHO, Dr Pierre Dorolle, had explained to the Assembly that the rules of procedure regarding Executive Board membership

8. In 1949, the Eastern Mediterranean Region only nominated one of the eighteen members of the EB. The same was true of the Southeast Asia and Africa regions. See *Yearbook of the United Nations*, New York, 1949, p. 944.

9. OR 21, 1949, p. 125.

10. Berkov, *op. cit.*, p. 146.

11. OR 25, 1950, pp. 48–9.

12. OR 28, 1950, p. 182.

13. OR 35, 1951, p. 97.

14. *Ibid.*

referred to 'equitable geographical distribution' and 'a balanced distribution of the Board as a whole', but not to regional representation.[15] However, the issue was far from dead.

The WHA of 1953 witnessed a revolt against that year's list of nominations for the Board, from which the Southeast Asia Region had been excluded. A new list of nominees had to be drafted to correct the perceived injustice.[16]

The issue of Executive Board representation has yet to be satisfactorily settled. In the history of the WHO, various proposals have suggested an increase in the size of the Board to reflect a fair balance from the various WHO regions. The steadily increasing membership of the Organization in the past forty years alone is considered by some to be adequate justification for a larger Board. Complaints of under-representation by various regions, while of considerable importance to some states, have been accorded less significance by others.

When a proposal was presented to the ninth WHA (1956) to enlarge the Board from eighteen to twenty-four members, the US delegate said that with regard to the constitutional goal of equitable geographic distribution, proposals for a larger Executive Board were 'too often related to the grouping of the member states into regions for the purposes of the Regional Offices, which did not necessarily require the same distribution as would be desirable in the Board'.[17] Further opposition came from the Indian delegate, who warned that an increase in the size of the Board would create undesirable strife and competition between regions for the additional seats.[18]

Other delegates were ambivalent. For instance, the Liberian delegate opposed the increase in Board membership on the grounds that it 'would seem to indicate that certain members were interested only in their own region'.[19] A few days earlier, following the election of three associate members to the Africa Region, the same delegate said to the World Health Assembly in plenary session:

> We hope the day will come when there will be others who will be able to join that region so that we may have a greater body in the African Regional Organization and can compete with other regions whose votes require three, four or five seats on the EB, as we know from experience.[20]

15. *Ibid.*, p. 159.
16. OR 48, 1953, p. 25.
17. OR 71, 1956, p. 10.
18. *Ibid.*, p. 12.
19. *Ibid.*, p. 15.
20. OR 71, 1956, pp. 25–6. Also quoted in Berkov, *op. cit.*, p. 147.

Although the ninth World Health Assembly decided against any enlargement of Board membership, by the time the twelfth Assembly took place (1959), there was sufficient support among member states (partly due to great pressure from Britain) to increase the size of the Executive Board from eighteen to twenty-four.[21] The increase in WHO membership since 1948 was the official reason given for the change, which was implemented in 1961.[22]

In 1975 the Health Assembly again decided to increase the size of the EB – this time from twenty-four to thirty members. This was justified by the fact that membership of the Organization had grown from eighty-seven in 1959 to 146 in 1975. A new condition was added at this time: 'the Board must contain at least three persons designated by as many Member States from each region.'[23]

As of 1984, each of the regions had at least three members on the Board, except the Southeast Asia Region, which had only two. Accordingly, in order to meet the 1975 constitutional requirement (Article 24) and ensure that the Southeast Asia Region had at least three members on the Board, the 37th WHA increased the Executive Board membership from thirty to thirty-one.[24] A similar increase in Board membership was implemented in 1985 so as to increase the number of Western Pacific Region members on the Board from three to four, and its overall membership from thirty-one to thirty-two.[25] The last two increases in Board membership were approved by the Assembly without any significant deliberation or debate.

The insistence of the regions on greater representation on the Executive Board seems to indicate both bloc sentiments and lack of explicit faith in technical experts. This is disturbing because the nominees to the Board are expected to function free of national or regional loyalties, and because it undermines the theoretical possibility that a government may nominate the national of another country. In practice, the nomination of a Dutch national by Belgium is the only example in WHO history of complete faith in foreign experts.

21. OR 95, 1959, Annex 12.

22. The time-lag between the resolution's passage in 1959 and its implementation in 1961 was due to the requirement for any amendment to the WHO's constitution to be ratified by at least two-thirds of the member governments before it can come into effect.

23. This change was brought about by an amendment to Articles 24 and 25 of the WHO's constitution. See WHA37/1984/REC/1, p. 34.

24. WHA37/1984/REC/1, p. 1.

25. Resolution WHA38.14; see WHO, *Handbook of Resolutions and Decisions, 1985–1986*, vol. III, Geneva, p. 46.

Furthermore, while individual Board members have been known to disagree with their country's position on a given issue, this is certainly not the norm. There have also been occasions when, for example, US members have taken one position when serving on the Board and another when they later represented their government at the Assembly. While it is uncommon overall, it appears that Board members from developed Western countries are more in a position to exercise their personal judgement than are their colleagues from the developing world. Independent action by some members has been taken seriously enough by Western states to attempt, albeit unsuccessfully, a fundamental alteration by constitutional amendment.[26]

Most commonly, Board members reflect the viewpoints of their governments. As Cox and Jacobson have noted, some 'clearly act as instructed representatives'.[27] Since many of them are the architects of their national health policies as Ministers of Health, it would be surprising if this were otherwise. In the 1993 Executive Board, only three members did not hold positions in their own national Health Ministries. The use of the Board as a platform to present purely national or regional viewpoints in an international organization may cause difficulties in presenting unified 'technical' or functional solutions to international health problems. One example of a potential conflict of interest was evident in the late 1970s in Tunisia, where the same person was the director of international relations in the Ministry of Health, the country representative to the WHO and a member of the Executive Board of the WHO. Eventually, this was seen to present constitutional anomalies and was corrected.[28]

Problems with Political Blocs

In 1993, WHO membership comprised 183 full members and two associate members (Puerto Rico and Tokelau). This is a dramatic increase in membership from forty-eight in 1948 and it has led to reorganization among the members, not only in regional blocs but also in political blocs. The members of WHO have organized themselves into the non-aligned group, the Caricom group, the Comecon group, the African group and the Western group. These

26. See R. Cox and H. Jacobson (eds), *The Anatomy of Influence*, Yale University Press, New Haven, Conn., 1973, p. 195.
27. *Ibid.*
28. Personal communication from Richard Symonds, former UNDP Resident Representative in Tunisia, Oxford, 20 Aug. 1988.

groups meet during the WHA to decide common stands on both political and technical health issues that may arise during the Assembly. For example, depending on the issue before the Assembly, the African group of countries can produce as many as thirty or thirty-five votes, compared with one vote for the United States or even some twenty votes for the major, developed states which supply most of the funds of the WHO. In 1985, the fifteen NATO countries paid approximately US$135 million, or 56 per cent of the overall budget of the WHO. Of this figure, the United States alone paid around $61 million, or 25 per cent of the overall budget. The seven Warsaw Pact countries paid about $32 million, or 14 per cent of the total (the USSR being the greatest contributor among these, providing $24 million). Thus the developing countries combined only paid 30 per cent of the total WHO budget.[29]

Numerically, the developing countries are assured predominance in the WHA because it is the only principal organ of the WHO where all member states participate on an equal basis. Each has one vote, and most decisions can be made by a simple majority. Because there exist few barriers to the inclusion of items on its agenda, the WHA has often provided a forum for the discussion of highly controversial issues.

As with the General Assembly of the UN, the egalitarian nature of the Assembly in the WHO makes it the favourite organ of weak states, because it gives them an influence over decisions that they lack in other fora. Thus, whether or not the question before the Assembly involves the WHO's budget, or some specific programmes that these states would prefer to see implemented, the African group becomes a political force when it votes as a bloc. As a response to the increasing Third World membership in the WHA, a number of the Western developed countries have organized themselves outside the WHO's administrative structure into a so-called 'Geneva group'.

The Geneva group is an informal body comprising the following thirteen states: the United States, Japan, Germany, France, Britain, Italy, Canada, Spain, Australia, Sweden, Belgium, Switzerland and the Netherlands. It was first convened in 1964 and is concerned with administrative and fiscal matters relating to the UN specialized agencies.[30] It is believed that the group has striven for a determination of priorities of the WHO's activities. One justification that has

29. See the 38th WHA report, *Status of Collection of Assessed Contributions and Status Advances to the Working Capital Fund*, May 1985.

30. See Jean-Pierre Masset, 'Une non-institution: Le Groupe de Genève', in Société Française pour le Droit International, *Les Organisations internationales contemporaines*, Pedone, Paris, 1988, pp. 205–19.

been offered for the existence of such a group of developed nations outside the WHO's formal organizational structure is that the technical and management skills of those states has become lost in the massive World Health Assembly.[31]

There are other groups too. The Organization of American States was founded in 1948; the Comecon group in 1949. In previous sections we have discussed instances of these groups working as political blocs within the WHO - the former in its obstruction of the integration of the PAHO into the WHO; the latter in the case of the mass withdrawals of the socialist states in 1949–50. Regarding the Comecon bloc within the WHO, Chris Osakwe has observed:

> Ever since their return to the WHO they have never made any secret of their preference for their regional health alliance or of the fact that their continued presence inside the WHO shall to a great extent depend on what the WHO has to offer them in terms of political considerations.[32]

Previous experience has shown that the Comecon bloc lacks sufficient strength to change WHO policy on its own.[33] Thus it has often backed the non-aligned bloc. With the demise of the Soviet Union, the Comecon group faded away.

The Geneva group also does not have enough votes to change Assembly decisions. However, since members of this bloc pay over half the WHO budget, they retain a strong voice in setting limits to certain WHO programmes, such as the Essential Drugs Programme, in lieu of having absolute authority to stop or start the programmes.

Despite their own membership of the Geneva group, the USA has been very critical of the other blocs in the WHO. The political aspects of the blocs, so far as the USA is concerned, permeate the entire UN system: the WHO simply shares this defect because it is part of that system. Henry Cabot Lodge has suggested that the power of the non-aligned bloc, and other such blocs of developing countries, emphasizes the root of the problem: 'the disparity between voting power and financial responsibility'.[34]

31. See F. Quimby, *Science, Technology and the American Government*, Congressional Record Service, Washington, DC, 1971, p. 32.
32. See C. Osakwe, *The Participation of the Soviet Union in Universal International Organizations*, A.W. Sijthoff, Leiden, 1972, p. 122.
33. For some idea of the Soviet bloc view of their role in the WHO and other international organizations, see Wojciech Morawiecki, 'Institutional and Political Conditions of Participation of Socialist States in International Organizations: a Polish View', *International Organization*, vol. 22, no. 2 (Spring 1968), pp. 494–507; and, by the same author, 'Some Problems Connected with the Organs of International Organizations', *International Organization*, vol. 19, no. 4 (Autumn 1965), pp. 913–28.
34. 'UN Weak, Nixon told by Lodge', *Detroit Free Press*, Sept. 14, 1970, p. 2B.

Even if the coalitions discussed above are not as cohesive as the term 'bloc' suggests, and even if they are primarily interested in improving the world health situation, a principal argument against them is the absence of public records of their proceedings. It is feared that, under such circumstances, a self-proclaimed non-political organization can very rapidly become a political one. In 1967 Dr Evang of Norway, an international health expert, criticized the development of blocs in the WHO at the Ciba Foundation Symposium on the Health of Mankind:

> Generally speaking, formation of political blocs of countries operating as such within WHO is not conducive to international health work, regardless of whether such a bloc is composed of developing African countries or of highly developed western countries. A number of the richest countries in the world have set a bad example by forming in Geneva a permanent committee which discusses the problems of international health at a non-technical and political level before the same problems reach the proper bodies of WHO.[35]

Other health specialists, however, do not share this opinion.

While blocs in the WHO have at times been obviously detrimental to the interests of the Organization, senior WHO officials do not consider them wholly undesirable. For instance, the Geneva group is considered by many as a way of reconciling the complaints of the main contributors about the one-member-one-vote situation in the World Health Assembly.

Certain senior WHO officials argue that it is preferable that any political or technical discussion of health-related issues takes place in these blocs rather than appearing *de novo* in the WHA as an unorganized and politically charged motion, completely unfettered by previous discussion. Indeed, there is no question that the bloc discussions previous to, or during, the WHA meetings do play an important role in diluting the political or extremist content of motions put from the floor in the Assembly.[36] With this in mind, the WHO's Secretariat has provided its facilities for these blocs to meet.[37]

The physical proximity of the Secretariat and the bloc meetings

35. K. Evang, *Health of Mankind*, Ciba Foundation Symposium, Boston, Mass., 1967, p. 208.

36. This is one reason why no motion has yet been put forward to expel Israel. The threat in 1982 by the then Secretary of State, George Shultz, to withdraw from, and withold contributions to, any UN organization that expels Israel has undoubtedly also put an end to any attempts to do so. See 'Playing International Hardball – an Aggressive US Stance Begins to Produce Results', *Time*, 1 Nov. 1982, p. 13.

37. Personal communication with a senior WHO administrator

has played a role in keeping the former informed (though usually off the record) of any controversial or unexpected motions about to be raised in the Assembly. This allows time for the Secretariat to prepare for the debate, and/or attempt to dissuade the group from submitting the motion.

13
THE ARAB–ISRAELI DISPUTE

Challenges to Israeli legitimacy in the World Health Organization and in other specialized agencies have stimulated many contemporary charges of politicization against these organizations. Clare Wells has suggested that such challenges have 'become a defining characteristic of the phenomenon [or politicization] as seen from the Western perspective'.[1] As is evident in the discussion that follows, politicization has been present in the WHO from its inception and did not start in the 1970s, as some Western observers claim.[2]

The most persistent political quarrels within the WHO concern the Regional Committee for the Eastern Mediterranean Region. The difficulties faced in that region have intermittently paralysed the operation of its Regional Committee. Two problems, both strictly political and both having their roots in the animosity between Israel and its Arab neighbours, are discussed in this chapter and the next.

The first Arab–Israeli conflict within the WHO began in 1951 when the members of the Arab League decided not to cooperate with Israel in the Eastern Mediterranean Region. The disputants did not bring specifics of the conflict into the WHA, and there was no argument in the Regional Committee, because it had been rendered essentially toothless by the refusal of Arab states to meet with Israel in its sessions. According to Berkov, the problem arose in the following manner:

> When the first WHA delineated the area of the Eastern Mediterranean, it included in that area the territory known as Palestine, then under British mandate. When Israel emerged as a state and was duly admitted to membership in the United Nations, she also sought admission to WHO and was accepted without debate. Even when she requested assignment to the Eastern Mediterranean Region, no objection was raised in the Health Assembly, and the action was completed by the Assembly on June 21, 1949. Israeli representatives attended the meeting of the Regional Committee for the EMed at Geneva in October of 1949, and again in Istanbul in 1950, and the record gives no indication of any controversy in regard to such attendance.

In 1951, however, the Arab League states decided not to cooperate with

1. Clare Wells, *The UN, UNESCO and the Politics of Knowledge*, Macmillan, London, 1987, p. 3.

2. See Victor-Yves Ghebali, 'The Politicization of UN Specialized Agencies: a Preliminary Analysis', *Millennium: Journal of International Studies*, vol. 14, no. 3 (Winter 1985), pp. 317–35. Also refer back to Chapter 1 of the present work.

Israel in any manner, and the Arab state representatives in the WHO region for the EMed declined to meet with Israeli representatives in sessions of the Regional Committee. The Committee held no session in 1951.[3]

This problem remained unresolved until 1985, and it forced the Executive Board and the WHA to experiment with various solutions.

The failure of the Regional Committee to convene deprived the region of a body to review the Regional Director's programme and budget prior to submission to headquarters. Unsurprisingly, this dilemma altered WHO operations in a manner inconceivable to its founders.

As an early solution to the problem, the Arab states proposed that Israel be transferred to the WHO's European Region. Israel rejected this idea on the grounds that it was motivated by political considerations rather than health concerns.

For the first time in the history of the Organization, it was apparent that the question of assignment to regions was intimately related to that of delineation of areas. Since Article 44 of the WHO's constitution required 'the consent of a majority of the Members within each area' for the establishment of a regional organization, a new region could not be created (by the Arab states in this case) until the World Health Assembly had formally delineated a new area.

From 1951 till 1953, no solution was agreeable to all parties concerned. Accordingly, the Regional Committee did not meet in 1951, 1952 or 1953. The sixth WHA, in responding to the Executive Board's recommendation that the Assembly should consider measures to end the stand-off, adopted a resolution which stated that the WHO is 'a technical organization and should not be called upon to determine questions of political character, the settlement of which will not be obtained by a decision of the Assembly'.[4]

Although the Assembly had the option of delineating a new Eastern Mediterranean Region in such a way as to exclude Israel for political convenience or expedience, it did not choose to do so. One author has referred to this incident as another one in a series in which 'the WHA had exercised diplomacy in handling political problems related to health; it continues to reject political solutions to political problems.'[5] The sixth Assembly in fact proposed a novel

3. Robert Berkov, 'The World Health Organization: a Study in Decentralized International Administration', Ph.D. thesis, University of Geneva, 1957, p. 34.
4. OR 48, 1953, p. 35.
5. F. Quimby, *Science, Technology and the American Government*, Congressional Record Service, Washington, DC, 1971, p. 34.

solution in suggesting that the 'regional committee for the EMed should provisionally carry out its duties through being divided into two sub-committees, the constitution of which would be fixed in accordance with the wishes of the countries concerned'.[6] The WHA's intention was that each sub-committee should produce a report which could subsequently be consolidated into a unified report for the region.

Of the two sub-committees, one was to be Arab and the other Israeli in its membership. In addition, each would include any other states from the region that wished to join. The establishment of the two sub-committees was to be carried out by correspondence and consultation, since the Arab states refused to meet with Israel.

To establish the sub-committees, the Director-General was authorized by the World Health Assembly to ask each member state of the region whether it found the two sub-committee idea feasible and, if so, which sub-committee, A or B, it preferred to join. Provisions were made for those member states wishing to participate in both sub-committees, while retaining only one vote, to be cast in one or the other sub-committee.

Ten Arab states accepted the proposal and chose to join sub-committee A, which was to meet in Alexandria, an Egyptian city from which the Israelis would be barred. Britain, France and Italy, which were members of the Eastern Mediterranean Region by virtue of their dependent territories in the area, chose to attend meetings of both sub-committees.

Initially Israel made no objection to the passage of the proposal for two sub-committees at the sixth WHA; however, later the Director-General received a letter from Israel objecting to the procedure adopted for implementation of the sub-committees and making it clear that Israel would not join sub-committee B. The objection was made on constitutional grounds, based on Israel's belief that a Regional Committee meeting 'by correspondence' was contrary to the spirit of the WHO constitution.[7]

Both the French and British governments, when informed of the Israeli refusal to join sub-committee B, withdrew their offer to participate in it. The British felt that without Israel, a member state of the region, neither sub-committee could be considered to comprise the full committee. Only Italy was left willing to participate in sub-committee B.

After these developments, the Director-General concurred with

6. OR 48, 1953, p. 35.
7. For full details, see 'Report by the Director General on the Regional Committee for the Eastern Mediterranean', OR 52, 1954, document EB13/49.

the British opinion that it was impossible for a meeting of sub-committee A to take place without a meeting of sub-committee B. Therefore, on 15 September 1953 he postponed the meeting of sub-committee A until such time as a meeting of sub-committee B was also possible.[8]

Egypt, Iraq, Jordan and Syria took great offence at the DG's decision, accusing him of exceeding his authority and enabling Israel to impose a 'veto' on the action of the Assembly.[9]

The seventh WHA, which met in May 1954, reintroduced the sixth Assembly's suggestion, but with a new twist: it proposed the establishment of two sub-committees, arrived at a procedure for the two meetings and declared that if only one of the sub-committees was able to meet, its 'opinion' should be transmitted to the Executive Board.[10]

Eleven members of the region, including the Arab states, opted to attend the meeting of sub-committee A in Alexandria. Israel was to attend the meeting of sub-committee B at Mogadishu, Somalia. France, Italy and Britain decided to attend both meetings.

Finally, however, Israel chose not to attend the sub-committee B meeting.[11] As a result, the representatives of France, Italy and Britain decided not to attend the meeting either, and chose to exercise their right to vote at the meeting of sub-committee A instead.[12]

Next year these events were repeated. Once more, a majority of the states insisted on convening sub-committee A in Beirut, where Israel would not be welcome. Britain, France and Italy were once more willing to participate in both sub-committees, and agreed that the two meetings should coincide in time and place.[13] The meeting of sub-committee B was again scheduled to convene in Mogadishu, and again Israel chose not to take part. Britain, France and Italy once more exercised their right to vote in sub-committee A, and the meeting of B was cancelled.[14]

The eighth WHA attempted one other permutation of the idea of two sub-committees: the Director-General tried to end the impasse

8. *Ibid.*
9. Letters from Egypt, Iraq, Jordan and Syria are reproduced in document EB13/49, *op. cit.*, pp. 18–23.
10. OR 55, 1954, p. 29.
11. In fact sub-committee B, which included Israel, did not meet at all in 1954, 1955, 1956 or 1957.
12. The meeting of sub-committee A was held as scheduled, from 27 September to 1 October, with fourteen of the fifteen member states of the region represented. See OR 59, 1954, p. 97.
13. OR 67, 1955, p. 97.
14. *Ibid.*

by offering facilities for both sub-committees to meet in Geneva. Israel agreed to this plan, but the Arab states were determined to meet in Beirut. With the Geneva possibility exhausted, Israel subsequently declined to go to Mogadishu and thus once again there was no meeting of sub-committee B.[15]

The ninth World Health Assembly had no new ideas on how to resolve the problem; it simply requested all concerned 'to continue their efforts with a view to giving the resolution full effect'.[16] It was not likely that the Assembly's hope would be realized in the near future, especially since the Arab states had successfully excluded Israel from regional deliberations in which all other states in the Eastern Mediterranean Region had participated.

There was no meeting of sub-committee B until 1958, primarily because Israel had questioned the legality of the arrangement and was unwilling to meet unless one or more of the member states in the region met with its representative.[17] However, as before, the meetings of the two sub-committees could not be coordinated geographically or temporally. The political polemics between the two sides continued. Sub-committee B met every year from 1958 till 1967, inclusive. It did not meet at all from 1968 onwards.

Although the WHA did not *de jure* accept the deliberations of sub-committee A as those of the Eastern Mediterranean Regional Committee, this was the case *de facto*. As early as 1955, a Lebanese delegate to the World Health Assembly had expressed the view that: 'we can now conclude that this subcommittee represents the Regional Organization of the EMed as a whole, mainly due to the absence of subcommittee B, and that its resolutions should be considered as coming from the Regional Committee itself.'[18] In fact, as of 1954 onwards, the Regional Director of the EMed presented an 'opinion' to the WHA that was basically a sub-committee A document but was treated as a Regional Committee report.

This situation continued until October 1984, when Israel demanded to be allowed to attend meetings of sub-committee A in Tunis. However, the Director-General informed Israel that this would not be possible due to political exigences, and after some communication the Israeli government decided to give up its demand. In a letter addressed to the Director-General, the Israeli

15. OR 69, 1956, pp. 39–40.
16. OR 71, 1956, p. 38.
17. Howard B. Calderwood, 'The WHO and Its Regional Organizations', *Temple Law Quarterly*, vol. 37, no. 1 (1963), p. 21.
18. OR 63, 1955, pp. 426–7.

Permanent Representative expressed the views of his government:

> [although] Israel strongly believes that its natural place is in the EMed region, at this stage, it has no alternative but to request you formally to present to the next WHA the necessity to transfer Israel to the European region where many of its medical organizations are already active and where it would be allowed, at long last, to participate on equal footing in regional activities as all other WHO Member States.[19]

Thus, what Israel had refused to do in 1951 it asked to be done in 1984.

The 38th WHA, which met in May 1985, considered the Israeli request for transfer. Other than a brief comment by the Soviet delegate, no discussion or debate was offered by the other delegates and the resolution was passed within minutes.[20]

19. Letter to the WHO Director-General, Halfdan Mahler, dated 7 Sept. 1984, annex to document A38/4, 38th WHA, 1985.
20. Resolution WHA38.1, *Handbook of Resolutions and Decisions, 1985–1986*, vol. III, WHO, Geneva, p. 44.

14

TRANSFER OF REGIONAL HEADQUARTERS FROM EGYPT

Following the 1978 Camp David Accords between the United States, Egypt and Israel, several Arab and Muslim states severed diplomatic relations with Egypt. This also affected the workings of the EMed regional office, as it had been located in Alexandria since 1951. As of 1979, all the Arab states in the region boycotted the meetings of sub-committee A in Alexandria, and in the 32nd WHA (1979) a decision was made to study the effects of a possible transfer of the regional headquarters from Alexandria to another of the countries in the region, as requested by nineteen members of the EMed Region. There was no doubt as to the political motivation behind this request.

Relocation of the regional office from Alexandria required the consideration of a number of legal, operational, financial and technical aspects. In particular, the following points were examined by a Working Group established by the WHA in 1979:

- authority and procedure for determining the site of the regional office of a regional organization;
- coordination with the UN and interested specialized agencies;
- termination of staff contracts;
- transitional difficulties for operations; and
- questions arising from the abrogation of the existing Host Agreement with Egypt.

The first of these has been discussed earlier. Suffice it to say that Article 44 of the WHO's constitution allows the majority of states within a region to decide the location of its headquarters. The second question was more complicated. The Organization has always consulted with the UN, through the Administrative Committee on Coordination (ACC), on the location of any of its regional offices.[1] This is required under Article XI (2) of the agreement between the United Nations and the WHO, which states that: 'Any

1. The ACC was set up in 1947 to assist in the 'taking [of] all appropriate steps, under the leadership of the Secretary-General, to ensure the fullest and most effective implementation of the agreements entered into between the United Nations and the specialized agencies'. For greater detail about the ACC, see Martin Hill on 'The Administrative Committee on Co-ordination', in Evan Luard (ed.), *The Evolution of International Organizations*, Thames and Hudson, London, 1966, p. 104.

regional branch offices which the World Health Organization may establish shall, so far as practicable, be closely associated with such regional or branch offices as the United Nations may establish.'[2] Similarly, the cooperation agreement concluded by the WHO with the FAO and UNESCO provides that these agencies:

> agree to keep each other informed of plans for the initial establishment and relocation of regional and branch offices and to consult together with a view, where practicable, to entering into cooperative arrangements as to location, staffing and use of common services.[3]

Since it was not clear why a transfer of the WHO's EMed regional office to a neighbouring country should inconvenience any other UN agency, no conflict with the cooperation agreements was anticipated by the member states insisting on the move. Neither was the question of termination of staff contracts considered a major obstacle to the transfer. It was expected that most of the professional staff in Alexandria would be offered, and would accept, reassignment to the new site of the regional office, if the move were decided. Many of the general service staff would probably not be able to accept reassignment to the new location even if reassignments were offered, as the UN had done in the case of the transfer of the Economic Commission for Western Asia (ECWA) from Beirut to Baghdad.[4]

There would undoubtedly be important repercussions on the work of the regional office for some time before, during and after the move. Over the thirty years that the regional office had been operating in Alexandria, the Organization had built up a well-trained, experienced, loyal and dedicated general service staff whose cumulative knowledge and experience could not be replaced in a short time. Thus the Working Group concluded that should a definite decision concerning the transfer of the regional office to another country be taken, some disruption of its work was likely to arise in the interim period because of staff resignations and other hitherto unforseen reasons. Such disruption, even if restricted to a minimum, could exert a significant negative impact on the implementation of the technical cooperation programme in the region.[5]

2. See *Repertory of Practice of UN Organs*, vol. III, Article 63, para. 182.
3. Article X of the Agreement with FAO: WHO, *Basic Documents*, 36th edn., Geneva, 1986, pp. 54–7.
4. See UN Document A/34/7 Add. 5, para. 4(b). The termination of the general service staff contracts at Alexandria was estimated to imply an expense of US$400,000, according to the Egyptian delegate.
5. WHA32/1979/REC/1, p. 48.

The most important consideration for the Working Group, however, was that of the Host Agreement with Egypt.[6] At the time, there was no precedent in WHO history for the renegotiation or abrogation of clauses of the Host Agreements. In treading new ground, the Working Group was unable to decide whether or not the WHO had any legal obligations to the host state with regard to leases, staff contracts and so on before a transfer could be implemented. The Working Group recommended that the final decision be made by the Health Assembly or, if that body wished, by the International Court of Justice.[7]

Having boycotted meetings in Egypt, the states interested in moving the regional office convoked a meeting of sub-committee A in Geneva in May 1980. Twenty EMed member states attended the meeting and, after considering Cyprus, Iran and Pakistan as possible locations for the new regional office, agreed on Amman in Jordan as the ideal site.[8] Moreover, in view of the fact that the majority of the states in the region had severed diplomatic relations with Egypt, they voted to: 'completely boycott the Regional Office in its present location and not have any dealings with it, as from today, 19 May 1980'. The resolution added that in future the countries in the region would deal directly with WHO headquarters in Geneva, through the Director-General, for the implementation of the health projects approved by the states, without any 'interference from the Regional Office' till the transfer was complete.[9]

Following this move, the 33rd WHA decided to submit the question of the transfer (originally considered by the Working Group) to the International Court of Justice for its advisory opinion. The Court delivered its opinion on 20 December 1980:

> The present [Host] Agreement may be revised at the request of either party. In this event the two parties shall consult each other concerning the modifications to be made in its provisions. If the negotiations do not result in an understanding within one year, the present Agreement may be denounced by either party giving two years' notice.[10]

6. The agreement between the WHO and Egypt in 1951, commonly called the 'Host Agreement', corresponds to Article 29 of the Headquarters Agreement concluded in 1948/9 between the WHO and the Swiss government. The latter served as a model for the former.
7. This option is explicitly spelled out in Article 76 of the WHO's constitution: 'the Organization may request the International Court of Justice for an advisory opinion on any legal question arising with the competence of the Organization.' See *Basic Documents*, *op. cit.*, p. 17.
8. Resolution EM/RC-SSA 2/R.1.
9. WHA33/1980/REC/1, p. 81.
10. For a summary of the Court's opinion, see WHA34/1981/REC/1, annex 2.

Naturally, with the exception of Egypt, the requirement of a two-year notice was not well received by the sub-committee A states, who persisted in attempts towards a speedier resolution of their wishes.

At the World Health Assembly which followed a few months after the Court's opinion, nineteen members of the Eastern Mediterranean Region submitted a draft resolution asking formally for permission to transfer the regional office to Amman. There followed heated argument on whether a majority of countries in a region could transfer their regional office for purely political reasons. Mr El Reedy, the Egyptian delegate, warned against hasty action, adding that 'the present rift in the Arab Nation is only temporary'. He went on to say that Alexandria was the most suitable and least expensive site for the regional office.[11] Egypt estimated that a transfer of the office would entail an additional expenditure of US$3 million in the first year alone.[12]

Perhaps the most compelling argument offered by the Egyptian delegate against the transfer dealt with the motivation behind the action:

> if WHO were to commit itself to a course with far-reaching consequences merely in order to meet a politically motivated demand, it would be setting a precedent for yet another transfer of the Regional Office, if political vicissitudes in the new host country should suggest it. A precedent would also be established for other organizations; and potential host countries would lose confidence in the face of such a decision.[13]

The American delegate stated that

> there was no reason in international law or international practice, no technical reason, and no reason in the attitude of the Egyptian Government to prevent the Regional Office in Alexandria from being used fully by all Member States of the Region.[14]

Arguments in favour of the proposed move were forwarded mainly by the nineteen sponsors of the draft resolution, but they were supported by the Soviet Union and many developing countries. The delegate from Kuwait questioned the jurisdiction of the International Court over what he referred to as a 'purely regional matter'. The Libyan delegate supported his Kuwaiti colleague, saying that because the regional office was located in Alexandria, the Regional Committee had been unable to meet in 1980 and its functions

11. WHA34/1981/REC/3, p. 255.
12. *Ibid.*, p. 256.
13. *Ibid.*
14. *Ibid.*, p. 261.

had consequently been paralysed.[15] He added that 'the arguments advanced against the transfer were specious and paternalistic, and they showed some contempt for the judgement of the majority of sovereign states in the Region.'[16]

Iran was the only country which openly admitted that, 'because of the Camp David agreements', it was strongly in favour of the transfer of the regional office from Alexandria; but it was not willing to support the transfer to Amman because 'there could be no guarantee that the Jordanian government would not in the future adhere to the Camp David agreements.' He said that right from the outset of the Iran–Iraq war, Jordan had supported the latter and so could not be trusted.[17]

The transfer debate produced a deadlock at the World Health Assembly of 1980; however, at the 34th Assembly the next year a second draft resolution on the issue was tabled by fourteen countries, none of which were members of the Eastern Mediterranean Region. The resolution proposed a further study of the opinion of the International Court for consideration and recommendation to the 35th WHA in 1982. This was an obvious delaying tactic and was recognized as such by the Iraqi delegate, who stated that

> it was to be regretted that, after a delay of two years, 14 countries not concerned with the Eastern Mediterranean Region should have submitted a draft resolution which was contrary to the wishes and interests of the States in the Region.

He accused the sponsors of the resolution of wanting to 'cause delays which would dilute the issue'.[18]

The Egyptian delegate, as expected, approved of the new draft resolution, calling the original resolution undemocratic. He pointed out that Egypt represented one-third of the Arab world and its one vote had much greater symbolic and practical significance than was appreciated by the states calling for a transfer. He continued on the demographic theme, observing that

> since Iran had made it known that it wished the Regional Office to be transferred not to Amman but to some other location, it could be concluded that at least half of the population in the Eastern Mediterranean region opposed the transfer as recommended.[19]

15. The fact that the 'Regional Committee' and 'sub-committee B' were being treated in this discussion as one and the same is relevant to the Arab–Israeli issue discussed in the previous section. In fact sub-committee A had met in Geneva in 1980.
16. WHA34/1981/REC/3, p. 258.
17. *Ibid.*
18. *Ibid.*, p. 274.
19. *Ibid.*, p. 278.

The discussion was finally drawn to a conclusion with a compromise at the next meeting. The draft resolution of the fourteen states was amended so that it instructed the Director-General to 'initiate action' on the 'negotiations' with Egypt for the transfer and 'report the results to the 69th session of the Executive Board in January 1982 for consideration and recommendation to the 35th WHA in May of the same year'.[20]

The Director-General accordingly sent the WHO's legal counsel as his personal representative (PR) to Egypt to discuss the issue. The PR pointed out to the Egyptians that the consultations required under paragraph 51 (of the opinion of the International Court) related to four points: the conditions, the modalities, the practical arrangements and the period of notice for the transfer of the regional office to a new site. Recognizing opportunities for legal gymnastics, the Egyptian government expressed its unwillingness to discuss anything except the theoretical modalities under which the regional office might be transferred out of Egypt. The absence of a clear decision from the Health Assembly regarding a transfer was given as the reason for Egypt's reluctance even to consider all four points raised by the Director-General's PR.

Not only did Egypt undermine the PR's mission, it also preempted any possibility of a clear-cut directive from the WHA in favour of transfer. The Egyptian government added further legal obstacles to transfer by listing criteria that had to be met prior to any cancellation of the Host Agreement or violation of the spirit of international health cooperation. It envisaged the following conditions as necessary before any legal transfer of the regional office:

- technical failure of the office to carry out its duties;
- failure on the part of the host country to meet obligations laid down in the Host Agreement;
- global restructuring of the Organization; and
- a unanimous understanding between all members of the region that, for technical reasons, a transfer would lead to a better performance of the office.

The Egyptian government also stressed the necessity of obtaining from the new host government formal assurances which would safeguard the stability of the Organization and maintain the continued proper performance of its functions. Without a comprehensive feasibility study which would cover these issues, and provide

20. WHA34/1981/REC/1, p. 54.

possible solutions, the government felt that the WHA was not competent to pronounce judgement on questions of a possible transfer.[21]

The Egyptian position generated three different draft resolutions at the 35th WHA in 1982. The first was sponsored by the Arab states and called for a transfer of the EMed regional office from Alexandria to Amman, giving the Director-General a period not longer than six months to effect the transfer. The second was sponsored by Belgium, the Central African Republic, Colombia, West Germany, Ivory Coast, Luxembourg, Malawi, Norway, Peru, Swaziland, Tonga and Zaire. It called for a 'comprehensive study on all the implications and consequences of relocating the Regional Office for the Eastern Mediterranean from its present site in Alexandria to another site in the region'. The third draft resolution was sponsored by Botswana, Rwanda, Samoa and Zambia, and called for the continuation of consultations with the government of Egypt regarding the transfer, while at the same time asking the Director-General to initiate *ad hoc* temporary arrangements, including the setting up of an operational sub-office in a suitable place in the region.[22]

The American delegate, Dr John Bryant, called the first draft resolution undesirable and the third impractical. He summarized the main arguments against any proposal to set up an interim subsidiary office by saying that: such a measure was unnecessary, since headquarters provided support functions; the decision would explicitly acknowledge the validity of the proposal to move the regional office; Article 44 of the WHO's constitution specified that there should not be more than one regional office in each area; and confusion would result from any attempt to have a subsidiary office assume functions properly carried out by the regional office. Therefore he favoured the second draft resolution, calling for an in-depth study of the problem.

The Arab countries made their dissatisfaction with the compromise (second) resolution evident. However, a secret ballot vote resulted in that same resolution being approved by 57 votes to 37, with 21 abstentions.

The Director-General submitted a comprehensive report on the implications of the transfer to the 36th WHA in 1983. At that time, another resolution was passed which asked the Director-General to continue yet more consultations with Egypt about the transfer and

21. WHA35/1982/REC/1, annex 2, p. 56.
22. WHA35/1982/REC/3, pp. 206–7.

to report back to the 37th WHA. There was no discussion on the matter.[23]

The next year, at the 37th WHA, the Director-General was again asked to continue his discussions with the Egyptian government, but no specific time was mentioned for him to report back to the Health Assembly. Having dragged on for five years, the perpetual 'discussions with the Egyptian government' served to wither away the resolve for transfer, a process that was reinforced as many Arab states re-established diplomatic relations with Egypt.

23. See Resolution WHA36.18, *Handbook of Resolution and Decisions, 1973–84*, vol. II, WHO, Geneva, 1985, p. 260.

15

AMERICAN AND SOVIET PARTICIPATION

Membership of the WHO has almost always been greater than that of the United Nations proper. The greatest difference between the size of the two memberships was in the period 1950–4, when the WHO had twelve more members that the UN in 1950 – and nineteen more in 1954. At other times, the WHO has had at most four more members than the UN.[1] As of 1993, the WHO has 183 full members and two associate members (Puerto Rico and Tokelau).[2] Since the end of 1991 alone, the former Soviet Union, Czechoslovakia and Yugoslavia have dissolved, resulting in sixteen new member states for the WHO. The fact that today virtually every nation-state is a member of the WHO is not something that was achieved easily. The most serious instances of politics and controversy entering the work of the World Health Organization are evident in issues involving the withdrawal, or exclusion, of states from membership.

As indicated earlier, the aspiration of public health experts to create a single international health organization with universal membership was undisputed at the Technical Preparatory Committee.[3] It was feared that any failure by the WHO to achieve universal membership could lead to a situation like the one in which the League of Nations Health Organization had found itself: the United States was not a member, and member states such as Germany and Japan withdrew from the Health Organization when they cut ties with the League itself.[4] Thus it seemed crucial for the World Health Organization to deal with any problems over membership in a very flexible, if not relaxed, manner. As will become clear, ideology and politics did not make this easy.

1. See WHO, *Basic Documents*, 36th edn., Geneva, 1986, pp. 155–8; A. Roberts and B. Kingsbury (eds), *United Nations: Divided World*, Oxford University Press, 1988, pp. 261–5.
2. See Appendix 1 for a full list of WHO member states with their dates of admission to the Organization.
3. In fact, the four draft proposals of the future WHO constitution submitted by Britain, the United States, France and Yugoslavia to the Technical Preparatory Committee showed remarkable similarity in this respect. See Howard Calderwood, 'The Founding of a Single International Health Organization', *WHO Chronicle*, vol. 29 (1975), p. 435.
4. See Charles Allen, 'World Health and World Politics', *International Organization*, vol. 14, no. 1 (1950), p. 33.

Early Obstacles to American Membership

Despite the functionalist separation of the health and political spheres by numerous delegates during the early deliberations to establish the World Health Organization, the two spheres frequently overlapped. Even as early as the International Health Conference of 1946, ideological concerns were prominent in national perceptions of the responsibilities of the new Organization. One example of such concerns at the IHC was the debate over health insurance.

Although there was general agreement about the role of the World Health Organization in improving health-care for the poor, the United States vehemently opposed WHO involvement in what was referred to as 'socialized' medicine.[5] The American delegate felt that health insurance should be left to the exclusive jurisdiction of the International Labour Organization. However, the Soviet Union and several Scandinavian and other European countries with national health insurance programmes argued that health and social security were inter-related, and thus a concern for the World Health Organization.

A compromise was reached by limiting the role of the WHO in social security matters to fact-finding, analysis and reporting in collaboration with other interested agencies. Yet even this degree of involvement was not acceptable to some American groups, and 'evidently contributed to the two-year delay in US ratification of the WHO Constitution'.[6]

There were other obstacles to American ratification too. The fact that the WHO's constitution could be amended without concurrence from the United States, merely by a two-thirds vote in the WHA and acceptance by two-thirds of WHO members, was a cause of concern for the US Congress.[7] Unsurprisingly, therefore, and in contrast to the decision of all other countries who became members of the WHO, the ultimate American ratification was not unconditional - the USA reserved the right to withdraw from the WHO at a year's notice, and made it clear that the Organization's constitution would not commit the country to enact any specific legislative programme:

5. The Americans were very sensitive to the term 'social medicine', and for ideological reasons preferred to refer to 'public health'.
6. See Allen, *op. cit.*, p. 38.
7. See US Congress, 'Providing for Membership and Participation by the US in the World Health Organization and Authorizing an Appropriation Therefor', 80th Congress, 1st session, 1947, S. Report 421, p. 7.

> The President is hereby authorized to accept membership for the United States in the World Health Organization. The Congress does so with the understanding that, in the absence of any provision for withdrawal from the Organization, the United States reserves its rights to withdraw from the Organization on a one-year notice: Provided, however, that the financial obligations of the United States to the Organization shall be met in full for the Organization's current fiscal year. [Also] the Congress does so with the understanding that nothing in the Constitution of the World Health Organization in any manner commits the United States to enact any specific legislative program regarding any matters referred to in said Constitution.[8]

The US reservations were significant in the light of the absence from the WHO constitution of any provision for terminating membership.

The Credentials Committee of the WHO was undisturbed by the US reservation.[9] On 2 July 1948 the issue came up for discussion in the first WHA. Other countries who were already members avoided legalistic stances in favour of realistic ones with regard to American membership. Sir William Jameson of Britain and Sir Dhiren Mitra of India emphasized the importance of US participation in international health activities. They accepted at face value the assurances given by the American delegate, Dr Parran, of his government's sincere commitment to the World Health Organization. Sir Dhiren even suggested that an 'unwilling Member might withdraw in one of many ways [and the US] provision for termination on a year's notice [might] be considered a more straightforward method than other possibilities'.[10] The Soviet delegate, Dr N. Vinogradov, 'in a speech that kept everyone on tenterhooks until its concluding sentence',[11] proposed that the United States 'be accepted for membership'.[12] Accordingly, it was admitted as a full member.

The fact that the United States, in setting a precedent by creating an exception for itself, did not rouse controversy reflected the importance attributed to US participation in the WHO. An obvious attempt was made by the World Health Assembly to strive for

8. United States Code, title 22, Government Record Office, Washington, DC, pp. 4477–8. Also see Legal Note, 'The US Reservation to the Constitution of the WHO', *American Journal of International Law*, vol. 44 (1950), p. 122.

9. Howard B. Calderwood, 'The WHO and Its Regional Organizations', *Temple Law Quarterly*, vol. 37, no. 1 (Fall 1963), p. 10. Also see F. Quimby, *Science, Technology and the American Government*, Congressional Record Service, Washington, DC, 1971, p. 26.

10. OR 13, 1948, p. 78.

11. See Neville Goodman, *International Health Organizations and Their Work*, Churchill Livingstone, London, 1971, p. 202.

12. OR 13, 1948, p. 77.

universality in membership. Practically speaking, the new organization could not afford to lose the technical and financial contribution that the United States could offer; by approving full membership for the United States, it acknowledged the American reservations while at the same time rejecting any formal provisions entrenching them into its constitution.

Why such practicality? In his analysis of the Credentials Committee debate on US membership, Chris Osakwe suggests that the 'US got away with its reservation' because the WHA was dominated by medical doctors who preferred practical solutions to any strictly legal considerations.[13] Nothing came of the Indian proposal mentioned earlier, and when withdrawals did occur, neither the departing member states nor the WHA of the day acknowledged that any precedent had been set by the US reservations.

Soviet Bloc Withdrawal and Return

The Soviet Union had joined the WHO in 1948, by which time it was a member of only three other specialized agencies: the Universal Postal Union (UPU), the World Meteorological Organization (WMO) and the International Telecommunication Union (ITU). In other words, the Soviet Union largely abstained from UN work in social and economic fields in the early years of the United Nations system.[14]

Within six months of its foundation, the World Health Organization suffered a severe political blow to its desire for universal membership. The withdrawal of the Soviet Union and the other Cominform countries in 1949/50 and their re-entry several years later is summarized here.[15]

Immediately before the start of the third session of the Executive Board on 21 February 1949, virtually identical telegrams were received from the Deputy Ministers of Public Health of the Soviet Union, the Ukraine and Byelorussia, announcing that their governments no longer considered themselves members of the WHO. There was no apparent forewarning of these drastic actions. The text of the Soviet telegram ran as follows:

> I have the honour to inform you that the Health Ministry of the USSR and the medical institutions and organizations under it are not satisfied

13. See *The Participation of the Soviet Union in Universal International Organization*, A.W. Sijthoff, Leiden 1972, p. 109.

14. See Harold K. Jacobson, *The USSR and the UN's Economic and Social Activities*, University of Notre Dame, Ind., 1963, p. 13.

15. Also see *ibid.*, pp. 142–4.

with the work of the WHO. Tasks connected with international measures for prevention and control of diseases and with the spread of medical science achievements are not being accomplished by the Organization satisfactorily. At the same time maintenance of the Organization's swollen administrative machinery involves expenses which are too heavy for Member States to bear. All this shows that the direction taken by the activities of the Organization does not correspond to those tasks which were set before it in 1946 at the inaugural conference of the Organization. In view of the above, the USSR no longer considers itself a member of this Organization. Yours, etc. [signed] Vinogradov, Deputy Minister of Public Health of the USSR.[16]

The three withdrawals comprised the early stage of a domino effect, and a long series followed. Between November 1949 and August 1950 Albania, Bulgaria, Czechoslovakia, Hungary, Poland and Romania all withdrew, giving reasons similar to those in the telegram from the Soviet Union, but adding that the Organization had come under American domination.[17]

An immediate reply from the WHO came in the form of telegrams from the Chairman of the Executive Board and from the Director-General, Dr Brock Chisholm, expressing deep regret at the withdrawals. The latter pointed out that the constitution made no provision for withdrawal and suggested it was 'premature to have expressed dissatisfaction with the implementation of aims of the Constitution by WHO after only four months of organizational work in 1948 and a few weeks of 1949'.[18] The Soviets turned a cold shoulder to the request by the Director-General and the Executive Board Chairman to visit Moscow to dispel any misunderstandings. Nonetheless, the WHA continued unsuccessfully to appeal to the absent states to return to full membership.

During the first few months of the World Health Organization's existence, the East European members of the Soviet bloc criticized the Organization for not providing sufficient material assistance to the countries that had suffered German occupation. They called for more insecticides, vaccines, antibiotics, drugs and materials for research and education.[19] The WHA, however, took the view that it was not financially practical for the WHO to become a supply

16. Quote from Goodman, *op. cit.*, p. 203.
17. OR 28, 1950, pp. 553–5, OR 35, 1951, pp. 380–1. See also OR 25, 1950, p. 28. The charge of US domination, though perhaps true, does not follow from the Soviet delegate's comments a few months earlier in the Health Assembly in favour of allowing the US membership of the WHO, despite that country's reservations about the WHO's constitution.
18. See OR 17, 1949, p. 52. Also see *The First Ten Years of the World Health Organization*, WHO, Geneva, 1958, p. 79.
19. See, for instance, OR 13, 1948, pp. 39–72 and 120–47.

house; it had to devote its scarce resources to technical, advisory and educational functions.

Harold Jacobson has pointed out that in 1947 Byelorussia, Poland, the Ukraine and Yugoslavia received roughly one-third of the funds under the control of the Interim Commission of the WHO. Later exigencies, however, dictated that this figure had to decline precipitously.[20] It was clear that the WHO had not met the material expectations of the socialist countries.[21] Thus, in their telegrams, the withdrawing states had claimed that, despite their heavy contributions, the Organization's work did not 'correspond to the actual needs'.[22] They also claimed that this was due to the 'discriminative attitude' that the Organization had adopted towards them,[23] as a result of it being 'subject to political influences'.[24] With regard to the latter complaint, Alexander Dallin has noted that by 1950–1, the Soviet Union and its allies 'had clearly come to view most specialized agencies as enemy tools in the Cold War'.[25]

The Soviet Union's unhappiness with the WHO and other specialized agencies was unsurprising in view of the traditional Soviet lack of support for functional enterprises.[26] The Soviets had been unenthusiastic about economic and social activities even in the League. In the early days of the UN and its agencies, the Soviet Union saw the UN system in terms of its interpretation of the League experience. The demise of the League, as well as its expulsion of the Soviet Union, undoubtedly had a profound impact upon Soviet leaders, who 'probably regarded the Bruce report as a final diversionary attempt to deflect the [League] from its principal

20. See H. Jacobson, 'WHO: Medicine, Regionalism, and Managed Politics', in R. Cox and H. Jacobson (eds), *The Anatomy of Influence*, Yale University Press, New Haven, Conn., 1973, p. 183.
21. OR 13, 1948, pp. 39–72.
22. Communication from the Minister of Health of Romania to the Director-General of the WHO. See OR 28, 1950, p. 553.
23. Communication for the Deputy Minister of Foreign Affairs of Albania to the Director-General of the WHO. See OR 28, 1950, p. 554.
24. Communication from the Minister of Foreign Affairs of Czechoslovakia to the Director-General of the WHO. See OR, 1950, p. 554.
25. See Alexander Dallin, *The Soviet Union at the United Nations*, Methuen, London, 1962, p. 64.
26. For instance, Victor-Yves Ghebali has pointed out that the Soviet Union was hostile to the ILO, 'which it regarded as a tool of capitalism designed to wean the working masses away from the defence of their class interests'. See Victor-Yves Ghebali, *The International Labour Organization: a Case Study on the Evolution of UN Specialized Agencies*, Martinus Nijhoff, Dordrecht, 1989, p. 104. Also see Harold K. Jacobson, 'The USSR and ILO', *International Organization*, vol. XIV, no. 3 (Summer 1960), p. 404; and J. Harrod and N. Schrijver (eds), *The United Nations under Attack*, Gower, Aldershot, 1988, p. 23.

purposes [of peace and security]'.[27] With their withdrawal from the WHO, the Soviet distrust of the League was extrapolated to the UN's social and economic activities. The inability of the WHO to provide material aid to the Soviet Union added to their distrust of the Organization, which they already considered a Western tool.

A conclusion reached by many observers about the withdrawals was that the Eastern European countries really wished to continue to cooperate and derive assistance from the WHO, but not to pay for it. As Charles Allen puts it: 'The Soviet bloc made clear that it wanted more goods and money, and less advice.'[28] Goodman has referred to the withdrawals as being related to 'some turn of the political screw rather than to the reasons given'.[29] The decision of the Soviet Union and Eastern European states to withdraw from the WHO, and not to join other international organizations, betrayed an obvious and 'growing cleavage between East and West and the general isolationist bent of Soviet foreign policy'.[30]

Whatever the motivations for the withdrawals, the official WHO reaction was very subdued: a World Health Assembly resolution urged the 'inactive members' to reconsider their decisions and resume active participation.[31] No further action was deemed necessary by the third Assembly, which maintained complete silence on the implications that the withdrawals had on the financial condition of the Organization.[32]

The withdrawals meant that the WHO's expenditure levels had to be adjusted; but since the WHO constitution did not provide for withdrawal, the Assembly persisted in denying the reality of the withdrawals and continued to assume that the contributions of the 'inactive members' would eventually be paid. In the same vein, members were opposed to taking any formal steps to suspend services to these states. As Quimby has noted: 'It was difficult to get any proposals through the Assembly which assumed that the inactive Members would not eventually renew their participation in WHO.'[33]

27. See Jacobson, *The USSR and the UN's Economic and Social Activities*, *op. cit.*, p. 269.

28. See Allen, *op. cit.*, p. 41.

29. Goodman, *op. cit.*, p. 203. For a comprehensive discussion of the Soviet participation in the WHO, see Osakwe, *op. cit.*, pp. 101–32.

30. Alvin Rubinstein, *The Soviets in International Organization*, Princeton University Press, 1964, p. 30.

31. Resolution WHA3.84 in *Handbook of Resolutions and Decisions, 1948–1972*, vol. I, WHO, Geneva, 1973, p. 351. See OR 28, 1950, p. 52.

32. See, for instance, OR 28, 1950, p. 55. Also consult Howard Calderwood, 'Membership in the WHO', as cited by Quimby, *op. cit.*, p. 27.

33. Quimby, *op. cit.*, p. 28.

Victor-Yves Ghebali has observed that Soviet hostility did not abate until after Stalin's death, with the shift in Soviet foreign policy that followed this event.[34] Just as suddenly as the socialist countries had withdrawn from the WHO, which Andrei Gromyko, the Soviet Vice-Minister of Foreign Affairs, had referred to as 'useless',[35] they returned to full membership. In July 1955 the Russian delegate to the UN ECOSOC stated that the WHO 'was doing useful work' and that the Soviet Union was joining it.

The Soviet Union's participation in the UN system expanded markedly in the post-Stalin era. By 1959 it had become a member of the International Labour Organization (ILO), UNESCO, the Inter-Governmental Maritime Consultative Organization (IMCO) and the International Atomic Energy Agency (IAEA). By 1989 there were only six UN specialized agencies to which the Soviet Union did not belong: the Food and Agriculture Organization (FAO), the International Monetary Fund (IMF), the International Bank for Reconstruction and Development (IBRD), the International Finance Corporation (IFC), the International Development Association (IDA) and the International Civil Aviation Organization (ICAO).[36]

Albania, Bulgaria, Poland and the Soviet Union were represented at the tenth WHA in May 1957. Czechoslovakia and Romania resumed active participation in 1958, and Hungary in 1963. Just as Rubinstein felt that the original withdrawals were dictated by Cold War considerations, Osakwe attributed similar motives to the returns.[37]

Since there was no provision for withdrawal in the WHO constitution, the Soviet Union and other returning states were technically in arrears with their payments to the WHO's budget. Consequently, they were not only subject to having their voting privileges suspended, they were also ineligible to benefit from the WHO's services. Problems concerning contributions for the years of inactive membership were discussed during the seventeenth Executive Board, which was attended by a representative Soviet. The ninth WHA decided that states resuming active membership should pay in full their arrears for years when they had participated actively, with a token payment of 5 per cent for their inactive years. Such

34. See Ghebali, *The International Labour Organization*, *op. cit.*, p. 106.
35. See Trygve Lie, *In the Cause of Peace*, Macmillan, New York, 1954, p. 304.
36. See Jacobson, *The USSR and the UN's Economic and Social Activities*, *op. cit.*, p. 14. Also see OR 68, 1956, p. 66.
37. See Osakwe, *op. cit.*, p. 116.

payments could be made in equal annual instalments over a period up to ten years. This was a significant move on the part of the WHO, in that it did not allow the previously inactive countries to return without some gesture of continued membership. This aim was achieved quite adequately by the 5 per cent rule, which yet did not appear to be a punitive measure. The Soviet Union (but not the Ukraine and Byelorussia) renewed active membership in April 1957. Within the year, the other Cominform countries followed suit.

There is little doubt that the repeated appeals by the Assembly and the member states, as well as deliberate inaction with regard to punitive measures, served to ease the return of the 'inactive members'. 'Little attention was given to the legal and other relevant aspects, although they were not completely ignored.'[38] Although all of the returning states considered themselves to be new members of the WHO, none objected to the Assembly's insistence that they were merely resuming active participation.[39]

The end of the Cold War has brought with it the dissolution of the Soviet Union, Yugoslavia and Czechoslovakia. Most, but not all, of the newly-created states were members of the WHO by early 1993.[40]

38. Calderwood, 'Membership in the WHO', as referenced by Quimby, *op. cit.*, p. 28.
39. See Calderwood, 'The WHO and Its Regional Organisations', *op. cit.*, p. 26.
40. See Calderwood, 'Membership in the WHO', *op. cit.*, p. 26.

16
THE POLITICS OF EXCLUSION

After the Second World War, the former enemies (Germany, Italy and Japan) were included in the new World Health Organization without controversy. However, in the first three decades of the WHO's lifetime certain states were prominent by their absence: the People's Republic of China, East Germany, North Korea and North Vietnam. Of these four, the question of the membership of the People's Republic was debated fairly regularly in the WHA during the report of the Credentials Committee. In addition, Spain's entry into full membership was controversial, and South Africa, though a full member since 1947, was effectively expelled from the WHO in 1964. Finally Palestine, occupied by Israeli forces since 1964, has been formally recognized as a state by much of the international community. It has made many attempts to apply for membership of the WHO, so far unsuccessfully.

The Representation of China

The question of representation of the Chinese people was a membership controversy that came up early in the history of the WHO. China was a member of the WHO right from the birth of the Organization in 1948. In fact Dr T. V. Soong, the Chinese delegate to the San Francisco Conference, was the first person to suggest the founding of a single international health organization. After the Chinese revolution in 1949, the area thus far referred to as 'China' broke up into the Republic of China (Formosa, now Taiwan) and the People's Republic of China (PRC). The debate over which of the two governments, Peking or Formosa, represented all China appeared repeatedly throughout the UN system.[1]

In May 1950 the government of the Republic of China (Taiwan) cabled to the WHO Director-General its intention to withdraw from the Organization as of 5 May 1950, because of difficulties in paying its contribution.[2] The telegram added that: 'despite China's with-

1. For a discussion of this issue in the UN General Assembly, see Kuo-chang Wang, *UN Voting on Chinese Representation*, Institute of American Culture, Taipei, 1984.
2. See F. Quimby, *Science, Technology and the American Government*, Congressional Record Service, Washington, DC, 1971, p. 28; Neville Goodman, *International Health Organizations and Their Work*, Churchill Livingstone, London, 1971, p. 204.

drawal from the Organization, it will continue to adhere to purposes and principles of the Organization, and cooperate to fullest possible extent with the Organization as a whole and with States Members.'[3] Evidently, this withdrawal was in no way related to the withdrawals of the East European states.

Soon after the telegram from Taipei, another was received from Chou En-lai, dated 13 May 1950, claiming that 'the People's Republic of China is the only legal government representing the Chinese people' and that 'the Chinese Kuomintang reactionary remnant clique have no longer any qualifications for participating in the World Health Organization and must be driven out from its various organs and meetings including the Third World Health Assembly.'[4]

The Taipei government had the support of the United States and other Western governments; nonetheless, it was somewhat surprising in retrospect that the telegram from the PRC was completely ignored by the third WHA. Indeed, when the WHA did take any action, it was contrary to its avowed goal of universal membership.

Two years later the government of Taiwan wrote to the WHO declaring itself competent to meet its financial obligations and asking to resume active membership. Taiwan proposed a mechanism for paying contributions now in arrears, together with those for the current and future years. The sixth WHA agreed to accept token payments, subject to future arrangements when Taiwan's financial situation had improved. The Assembly, without discussion or vote, also accepted a resolution which substituted the term 'China' for the previous designation of the 'Republic of China' and which stated that 'the resumption by China of full participation in the work of the Organization will be welcomed.'[5]

Because of the prior withdrawal of the East European states, there were very few states in the WHO which had formally recognized the PRC. This, together with the fact that the United States was the main ally of the government in Formosa, meant that little opposition materialized when the majority of the Chinese population (those in the PRC) were ignored as far as health was concerned. In fact, as Calderwood has observed:

> By treating the communication from Formosa as a communication from a Member of the Assembly, in effect [the action] recognized the Government

3. OR 28, 1950, p. 555.
4. *Ibid*. pp. 555–6.
5. Resolution WHA6.6, *Handbook of Resolutions and Decisions, 1948–1972*, vol. I, WHO, Geneva, 1973, pp. 351 and 375. OR 48, 1953, p. 18.

in Formosa as the Government of [all] China. The Assembly's subsequent decision . . . in regard to the settlement of China's financial obligations to the Organization when China resumed active participation, had the same effect.[6]

As long as the Western coalition of states controlled the WHO's political priorities, the Republic of China remained the only representative of the Chinese people. During the Credentials Committee report of the WHA, various states expressed the opinion that the PRC should be included in the work of the WHO, but did not advance the issue any further. The Credentials Committee continued to recommend the acceptance of the credentials of the delegates of the Republic of China, and the recommendation was accepted without recorded vote. This situation continued for over twenty years.

The return of the Soviet Union and the other socialist states to full membership, as well as the later entry of numerous developing countries, served to dilute the influence that the Western coalition had, at least with regard to the question of membership of the PRC. When the twenty-sixth session of the UN General Assembly (1971) recognized the representatives of the government of the People's Republic of China as the only legitimate representatives of China to the United Nations, it recommended expulsion of the 'representatives of Chiang Kai-shek from the place which they unlawfully occupied at the UN and in all organizations related to it'.[7] The WHO carried out this recommendation.[8] Thus the decision that the American coalition of states had approved in 1950 was revoked by the coalition of developing countries in 1971.[9]

North Korea, North Vietnam and East Germany

Following the Korean War, the original seat of Korea was given to the Republic of (South) Korea. This situation continued till 1973, when North Korea was allowed full membership as well. An analagous loss of representation by the socialist half of divided states took place in Vietnam and Germany.

6. Howard Calderwood, 'Membership in the WHO', as referenced in Quimby, *op. cit.*, p. 28.
7. UN General Assembly Resolution 2758 (XXVI) of 25 Oct. 1971.
8. OR 201, 1972, p. 1.
9. For a comprehensive review of the role of the PRC in the WHO, see Bruno Munier, 'La Chine et l'OMS', in Harish Kapur (ed.), *China and the Specialized Agencies*, Graduate Institute of International Studies, Geneva, 1986, pp. 104–29.

Vietnam became a member of the WHO in 1950; however, following the Vietnam War, which divided the country into two separate states, only South Vietnam was left as the effective member. The Western powers which actively excluded the PRC from the WHO also kept North Vietnam from joining the Organization. Such was the case until 1975, when the Democratic Republic of (North) Vietnam was admitted to membership of the WHO.[10] The next year, North and South Vietnam were unified under the name of the Socialist Republic of Vietnam, which now retains one seat in the WHO.

After the division of Germany into the Federal Republic (West) and Democratic Republic (East), the latter was also denied membership of the WHO. From 1970, the USA and other Western powers used their influence in the WHO to postpone East German admission to the Organization for three consecutive years. In each of these three years, the World Health Assembly chose to 'defer consideration of the participation of the German Democratic Republic' to the next year. This situation was finally reversed in 1973, when the Democratic Republic of Germany became a full member of the WHO. Subsequent to the merging of East and West Germany in 1989, reunified Germany has one seat in the Organization.[11]

Spain and South Africa

At the debate in the IHC concerning the criteria for membership of the WHO, controversy arose over Franco's Spain. As Charles Allen has noted, 'the injection of the Spanish matter transformed the relatively innocuous constitutional question of how new members should be admitted to WHO into a serious ideological issue.'[12] This issue split the IHC into two camps, reflecting the ideological divide on the Spanish question.

The Latin American countries, whose sympathies lay with Spain, suggested that new members be admitted by a simple majority in the Health Assembly. Such a rule would have facilitated future Spanish admission to the WHO. Another group, led by the Soviet Union, urged a two-thirds majority rule on membership questions. This requirement would effectively have created an anti-Franco veto in the Health Assembly. Some countries, such as Canada, despite their

10. OR 226, 1975, p. 1.
11. See OR 184, 1970, p. 6; OR 193, 1971, p. 11; OR 201, 1972, p. 10; and OR 209, 1973, p. 2.
12. See C. Allen, 'World Health and World Politics', *International Organization*, vol. 14, no. 1 (1950), p. 39.

dislike for the Franco regime, espoused the simple majority proposal on the grounds that universal membership was essential for the work of the Organization.

The issue was sufficiently contentious to merit a roll-call vote. By the narrow margin of twenty-five to twenty-two, the IHC adopted the simple majority provision. However, this was a pyrrhic victory for the pro-Franco group because the UN General Assembly subsequently (1946) recommended that the Franco government be denied membership of UN agencies. Only when this UN resolution was rescinded in 1951 was Spain admitted to WHO membership.[13]

In 1964, when the South African government declared apartheid to be its official policy, the seventeenth World Health Assembly referred to this as a 'special circumstance of failure to adhere to the humanitarian principles governing the World Health Organization'.[14] The Assembly decided to deprive South Africa of its voting privileges on the basis of Article 7 of the constitution, which allows it 'on such conditions as it thinks proper, [to] suspend the voting privileges and services to which a Member is entitled'.[15] After this action, South Africa withdrew from the Organization and became an inactive member. It was restored to full membership rights, including voting rights, at the May 1994 Assembly.

Palestine in the World Health Organization

In the early 1970s the WHA has recognized national liberation movements, including the Palestine Liberation Organization (PLO), the African National Congress and the Pan African Congress of Azania. These three liberation movements obtained observer status in the WHO, and the latter two also participated in the Regional Committee for Africa, but ceased to be observers with the end of the apartheid regime.[16]

In early 1989 the PLO declared its intention to seek full membership of WHO. It had declared the formation of a Palestinian state in the occupied West Bank and Gaza a few months earlier. Since ninety-eight countries had recognized the PLO's self-proclaimed Palestinian state, there was a fair chance that it would gain the simple majority of WHO members needed to gain admission.

The United States reacted strongly to the PLO's bid to join the

13. OR 35, 1951, p. 35.
14. OR 135, 1964, p. 23.
15. WHO constitution, Article 7, in WHO, *Basic Documents*, 36th edn., Geneva, 1986, p. 4.
16. See WHA38/15, p. 3.

WHO. Secretary of State James Baker warned that he would recommend to President Bush that the United States cut off all financial support to any UN agency that voted to admit Palestine as a full member. Saying that the 'United States vigorously opposes the admission of the PLO to membership in the World Health Organization or any other UN agency', Baker added that 'Political questions such as this should not be raised in specialized agencies because such politicization detracts from the important technical work of these organizations.'[17]

The American warning was also delivered to the PLO representative in Tunis, Hakam Ballaoui, in a meeting with the US Embassy's *chargé d'affaires*, Gordon Brown. The US State Department reportedly asked the PLO to withdraw its request for membership.[18]

The threatened withdrawal of US funds from the WHO was treated very seriously by the Organization. The WHO's Director-General, Hiroshi Nakajima, went to the United States for talks with administration officials and Congress days before the WHA meeting (which was to take place on 8 May) to discuss what was by then widely perceived as a crisis.[19]

In two meetings with the Chairman of the PLO, Yasser Arafat,[20] Nakajima pleaded with him to withdraw Palestine's application for membership, in order to diffuse a confrontation with the United States which, in his words, could 'stop most of the activity [for the rest] of this year'.[21] Nakajima also told the international press that it was 'most inappropriate' for the PLO to put WHO programmes in jeopardy by making the Organization its first target in a drive to win international recognition of its proclamation of statehood.[22]

The PLO refused to withdraw its application, leaving the forty-second WHA faced with a proposal to admit the Palestinian state to membership. The discussion in the WHA was, as expected, highly charged and thoroughly political. The debate was suspended twice, giving the delegates an extra forty-eight hours to reconsider their positions. Following the two suspensions, a 'compromise' proposal was co-sponsored by ten WHO members and introduced by Dr S. Tapa of Tonga, requesting the Director-General to study in detail the Palestinian request for membership and report the findings to

17. See David Ottaway, 'US Warns UN Units about PLO; Funds to be Cut if Agencies Admit Palestinian Group', *Washington Post*, 2 May 1989, p. A01.
18. *Ibid.*
19. WHA42/VR/10, p. 9.
20. *Ibid.*
21. See 'UN Unit Asks PLO to Drop Application', *Washington Post*, 3 May 1989, p. A09.
22. *Ibid.*

the 1990 WHA.[23] In a secret ballot, the compromise proposal was adopted by the WHA by 83 votes for, 47 against and 20 abstentions.[24]

The debate over the compromise proposal was of course animated. Countries such as India and Israel opposed the compromise for opposite reasons – the former felt that Palestine should be admitted to full membership immediately; the latter that the issue did not merit discussion, much less detailed study.[25] Canada, on the other hand, voted for the compromise because of what it considered its 'sense of constructive moderation'.[26]

Overall, the deferral of the question of Palestine's membership of the WHO was handled by the WHA in a manner similar to the way in which it approached other contentious issues. As the Canadian delegate, De Montigny Marchand, noted, the compromise 'enabled [the WHO] to avoid a confrontation' which could have been very disruptive to the Organization if taken to its logical extreme.[27]

23. See WHO Press Release WHA/13, 19 May 1989, p. 3.
24. See WHO Press Release WHA/5, 13 May 1989.
25. See WHA42/VR/10, p. 36 for the Israeli view, and p. 42 for the Indian position.
26. See WHA42/VR/10, p. 36.
27. *Ibid.*

17

HOW EFFECTIVE WAS THE W.H.O.'S ASPIRATION FOR A DECENTRALIZED, UNIVERSAL ORGANIZATION?

In Part II we have outlined two of the WHO's aspirations with regard to its attempts to entrench the machinery crucial for world-wide public health cooperation, or what may be referred to as an international infrastructure for health: the desire to achieve universal membership; and the establishment of a decentralized organization with regional offices. Difficulties faced by the WHO with regard to these two aims have been outlined and assessed; without doubt, these difficulties have involved largely political and ideological controversies and confrontations.

It appears that the Organization has had mixed results (early ineffectiveness and later effectiveness) in its attempts to achieve decentralization and universal membership. This conclusion is arrived at by the various effectiveness criteria established at the outset of this work.

The WHO has been effective in establishing its aims with regard to its structure. We have clearly established that the aims of the WHO concerning universal membership, decentralization and an efficient administrative structure were well entrenched in the early deliberations of the founders of the Organization at the TPC and the IHC. The WHO's constitution speaks of its objective being 'the attainment by all peoples of the highest possible level of health', explicitly signifying an interest in the universality of its appeal and thus of its membership. The fact that membership can be agreed by a simple majority in the WHA is a practical example of the Organization's open-door policy towards non-member states.[1] The fact that a small handful of communist states, the PRC most prominent among them, were actively excluded from membership of the WHO can be attributable to the overwhelming influence of the United States and its allies in the first two decades of the Organization's history.

As far as decentralization is concerned, this necessarily became an aim of the Organization and its founders because of the existence of regional health organizations when the WHO was established. The

1. The cases of the PRC and the Palestinian state are exceptions to this general observation.

saga of the difficult integration of the PAHO into the WHO serves to illustrate graphically how vested interests present in 1948 and after rendered any consideration of a purely centralized (that is, non-regional) organizational structure impracticable. The passionate loyalties among employees of existing regional health organizations inevitably played a crucial role in the preservation of those organizations in a decentralized WHO.

The desire for a decentralized Organization was also accepted for unselfish reasons. Many delegates to the TPC and the IHC sincerely believed that a decentralized organization would be closer to the people it served. This proximity was obviously preferable if not attractive to people like Szeming Sze, who did not have any transparent vested interest in calling for a decentralized structure.[2]

Thus the objectives of universal membership and decentralization were well entrenched in the early days of the WHO, and have not changed over time. In fact, past difficulties in realizing these aims have further strengthened the belief in their usefulness. We find mixed results with regard to targets hoped for and results achieved by the WHO in these structural areas. The targets of universal membership and decentralization have been reached over time. This effectiveness is largely due to the WHO's attempts to limit controversy, as was evident in its handling of the dispute over the transfer of regional headquarters from Alexandria. By the use of technical and legal means to delay any substantive action, the WHO dealt with the problem, which eventually faded away. Other potential difficulties in the decentralization issue were limited by the fact that the founders were at least largely agreed on the ends, although not on the means: they agreed on the need for decentralization, but not on its timing and extent.

In the case of attempts to achieve universality, the Organization has, from the outset, made membership fairly easy to acquire by any state wishing to join. For instance, states which were not members of the UN were invited to the International Health Conference, and membership of the UN was not a stipulation for membership of the WHO. The desire to cast aside technicalities in an attempt to achieve universality in membership was also obvious in the handling of US reservations on the WHO's constitution. By refusing to let semantics stand in the way of American membership, the WHA reinforced the significance it ascribed to universality.

In areas of WHO effectiveness and ineffectiveness alike, the

2. Dr Szeming Sze was the Resident Representative (in Washington, DC) of the National Health Administration of China. He was also the Vice-Chairman of the Interim Commission.

obstacles to the achievement of the Organization's aspirations regarding structure have been largely of the negative political type. For instance, the Organization has been effective in dealing with problems arising in the decentralized structure; however, these difficulties have originated mostly for political reasons, as the example of problems in the Eastern Mediterranean Region indicated. In areas where the Organization has been ineffective, as in the attempts to limit political blocs, negative politics has also been the main obstacle faced.

Our final criterion of effectiveness, namely the totality of measures used to pursue aims and targets, has been more than adequately met by the WHO. However, as formulated in Part I, three of the five components of this criterion do not apply to the structural areas of interest in this book. For instance, with the exception of Franco's Spain and the PRC, collaboration with other international organizations is not directly relevant for issues of universal membership and decentralization in the WHO.

In relation to the other two points, namely the Organization's commitment to its aims and flexibility to accommodate set-backs and successes, it is clear that the WHO has been highly effective. Part of this effectiveness can be attributed to the Organization's attempts to minimize the damage of politicization by adhering closely to its aims. For example, the Organization's commitment to universal membership was demonstrated in its refusal to use legalistic measures to deal with the socialist bloc withdrawal in 1949/50, in its repeated pleas to those countries to return to full membership, in its refusal to take punitive action against the states who had withdrawn, and in its indulgent attitude upon the return of these states by charging them only nominal dues for their period of absence.

The WHO's commitment to regional structure was evident in its refusal to let the Arab majority in the Eastern Mediterranean Region expel Israel. The WHO's insistence, on this occasion, on adhering to the strict letter of the law concerning membership of a regional organization set a precedent which worked against any future attempts of the sort.

The WHO exhibited flexibility in its handling of the Arab–Israeli conflict by accommodating the lack of a regional committee and by ensuring the progress of health programmes in the region. Moreover, the Organization has been flexible in handling the obstacles to its attempts to achieve an efficient administrative structure that persist. For example, the Organization has learned to live with the political blocs within it and to attempt to keep in contact with each one, in an attempt to prevent any further politicization other than that which has become absolutely inevitable.

To summarize our findings about the Organization's effectiveness in its structural areas of interest: ineffectiveness is found on the basis of one of the three sets of criteria established in Part I. The structural aspirations of the WHO have suffered mainly from weaknesses in the realization of hoped-for goals; with regard to its establishment of aims, and its use of the totality of measures in attempts to achieve such aims, the Organization has been effective.

We have also tried to demonstrate that the greatest obstacles to the WHO's structural aspirations have involved negative politics. Examples of such negative politics include the desire of the Arab states to exclude Israel from the Eastern Mediterranean Regional Committee, the attempts by Arab states to transfer the regional headquarters from Alexandria, the problems with the integration of the PAHO into the WHO, and the presence of political blocs within the WHO. We have shown that the influence of negative politics has been consistent and ever-present in the history of the Organization; it is not simply a phenomenon of the 1970s and 1980s.

Our demonstration of the prevalence of negative politics in a functional organization like the WHO also points to the conclusion that the political and technical spheres cannot be segregated, as the functionalists would have us believe. As evident in the problems with the integration of the PAHO, when personal and governmental interests are at stake health professionals prioritize politics as highly as their diplomatic colleagues are expected to do.

The fact that the World Health Organization has experienced, and at times mirrored, many of the political controversies that are present in its parent political Organization, the United Nations, also indicates the difficulty in segregating negative politics from inevitable, legitimate or positive politics.

It seems that functionalists were mistaken in the assumption that the value of international cooperation would be evident to all countries, despite their ideological bent. This did not turn out to be true. For instance, the withdrawal of the socialist states from the WHO demonstrated that communists have little in common ideologically with functionalists – the former call for radical transformation of society internally (by way of revolution) while the latter urge more international cooperation.[3] Thus it seems that functionalist theory underestimates the ability of a totalitarian state to isolate itself; it also underestimates the degree of ideological consensus and political agreement necessary for meaningful international cooperation in health issues. The insistence by the various regions of WHO on

3 See H.K. Jacobson, *The USSR and the UN's Economic and Social Activities*, University of Notre Dame, Notre Dame, Ind., 1963, p. 10.

greater representation in the Executive Board further contradicts the functionalist expectation of cooperation among technical experts, without regard for nationality.

Finally, in the light of the overwhelming consensus at the TPC and the IHC regarding the two aspirations of the WHO discussed in this chapter, it is arguable that contemporary critics of the UN system and functionalists would not have predicted the strong presence of negative politics that we have shown. Indeed, the early consensus about universality of membership, for instance, was seen as an essential component of an international infrastructure for health (which would encourage a universal outlook and approach in public health); yet universality has at times led to a breakdown of the very consensus that the founders of the WHO hoped it would foster.

Part III

CASE STUDY: THE MALARIA ERADICATION PROGRAMME

18

INTRODUCTION TO THE M.E.P.

As already discussed in Part II, the most pressing difficulties that the WHO faced soon after its birth in 1948 were structural issues concerning membership and decentralization. This case study deals with the malaria eradication programme (MEP) of the 1950s and 1960s,[1] and attempts to trace its rise and fall and evaluate its effectiveness.[2] The WHO launched the MEP in 1955, soon after recovering from its teething troubles and as the eight socialist countries which had withdrawn from the Organization were returning to full membership. Thus, with a legitimacy accorded by almost universal membership, with the decentralization of the Organization well entrenched and with the expectation that the universal membership could be united behind a truly universal health menace, the WHO now attempted to use its international infrastructure for health in organizing a battle against malaria.

Malaria represented the most persistent and prevalent public health menace that the WHO inherited from its predecessor organizations.[3] From prehistoric times, the disease had been unsuccessfully fought with various weapons, ranging from sorcery to chemotherapy. In view of the atmosphere of cooperation that prevailed in the ten or fifteen years after the Second World War, a

1. The Malaria Eradication Programme will also at times be referred to simply as the 'eradication programme'.
2. The MEP was chosen for study (as opposed to the Smallpox Eradication Programme) because it was the first and largest WHO mass campaign. Also, malaria was the greatest challenge that the WHO faced. A discussion of some of the factors that aided in smallpox eradication is presented in Appendix 4.
3. See Appendix 3 for essential definitions, and phases, of the MEP.

fresh effort against malaria was deemed necessary by health experts who wanted to exploit the type of international consensus which manifested itself in the formation of the United Nations and the World Health Organization.[4]

Malaria eradication was the first of the WHO's eradication programmes and the first attempt by the Organization to unify public health procedures on a truly universal scale. The MEP was also the WHO's first chance to operationalize its early 'vertical' health philosophy.

The functionalist disdain for the political, and preference for the 'technical', increased the faith of political leaders in experts, and of experts in themselves. The early structural problems in the WHO having been solved to some degree, its medical experts felt that the task of eradicating malaria was now largely technical. The idealism of the post-war era was clearly evident at the International Health Conference, where functionalist views were aired by medical experts who felt that the simplest path to welfare goals involved the avoidance of political and ideological conflicts, and the focusing of attention on possibilities for international cooperation on strictly 'technical' matters. Malaria eradication seemed ideal.

The WHO's Malaria Eradication Programme was remarkable for several reasons: first, it represented a departure from the traditional public health approach in that it was the first mass eradication programme to be coordinated by an international health organization; secondly, it required the active participation of dozens of countries in precisely following predetermined procedures with the final aim of the total disappearance of the disease;[5] thirdly, it represented the largest and most dramatic public health undertaking in the history of international health cooperation;[6] fourthly, while it represented only one of a series of WHO mass campaigns, including those against smallpox and yaws, the rise and fall of malaria eradication efforts ultimately had more of an influence on the WHO's overall health philosophy than did any of the other mass campaigns; and, finally, a close look at the MEP also offers the opportunity to analyse a programme which began with overwhelming support, in direct contrast to some of the WHO's previous and later efforts.

4. Much of the post-Second World War milieu of international cooperation that provided the impetus for the formation of organizations such as the WHO and UNESCO has been attributed to the wartime alliance and an anti-Nazi consensus. See B. F. E. Jenks, 'The Concept of International Organization: the Case of UNESCO', unpubl. D. Phil. thesis, Oxford University, 1982, p. 59.
5. See OR 65, 1955, p. 5; and OR 71, 1956, p. 44.
6. See 'Malaria Eradication: a Plea for Health', WHO, Geneva, 1958, p. 5.

The MEP represented an example of the increased significance of the WHO compared with its predecessor organizations. The advisory role mandated to the WHO by its constitution was one example of this greater significance - never before had an international health organization been given so clear a mandate to advise national governments, when requested, on planning, financing, implementing and evaluating health programmes.[7] The WHO was the 'executing agency' for the implementation of both the Malaria and Smallpox Eradication Programmes. This meant that it was trusted by the funding agencies and national governments to outline exactly how these programmes should be carried out. Generally, the WHO suggestions were considered by member states to represent the 'correct' way of approaching the problem. Essentially, the eradication programme represented an extreme case of the advisory and coordinating function of the WHO: most countries were expected to follow similar advice (often couched almost as instructions) about malaria eradication, in the same order and at the same time.

An evaluation of the effectiveness of the MEP, it is hoped, will shed light on how certain WHO priorities were established during the 1950s and 1960s, and on the philosophical leanings of the Organization before and after the programme. We also expect to draw some conclusions about the validity of functionalist ideas which were prevalent in the early days of the WHO and which persist in the Organization to this day.

This case study demonstrates that the MEP was largely ineffective. We show that many factors played a role in the downfall of the MEP at the levels of process and outcome. Among these factors were misconceptions as to the feasibility of eradicating malaria, as well as theoretical support from functionalist ideas. As will be evident in this section, factors relating to political influence, individual search for accolade, national prestige and misjudged priorities were also important in the rise and fall of the MEP.

Starting with a description of the seriousness of malaria worldwide, we go on briefly to discuss the international efforts against the disease before the WHO's eradication programme was launched in 1955. The reasons for and justifications of the rise and fall of the eradication programme are documented. Finally, an evaluation of the effectiveness of the programme is undertaken by reference to the criteria previously established.

7. On this advisory function, see the WHO's constitution, Article 2.

19

MALARIA: THE EXTENT OF THE PROBLEM

In 1955 Pampana and Russell estimated that the worldwide annual incidence of malaria was about 250 million cases, with 2.5 million people dying of the disease.[1] Johnson estimated the yearly figures to be 200 million and 2 million, respectively.[2] Despite these differences, however, there seemed little doubt that not only was malaria killing, and had killed, more people than any other disease, but that it also interfered with the development of agriculture and industry in the tropical countries where it was the greatest scourge.[3]

The extent of the malaria problem was so great, and the desire to eradicate the disease so strong, that the emergence of certain wartime discoveries such as DDT led public health leaders to abandon the control measures utilized thus far in favour of an all-out attempt at 'malaria eradication'. 'Malaria eradication' refers to the ending of the transmission of malaria and the elimination of the reservoir of infective cases in a campaign limited in time and carried to such a degree of perfection that, when it comes to an end, there is no resumption of transmission.[4] As Soper has said, 'for the first time there exists a single efficient and economical method of attack on malaria which can be standardized and applied with confidence to almost all malarious areas.'[5]

In 1955, the WHO felt that malaria eradication was feasible and officially launched a concerted international eradication effort. The focus and direction of this Malaria Eradication Programme was 're-evaluated' fourteen years later, in 1969, when it was abundantly clear that the Organization had failed to achieve its original objectives. Malaria eradication was abandoned and replaced by a policy of malaria control.[6] 'Malaria control' refers to an unending programme of limiting the danger of malaria, without any attempt to end it completely.

1. E. J. Pampana and P. F. Russell, 'Malaria – a World Problem', *WHO Chronicle*, vol. 9 (1955), p. 31.
2. See D. R. Johnson, 'Development of the Worldwide Malaria Eradication Programme', *Mosquito News*, June 1966, p. 114.
3. For a good history of malaria from classical times until the 1950s, see Paul Russell, *Man's Mastery of Malaria*, Oxford University Press, 1955.
4. See P. Russell, 'Malaria Eradication Defined', Mal/Exp. Com.8/WP/35, p. 1, June 1960. Also see Appendix 3 to the present work.
5. Fred L. Soper, 'General Principles of the Eradication Programmes in the Western Hemisphere', *Journal of the National Malaria Society*, vol. 10 (1951), p. 186.
6. See OR 176, 1969, Annex 13 and p. 18.

Despite certain impressive successes during the early years of the eradication programme, the world malaria situation has been deteriorating steadily since the early 1960s. In 1982, the most recent year for which reliable figures are available, the WHO reported that 365 million people were living in areas where malaria was endemic and where no specific anti-malaria measures were being applied. A further 2,217 million - 46 per cent of the world's population - were living in areas where malaria was still endemic but where some malaria control measures existed.[7] The worst situation was in the African Region of the WHO, where over 90 per cent of the total population lived in areas that were or had been malarious. From the mid-1960s onwards, it is estimated that at least 1 million infants and children have died of malaria annually on the African continent alone. In 1986 Ruebrush *et al.* estimated that the figure of between 6 and 11 million cases of malaria reported annually to the WHO (their data do not include Africa) may represent an underestimation of the actual incidence of malaria by a factor of ten. The data are considered grossly inaccurate because screening, diagnosis and notification efforts have declined over the past fifteen years.[8] Indeed, in 1982 the WHO's own estimates suggested the worldwide incidence of malaria to be 220 million cases a year.[9]

The eradication of malaria remains an elusive goal in much of the developing world. For instance, Venezuela was the first WHO member state to declare that it had eradicated malaria in 1961; in 1985 it had a substantial malaria problem.[10] The continuing epidemic resurgence of the disease has raised questions about the appropriateness of the original WHO efforts against the disease and about the negative political and non-technical reasons for the effort's failure; the WHO's record in the fight against malaria is further compromised by what is perceived by many contemporary critics as a level of commitment against malaria that is even lower now than it was in pre-eradication days. In 1985 the percentage of the WHO regular budget devoted to anti-malaria activities was 3 per cent, compared to 5 per cent in 1959.[11]

7. See *Tropical Disease Research*, Seventh Programme Report, WHO, Geneva, 1985, pp. 2–3.
8. See Ruebrush *et al.*, 'Malaria', in Julia A. Walsh and Kenneth Warren (eds), *Strategies for Primary Health Care*, Chicago University Press, 1986, p. 47.
9. See *Tropical Disease Research, op. cit.*, pp. 2–3.
10. See *World Health Statistics*, WHO, Geneva, 1985, p. 166.
11. See OR 97, 1961, p. 315 and PB/84–85, 1982, p. 235. Also see Harry Cleaver, 'Malaria and the Political Economy of Public Health', *International Journal of Health Services*, vol. 7, no. 4 (1977), pp. 557–79. Also see G.M. Jeffery, 'Malaria Control in the 20th Century', *American Journal of Tropical Medicine and Hygiene (Am. J. Trop. Med. and Hyg.)*, vol. 25. no. 3 (1976), pp. 361–71.

20
INTERNATIONAL ANTI-MALARIAL EFFORTS BEFORE 1955

The League of Nations and Malaria

Malaria was one of the health concerns of the League of Nations which continued to be a priority when the WHO was formed. The League's efforts against malaria were essentially limited to epidemiology and drugs; little attention was paid to anti-mosquito measures of malaria control and eradication that were later so popular with the WHO.[1]

Early Work in the WHO, 1949–1955

The importance of malaria as a public health problem and the need to give anti-malaria activities priority were recognized as early as 1946 by the Interim Commission of the WHO.[2] In some respects the functionalist notion of spillover had a strong influence in the Organization at this time, and continued to do so in malaria work until the late 1960s. This involved the assumption that cooperative experience gained in one functional area, in this case malaria control (later eradication) measures, could be transferred to a similar but more broadly defined area such as other eradication programmes or public health administrations in general.[3] The distant goals of spillover theory were more ambitious and would predict international cooperation in public health measures ultimately to spillover to political areas. While WHO officials may not have been explicitly aware of the theory of functionalism, their words implied an acceptance of notions such as spillover: in a speech at the US State Department regarding the American donation of US$5 million to the Malaria Eradication Programme, Dr Candau, the WHO Director-General, spoke of putting the money towards 'building a firmer foundation for permanent peace and security'.[4] Relying on spillover philosophy, the first World Health Assembly in 1948 decided

1. For a discussion of the League's role in malaria control, see Paul Russell, *Man's Mastery of Malaria*, Oxford University Press, 1955, pp. 198–208.
2. See OR 4, 1946, p. 32.
3. G. Abi-Saab (ed.), *The Concept of International Organization*, UNESCO, Paris, 1981, p. 18.
4. See *Department of State Bulletin*, vol. XXXVII, no. 965 (23 Dec. 1957), p. 1003.

to provide malaria control 'demonstration teams' to countries requesting assistance. These teams consisted of WHO consultants and advisors, as well as some national staff. The use of expatriate workers, even when local specialists were available (but were not connected with the WHO), was quite routine at the time, although it is now considered intrinsically condescending.[5] As early as 1950 a WHO Expert Committee on malaria had considered that 'the sending of these teams is one of the most efficient ways in which WHO may foster anti-malaria work throughout the world.'[6] By the end of 1949 seven such teams were in operation in different parts of Asia.[7]

The demonstration team approach presumed that a concentration of international effort against malaria in one non-randomly chosen section of a given country could provide national authorities with a training ground, as well as a model with which to replicate successes in the rest of the country, where the epidemiology of the disease was assumed to be the same or similar. The demonstration team concept implied a misunderstanding of resources and political realities at the national level. The eradication of malaria from a 50-square-mile patch of territory by a group of foreign specialists with almost unlimited amounts of funds and supplies was not imitable. Generally, when these WHO specialists left, malaria re-invaded even the 'demonstration patch' because of the country's inability to maintain a control programme of the required intensity, lacking the resources that were available to the demonstration team.[8]

As the Japanese occupied the Dutch Indies during the Second World War, the major source of the anti-malarial drug quinine was lost to the Allies and the search was on for other means of fighting malaria.[9] The advent of DDT in 1943 made it possible to undertake the control of the anopheline mosquito on a large scale. DDT had proved extremely valuable in the Mediterranean and Western Pacific theatres of war, and this added to its legitimacy as the ideal tool for the job. DDT came into widespread use among the Allies

5. Personal communication with Dr J. Hamon, Assistant Director-General of the WHO, Geneva, 26 Mar. 1986. Also see TRS 8, 1950, p. 5.

6. TRS 8, 1950, p. 33.

7. See OR 25, 1950, p. 10; Expert Committee on Malaria, WHO/Mal/70 Corr. 1, 17 Jan. 1951, p. 4; and, for an example of a report by a demonstration team, see G. Livadas, 'The Present Position of the Malaria Control Demonstration Project in Terai', WHO/Mal/76, 5 Feb. 1952.

8. Personal communication with Dr M. A. Farid, former Regional Malaria Advisor for WHO's Eastern Mediterranean Region, Geneva, 6 Aug. 1987. See also TRS 38, 1950, p. 42.

9. Fred L. Soper, 'General Principles of the Eradication Programmes in the Western Hemisphere', *J. of the National Malaria Society*, vol. 10 (1951), p. 185.

during the Second World War at a time when successful malaria control was crucial in determining victory or defeat. Anti-larval measures were useless for protecting troops who were not in fixed camps. An insecticide that could be easily applied at fairly long intervals so as not to interfere with the waging of war was required. Having fulfilled both these conditions during the emergency, DDT came to be popularly accepted as an ideal insecticide.[10]

The residual spraying of houses with DDT was the main method of control recommended and demonstrated by the demonstration teams. Experience in Ceylon, Greece, the Guianas and India in anti-malaria operations using residual insecticides in rural areas indicated that transmission could be interrupted by using this method. As of 1950, in the western hemisphere it was only in Mexico, Colombia and Jamaica that more people were protected from malaria by engineering projects than by residual insecticides.[11] It thus seemed possible to control malaria on a wide scale, including in rural areas where the disease was of the highest public health importance.

In the years 1949 to 1952, malaria-control demonstrations by joint WHO and national teams in eleven countries proved that the overall parasite rate, and particularly the infant parasite rate,[12] could be dramatically reduced by one or two years of residual spraying with DDT.[13] Earlier, in 1947, when Brazil decided to depend entirely on residual DDT, all other tools were flamboyantly discarded: it was felt necessary to stage an elaborate public burial (complete with funeral rites) of ditching and larvicidal equipment and materials to impress on the employees of the malaria service and on the public the dawning of a new era in malaria control.

Successes were reported. In less than four years Argentina practically eliminated the problem of endemic malaria, and the country's Division of Malaria and Endemic Diseases was dissolved and converted into the Department of Health for Northern Argentina. Although Argentina's malaria law did not use the word 'eradicate', eradication was obviously the objective.[14] In the endemic zone of

10. For a general discussion of DDT and war, see P.F. Russell, *op. cit.*, pp. 109–21.
11. See Soper, *op. cit.*, p. 192. For greater detail, see A. Brown, J. Haworth and A. Zahar, 'Malaria Eradication and Control from a Global Standpoint', *J. of Medical Entomology*, vol. 13, no. 1 (1976), pp. 3–4.
12. The infant parasite rate refers to the level of malaria parasites, plasmodia, found in blood samples of infants. The larger the number, the higher the chance of developing malaria.
13. See Brown *et al., op. cit.*, Table 2, p. 3. Also see TRS 39, 1976, p. 20.
14. Law 5195 modified by Law 13266, 24 Sept. 1948, and Decree 96249. See *International Digest of Health Legislation*, vol. 2 (1950), p. 8.

Argentina it was obligatory to spray all houses with insecticide at regular intervals and to report all suspected malaria cases within twenty-four hours.[15] Comparable national commitment was shown in Ecuador, where the government declared the 'eradication of malaria to be an urgent national problem' and established the national malaria service under the National Institute of Health. This service also concentrated its efforts on the use of residual DDT.[16] The government of Ecuador also increased its budget from 400,000 sucres in 1948 to 6,220,000 sucres in 1950 – a rise of more than 1,500 per cent. Health officials estimated that 68 per cent of the houses in the endemic zones had been sprayed at least once, if not twice, in 1950, and the programme aspired to complete coverage of dangerous areas.[17]

In South Africa (not one of the eleven countries mentioned above), operations with DDT between 1946 and 1950, utilizing larvicides as well as house spraying, reduced the average infant parasite rate to less than one-fifth of its former level and eliminated malaria from 42,000 square miles (108,780 km^2) of northern Transvaal;[18] moreover, control programmes were started in Natal and Swaziland.[19] Apart from operations in Rhodesia, no other national malaria control programmes were being undertaken in Africa, although much investigative work was being performed[20] and local pilot projects were undertaken.[21]

In South America, notable progress was achieved in British Guiana, where large-scale anti-malarial operations begun in 1947 succeeded in eradicating the vector *A. darlingi* from the coastal areas.[22] DDT spraying was also eliciting good results in Brazil and Argentina.

15. Soper, *op. cit.*, pp. 190–1.
16. Despite Ecuador's exceptional display of political will in the fight against malaria, the disease continues to be prevalent there to this day.
17. Soper, *op. cit.*, p. 191.
18. See S. Annecke, 'Report on Malaria Control in Transvaal', WHO/Mal/48, 3 Oct. 1950, p. 2; and 'Malaria Control in the Transvaal', WHO/Mal/90, 19 June 1953, pp. 4–5.
19. 'Malaria Control Measures in Africa', *WHO Chronicle*, vol. 11 (1957), pp. 133–6.
20. L. J. Bruce-Chwatt, 'Problems of Malaria Control in Tropical Africa', *British Medical Journal*, 23 Jan. 1954, p. 164.
21. J. Hamon, J. Mouchet, G. Chauvet and R. Lumaret, 'Bilan de quatorze années de lutte controle de paludisme dans les pays francophone d'Afrique tropicale', *Bulletin de la Société de pathologie exotique*, vol. 56 (1963), p. 933.
22. G. Giglioli, 'Eradication of *Anopheles darlingi* from the Inhabited Areas of British Guiana by DDT Residual Spraying', *J. of the National Malaria Society*, vol. 10 (1951), p. 142.

These early attempts resulted in spectacular successes; the exceptions received less attention and went largely undocumented. In sub-Saharan Africa the pilot projects using residual DDT spraying led to a significant reduction in malaria morbidity and mortality, but no interruption of transmission could be achieved.[23] The eagerness of some countries to report good results to the WHO led to an underestimation of the problem and an overestimation of the achievements. In his opening speech to the 1950 Malaria Conference in Equatorial Africa, Sir John Hathorn Hall, the Governor of Uganda, alluded to this: 'It is true that Kampala itself has been rendered virtually free from malaria, but you would not have to stray far afield . . . to find hyperendemic conditions which persist throughout the greater part of Uganda.'[24]

In many places, the effectiveness of DDT residual deposits was somewhat handicapped by the excito-repellent effect they had on some anophelines, notably *A. gambiae*. Excito-repellency in malaria eradication terminology refers to the property in an insecticide of stimulating irritability in mosquitoes, which then learn to avoid DDT-sprayed surfaces (rendering the spraying useless for malaria eradication).[25] Even though the anophelines were no longer found during searches made in the daytime after spray applications, this did not necessarily represent the true situation at night, when the anophelines that are present may leave the dwelling soon after biting, and survive.

It had been shown that in Uganda, 38 per cent of the *A. gambiae* entering mud huts treated with 2 grams per square metre did in fact survive. Similar results were seen in Mexico. Several malaria control and/or eradication schemes based on DDT or dieldrin house spraying were organized between 1953 and 1960 in the savannas of West Africa, from the northern Cameroons to Senegal. Despite an unusually good insecticide coverage obtained during several consecutive years, *A. funestus* was never eradicated in northern Cameroon, northern Nigeria or Upper Volta.[26]

23. This lack of interruption of malaria transmission was later referred to by the WHO as the reason why the malaria eradication programme was not extended to sub-Saharan Africa.
24. See TRS 38, 1950, p. 51.
25. See G. Davidson, 'Experiments on the Effect of Residual Insecticides in Houses against *Anopheles gambiae* and *A. funestus*', *Bulletin of Entomological Research*, vol. 44 (1953), p. 231.
26. For a summary, see J. Hamon, J. Brengues and G. Chauvet, 'Problems Facing Anopheline Vector Control', *Miscellaneous Publications of the Entomological Society of America*, vol. 7, no. 1 (1970) p. 30.

Most early difficulties were overshadowed by contemporaneous successes. The largest DDT residual spraying campaign in Latin America, in the highly endemic areas of Venezuela, led by Dr Gabaldon in the early 1950s, had spectacular success in eliminating malaria. As malaria eradication became imminent, Venezuelan authorities became increasingly sanguine in their assumption that theirs was a malaria-free country. Practical (non-medical) benefits of malaria eradication ensued: law enforcement officials were allowed to identify smugglers by blood tests for the malaria parasite, assuming that a positive test without formal documentation implied illicit foreign travel.[27] The Venezuelan experience also helped to suppress overt discussion of the potential failures of other campaigns, while at the same time convincing any sceptics of at least the potential efficacy of such campaigns.

Hence, in 1954, the fourteenth Pan American Sanitary Conference in Santiago, Chile, resolved 'to join efforts with the international organizations to face the enormous task of eradicating malaria from this hemisphere'.[28] One year later, in Mexico City, the eighth WHA (1955) passed a resolution marking the largest public health venture in history. The WHO urged governments to transform their malaria control schemes into programmes aiming at eradication.[29] This resolution was long overdue according to some eminent malariologists, who suggested that

> considering that it is only five years since DDT became available, and that approximately 75% of the habitations in the malarious regions of the Americas are in countries with nation-wide programs for the eradication of malaria, it is not too much to anticipate that the rest of the job can be done during the next five years, if full advantage is taken of the services of the international organizations responsible for coordination of health activities.[30]

The resolution of the eighth WHA reflected the belief that by 1955 the methodology of malaria control, with its house-to-house visits, spray crews, transport of insecticide, compression sprayers, and the dose and frequency of insecticide to be applied, had essentially become standardized.[31]

27. See Soper, *op. cit.*, p. 188.
28. See OR 61, 1955, Appendix 5.
29. Resolution WHA8.30 is discussed in OR 63, 1955, p. 31.
30. *Ibid.*, p. 192. For similar views, see also TRS 123, 1957, p. 16.
31. See TRS 80, 1954, p. 20. Also see M.E. Farinaud, 'Eradication of Malaria: Programmes and Organization', Expert Committee on Malaria, Inter-regional Conference on Malaria, Working Paper 1, 21 Mar. 1956, p. 17.

The timing of the resolution was no doubted also influenced by the presence of several eminent malariologists within senior WHO ranks. It was no coincidence that, at one time, five of the six WHO Regional Directors were ex-malariologists; even the then Director-General was a veteran of the Brazilian Malaria Eradication Service.

These public health leaders were convinced that in rallying public health opinion around one objective, such as malaria eradication, the Ministries of Health, particularly those of developing countries, would be roused from their apathy regarding public health and preventive medicine. There was some evidence for this view. For instance, soon after the WHO resolution of 1955, the concept of eradication was rapidly adopted by all the thirty-five malarious countries in the Americas region.[32]

The malaria control projects were also attracting international funding: by 1955 twenty-nine countries were being assisted with expertise from the WHO (which was partly funded under the UN Expanded Programme of Technical Assistance),[33] and by commodities such as insecticides and equipment from UNICEF.[34] While the WHO had provided great impetus for the programme, it lacked the financial resources to attempt worldwide malaria eradication on its own. With its large staff of malariologists, the WHO's major role was that of a coordinating authority. WHO funds for malaria were limited, and some fund-raising efforts of symbolic and practical significance were instituted: a postage stamp was issued commemorating the start of malaria eradication, while the Malaria Eradication Special Account, to which nations, organizations and individuals were encouraged to make contributions, was also established.[35]

32. See OR 176, 1969, p. 110.
33. See OR 63, 1955, p. 31.
34. See 'Report on Malaria Eradication by the Director-General of WHO', UNICEF document E/ICEF/386, 21 July 1959. See also OR 71, 1956. p. 43. Also consult E.J. Pampana and P.F. Russell, 'Malaria, a World Problem', *WHO Chronicle*, vol. 9 (1955), pp. 31–100.
35. See OR 63, 1955, p. 31, and OR 106, 1960, p. 7.

21
MALARIA ERADICATION *VS.* MALARIA CONTROL

By 1955 malariologists had begun to fear 'the potential danger of a development of resistance to insecticides in anopheline vector species'.[1] Indeed, resistance was already appearing in parts of the world.[2] A participant in the inter-regional conference on malaria in 1956 observed that the case for eradication was 'made primarily because more kinds of mosquitoes are becoming resistant: we have emphasized that there may be no choice between attempting eradication and living indefinitely with mosquitoes that have learned to live with DDT'.[3] Considerable social and economic advantages of malaria eradication were also presumed.[4] Prominent among these was the understanding that an eradication programme would need to be financed for a limited time only – during which its necessity would be understood by the people and by their representatives in the legislature, as well as by donor countries such as the USA – whereas sustaining successful control would call for continued financial support long after the disease had become largely a memory. As one WHO expert put it, one reason 'for proceeding at once to nation-wide eradication is the fact that international aid monies are available now to assist in such projects but may not be obtainable in later years'.[5]

Moreover, it was felt that in view of the apparent eradicability of malaria, mere control might no longer stimulate interest and support, and hence such a programme might be expected to fail in the

1. OR 60, 1955, p. 27.
2. Early resistance was evident in Greece, Indonesia and Saudi Arabia. See E. J. Pampana, 'The Control of Malaria Vectors in Regions where the Vector Has Become Resistant to DDT and Other Chlorinated Hydrocarbon Insecticides', Working Paper 4, Inter-regional Conference on Malaria, 21 May 1956; G. A. Livadas, 'Development of Resistance to DDT by Anopheles Sacharovi in Greece', WHO/Mal/80, 22 Jan. 1953; and M. A. Farid, 'Non-effectiveness of DDT Residual Spraying in Stopping Malaria Transmission in the Jordan Valley', WHO/Mal/82, 10 Feb. 1953.
3. See S. M. Keeny, 'Organizing for the Last Battle against Malaria', Working Paper 25, Inter-regional Conference on Malaria, 11 May 1956, p. 1.
4. See S. Annecke, 'Economic Importance of Malaria', WHO/Mal/57, 24 Oct. 1950, pp. 2–4.
5. See Paul F. Russell, 'Advisability and Practicability of Eradication', Working Paper 13, Inter-regional Conference on Malaria, 16 Apr. 1956, p. 4.

end.[6] Opinion veered strongly towards malaria eradication as a universal goal, and was further coaxed in this direction by what the international organizations such as UNICEF and the WHO considered to be increasing evidence of its practicability and value. UNICEF's Regional Director for Asia, S. Keeny, may have best summarized the prevailing view: 'this is the "golden moment" for an all-out attack on malaria', and 'if it is not seized it may never come again.'[7]

It was believed that an eradication programme would bring benefits which would far outweigh its cost or inconvenience: 'Eradication campaigns are costly affairs and require expert direction but once they have been brought to a successful conclusion the recurrent expenditure is negligible.'[8] Similar views were expressed in a WHO technical report:

> Eradication in itself is a literally invaluable benefit, both in terms of the increased expectation of life, health and well-being of the people and in terms of social and economic advantage. The programme, though intensive, is relatively brief; the money spent may be looked on as capital investment and not as a perpetually recurring item; in the existing state of our knowledge there is every reason to hope that the adaptation of the mosquito to insecticides can be kept at bay long enough to secure eradication, whereas unending successful reliance on insecticides is by no means foreseeable.[9]

The emphasis on short-term expenditure on MEPs (versus long-term expense on malaria control measures) was not directly aimed to appeal specifically to any country; however, as will be evident below, such an emphasis did affect the attitude of the US Congress.

It was argued that while malaria control programmes might be affected by negative political priorities, the economic benefits of an eradication programme would be obvious to politicians.[10] Whereas control was described by the WHO as merely 'good', eradication would be 'perfect'.[11] As one observer put it, 'control has become almost a dirty word, we use it with apologies.'[12]

In retrospect, it appears that even those arguments suggesting the impracticability of malaria eradication were presented in support of

6. See TRS 123, 1957, p. 6.
7. See Keeny, *op. cit.*, p. 7.
8. B. Meillon, 'Malaria Survey of South West Africa', WHO/Mal/61, 24 Nov. 1950, p. 92.
9. TRS 123, 1957, p. 10.
10. *Ibid.*, p. 9.
11. See WHO, *Malaria Eradication: a Plea for Health*, Geneva, 1958, p. 6.
12. See Keeny, *op. cit.*, p. 1.

eradication. Integration of anti-malaria measures with other insect-control programmes is a case in point: such integration is often convenient and feasible in an integrated public health programme but is not always feasible in an eradication programme, because the latter has a specific, well-defined objective to be attained within a limited time. A WHO Expert Committee argued, however, that

> in producing eradication, a government gains an asset in well-trained staff of all grades available for other services, and it also gains a new approach to the technique of communicable disease prevention which can be a valuable stimulus to similar progress in campaigns against other such diseases.[13]

This was basically the functionalist argument of spillover, which had also been made at the WHO Malaria Conference for the Eastern Mediterranean and European Regions in 1956:

> In countries where the public health service is not well developed, the development of an eradication service will be a pattern of an efficient service and will serve as a nucleus around which the public health service could be built.
>
> A group of public health personnel, well trained in the techniques of malaria eradication, would be, after a minimum of special training, particularly well qualified to deal with other rural health problems. Thus, while concentrating full attention on malaria eradication, it is necessary at the same time to look forward and to plan for the full utilization of the services of the malaria eradication staff once malaria has been eradicated.[14]

The predicted spillover was to start early on in the anti-malaria efforts, and to a peak with malaria eradication. Up until the end of the programme, the WHO recommended (in 1957):

> Eradication of malaria should be looked on as an urgent measure, outside the regular routine of health.
>
> Any country planning to eradicate malaria needs a special malaria service which should preferably be a primary division of the national health department.[15]

Even as late as 1967, when serious problems were evident in malaria eradication efforts, similar recommendations were made by the WHO: 'The government should accord the programme the

13. TRS 123, 1957, p. 10.
14. See E. B. Weeks, Chief, Planning and Programme, Division of Malaria Eradication, 'Minimum Conditions to be Met before Initiating a Malaria Eradication Programme', Geneva, Mal/Exp. Com.14/67.2, 12 Sept. 1967, p. 5.
15. See TRS 123, 1957, p. 10. Also see G. Gramiccia, 'The Organization of Malaria Eradication within the Framework of General Public Health and Administration', Working Paper 29, Expert Committee on Malaria, 26 Aug. 1958, pp. 1–7.

necessary priority, recognizing that a malaria eradication programme will not only remove one of the most important public health problems but will also provide an effective total coverage basis health service.'[16]

It appears that no particular level of health service was demanded as a prerequisite for a MEP,[17] and it was recommended that the eradication programme be organized in a vertical manner – that is, with the chain of command run from the top down and the programme as a specialist effort, independent from the rest of the public health infrastructure.[18]

Some of these suggestions are now seen as unrealistic. For instance, because public health specialists specialize in certain areas, experts from one field are not necessarily in a position to move easily into another.

Another instance of serious impracticability in the malaria eradication approach concerned case-finding. Case-finding refers to the identification of malaria-infected individuals, and their treatment. It offers a gauge of the extent of the disease. Active case-finding involves visiting, at regular intervals, all houses in the malarious area and taking blood specimens of any inhabitants who have, or have recently had, fever. Although this was of secondary importance in a malaria control programme, it was of primary importance in malaria eradication. The massive logistical problem involved in isolating every case of malaria in most developing countries necessitates a cautious estimation of success. The epidemiological investigation of individual cases, which would follow the case isolation, is also essential to an eradication approach and involves serious logistical problems as well. This investigation often involves an international investigation component, which depends on friendly relations between neighbouring countries. Such good relations are also presumed if the number of imported cases of malaria is to be limited: this is of minor interest (mostly academic) in malaria control programmes but is very important in malaria eradication efforts, especially when partial eradication is achieved.[19]

Despite this list of potential difficulties in achieving successful malaria eradication, it was presumed by WHO officials, and by public health officials in general, that despite past experience of international cooperation in public health (which has been rife with

16. See TRS 357, 1967, p. 6.
17. See Weeks, *op. cit.*, p. 5.
18. See A. Ray, 'Maintenance of Achieved Eradication', Mal/Exp. Com.12/WP/2.65, Sept. 1965, p. 13; Weeks, *op. cit.*, pp. 2–5.
19. TRS 132, 1956, p. 32.

examples of non-cooperation even between developed countries, let alone developing ones which typically face greater obstacles to effective cooperation), these problems were soluble. Furthermore, it was not appreciated that what little cooperation that existed among countries could easily be strained both by the increasing demands on already weak administrative machineries, and by the impatience engendered when those demands were frustrated.[20] Gauging progress involves the measurement of what has been accomplished in control programmes, and the measurement of what remains to be accomplished in eradication programmes. One can easily imagine how the latter is more open to despair, and mutual accusations of inefficiency, than the former.

The WHO commitment to malaria eradication was based on several factors. One of these factors was the observation by a WHO Expert Committee on malaria that 'in the countries concerned at least, reintroduction or reappearance [of malaria] has been very much rarer than had been expected by many.' It was also accepted that 'a control programme is a practical step towards eradication only if it shortens the duration of the spraying campaign necessary for eradication.'[21] As we will see later, many developing countries prematurely started eradication programmes on the presumption that their malaria control programmes, inadequate as they often were, were 'a practical step towards eradication'.

In any country where malaria was widespread, an eradication programme would normally start with an attack on the mosquito vector, based on the application of residual insecticides on a basis of total national coverage.[22] It would continue for a sufficient number of years to ensure that at least the vast majority of malaria cases underwent cure, natural or therapeutic, while transmission and endemicity were stopped. It was thought that, ideally, 'one year's spraying with residual DDT will stop malaria transmission in a given area', and that 'if this freedom from transmission was actively maintained for 3 years, the reservoir of infection in the human population would become empty', resulting in malaria eradication.[23] To add a further margin of safety against failure, it was considered that routine spraying would be necessary for a further four years.[24]

20. Even as early as 1956, some experts considered good administration of malaria eradication programmes to be 'the missing factor'. See Keeny, *op. cit.*, p. 2.
21. TRS 123, 1957, pp. 10, 16.
22. See 'Suggested Sequence of Events in Malaria Eradication Programs', Expert Committee on Malaria, Working Paper E. 3, 20 Apr. 1956.
23. See Paul F. Russell, *op. cit.*, p. 2.
24. *Ibid.*

Whatever the mechanism used in the original programme, a stage is reached where it is assumed, on the evidence of surveillance and particularly on a search for cases, that transmission is completely ended and that the number of infective human carriers is reduced, if not to zero at least to an insignificant level. This is the moment at which spraying is stopped.

However, the end of spraying does not mean the end of malaria transmission. The WHO theory of eradication assumed that any apparent interruption of transmission was not universal until three factors were examined: first, whether there remained any undiscovered foci in which transmission persisted; secondly, if there remained in the general population some carriers from whom dissemination might occur; and lastly, if human immigrants or infected mosquitos either from the residual foci or from outside the country might at any time re-introduce the disease.[25] Thus, to take into account the above concerns, the WHO methodology of malaria eradication required that surveillance and emergency mechanisms should be a crucial part of the eradication programme.[26]

25. See A. Gabaldon, 'Malaria Eradication: Definitions, Criteria, and Terminology', Expert Committee on Malaria, Working Paper E. 8, 25 May 1956, pp. 1–4.
26. P. Yekutiel, 'Notes on Basic Problems of Eradication and Surveillance in Malaria Eradication', Expert Committee on Malaria, Working Paper 9, 5 Aug. 1958, p. 2.

22
THE FUNDING OF MALARIA ERADICATION

As mentioned earlier, the initial impetus for the eradication programme was given by the Americas Region of the WHO, leading to the WHO declaring an international eradication effort against malaria. This response may have been due in part to the desire of the then Director-General, Dr Candau, to minimize any major regional initiatives. Dr Candau was Director-General for twenty years. He had previously held the position of Assistant Director of the Pan American Sanitary Bureau in 1952 and, like his predecessor at the WHO, fought to preserve central control and initiative in the WHO, an organization whose regional structure was conducive to divided loyalties.[1] Candau always felt that power should be kept at headquarters as much as possible and would not have wanted to allow the spotlight of attention to be diverted from the centre to the periphery. Also, as a malariologist from Brazil, where the disease was rampant, the idea of eradicating malaria undoubtedly appealed to him.

More importantly, Candau appears to have thought it opportune to declare an international eradication programme in 1955, secure in the knowledge that the American government, which paid up to 40 per cent of the budget of the PAHO and which had been a major proponent of the regional declaration of a malaria eradication policy, would also find it in its interests to fund the worldwide effort. Even though the United States had a special interest in malaria eradication in its own region,[2] it would have been a great inconsistency in US aid policy if malaria eradication had been funded exclusively in the Americas Region. As will be more evident later in this book, other than the desire to help eliminate a public health menace, the American support for malaria eradication represented a continuation of the wartime economic and psychological operations approach to Latin America.[3] When the MEP was

1. For a general discussion on executive heads of the WHO, see Harold K. Jacobson,' WHO: Medicine, Regionalism, and Managed Politics', in R. Cox and H. Jacobson (eds), *The Anatomy of Influence*, Yale University Press, New Haven, Conn., 1973, pp. 198–200.
2. As will be evident later in this chapter, most of the US aid for malaria was spent in the Americas Region of the WHO.
3. See J. B. Bingham, *Shirt-Sleeve Diplomacy: Point 4 in Action*, Freeport Books, New York, 1953, pp. 19–23.

declared, it was accompanied by pleas to national governments and institutions for support and was based on the assumption that the United States would be the biggest aid donor for the programme.[4] Thus the eradication programme, which had already gained much intellectual legitimacy from public health leaders such as Drs E. Pampana, L. J. Bruce-Chwatt, Fred Soper and Candau, now needed an operational legitimacy which could only come from a major financial backer. This is where the American support for malaria eradication was crucial.[5]

The year 1956 marked the watershed in American support for the fight against malaria, because in that year President Eisenhower decided to give substantial US financial backing to the WHO's malaria eradication campaign.[6] Although this decision was officially presented as another example of the humanitarianism of the US government, much less altruistic reasons were evident in a special 'official use only' report prepared for the President by the State Department.[7] Harry Cleaver has traced the impetus for the report to Cold War exigencies. The report was prepared in response to a State Department request to the International Development Advisory Board (IDAB) to come up with new American foreign aid programmes that could help counter what was then perceived as the expansion of Soviet aid efforts in the Third World. Malaria programmes seemed perfect for this. One of the contributors to the report, Dr Wilton Halverston, Associate Dean of the School of Public Health at UCLA and formerly Director of Public Health for the state of California, argued that American support for malaria programmes

> could be received throughout the world only as a humanitarian action on the part of the people of the United States and their government toward their fellow human beings. This would do much to counter the anti-United States sentiments which have been aroused by subversive methods in these countries. If properly carried out, programs like these will challenge the Russian approach.[8]

4. WHO, *Malaria Eradication: a Plea for Health*, Geneva, 1958, p. 6.
5. Even as early as 1942, US aid was given to eight Latin American countries for malaria control activities. These countries were Bolivia, Brazil, Ecuador, Guatemala, Haiti, Honduras, Nicaragua and Peru. See D. R. Johnson, 'Development of the Worldwide Malaria Eradication Programme', *Mosquito News*, June 1966, p. 115.
6. 'U.S. Gives 7 Million Dollars to Malaria Eradication Campaign', *US Dept. of State Bulletin*, 23 Dec. 1957, pp. 1000–3.
7. See Harry Cleaver, 'Malaria and the Political Economy of Public Health', *International J. of Health Services*, vol. 7, no. 4 (1977), p. 571.
8. From W. Halverston, 'Suggestions Regarding Malaria Eradication and Urban Sanitation', International Development Advisory Board, 20 Dec. 1955 (as referenced in Cleaver, *op. cit.*).

Dr Paul F. Russell, an eminent malariologist, also developed these arguments in testimony given to the IDAB:

Dr Russell pointed out that a malaria eradication programme was a dramatic undertaking that would penetrate into the homes of people and would benefit the US politically and financially.[9]

Such arguments were crucial in the resulting US support for malaria eradication, which in the first five years of the programme alone amounted to approximately US$150 million. This provided great impetus to the global programme, and malaria eradication activities were intensified substantially in many countries. From 1958 to 1966, the United States provided direct assistance to a total of twenty-eight countries, as well as to the WHO Special Malaria Fund.[10]

Following the spirit of the eighth World Health Assembly resolution on malaria eradication, many international and bilateral agencies which had been assisting governments in their control schemes became reluctant to support control operations.[11] In 1956 the US government recommended that all its malaria control activities be converted to MEPs, and that such activities be carried on both directly, through its own bilateral programmes overseas, and indirectly, through multilateral agencies such as the WHO. This identification of WHO and US priorities was one of the main driving forces behind the MEP.

After he had announced this anti-malaria support, the President put it to its originally planned Cold War use by magnanimously inviting 'the Soviets to join us in this great work of humanity'.[12] In a message to Congress, President Eisenhower referred to malaria as the 'World's foremost health problem'. In 1957 the US Congress acted positively on his request to increase spending on malaria and to convert control programmes to eradication ones:

The Congress of the United States, recognizing that the disease of malaria, because of its widespread prevalence, debilitating effects, and heavy toll on human life, constitutes a major deterrent to the efforts of many peoples to develop their economic resources and productive capacities and to improve

9. IDAB, Summary Minutes, 13 Apr. 1956.

10. 'Report on the Second Regional Conference on Malaria Eradication', WHO/Mal/265, 20 May 1959, p. 24, Also see Johnson, *op cit.*, p. 115.

11. See TRS 13, 1967, p. 24.

12. D. Eisenhower, 'Annual Message to Congress on the State of the Union', 9 Jan. 1958, *Public Papers of the Presidents: D. Eisenhower*, National Archives and Record Service, Washington, DC, 1958, p. 13.

their living conditions, and further recognizing that it appears now technically feasible to eradicate this disease, declares it to be the policy of the U.S. and the purpose of this section to assist other peoples in their efforts to eradicate malaria.[13]

This action by Congress made it possible to increase US support for malaria eradication programmes in many countries of the world, including India and Brazil. At the same time, the Malaria Eradication Special Account was augmented by a large US contribution.[14]

Starting in fiscal year 1958, the American anti-malaria assistance was made available exclusively for malaria eradication activities. UNICEF also began to give priority to eradication in its aid programmes, as did the American Public Health Association.[15] This made early reconsideration of the wisdom of the eradication programme inappropriate, and many developing countries made what even then were considered premature conversions of their already inadequate malaria control programmes into even more inadequate MEPs. According to an Expert Committee of the WHO which met in 1966, the premature conversions of control to eradication programmes were understandable: 'The governments . . . did not want to lose external assistance and interrupt the control operations that had already yielded [some] good results.'[16] In 1956 a more cynical view was expressed by a UNICEF official: 'country after country is coming forward with its request for aid. It is pleasant to be progressive – especially so when international aid is available more generously for eradication than for control.'[17]

Once the snowball effect took over, the WHO, which thus far had suggested that an effective control programme was a prerequisite for attempts at eradication,[18] now suggested that even countries without any control programmes could go straight to eradication.[19] Some countries, lacking in expertise to start anti-malaria programmes, were supplied by the WHO with a 'short-term consultant to assist . . . in preparing a plan of operations for malaria eradication'.[20]

13. From Johnson, *op. cit.*, p. 114.
14. See OR 90, 1958, p. 3, and OR 135, 1964, p. 98.
15. See P.F. Russell, 'Advisability and Practicability of Eradication', Working Paper 13, Inter-regional Conference of Malaria, 16 Apr. 1956, p. 5.
16. See TRS 13, 1967, p. 24.
17. S.M. Keeny, 'Organizing for the Last Battle against Malaria', Inter-regional Conference on Malaria, Working Paper 25, 11 May 1956, p. 2.
18. OR 71, 1956, p. 44.
19. See *WHO Chronicle*, vol. 13, nos. 9–10 (1959), p. 363.
20. See OR 90, 1958, p. 4.

As one malaria worker noted, among member states too the expectations were high:[21]

> In many governmental quarters it seems to be taken almost for granted that malaria is going to be eradicated without much reorganization of present [control] services. Five years have been mentioned as a possible goal: many are even thinking that all countries can eradicate all their malaria in the same five years.[22]

In 1960, however, the rush to declare eradication programmes was understood by a WHO Expert Committee, which recognized that 'most countries are naturally anxious to undertake malaria eradication in order to obtain its benefits and to fall in line with neighbouring states, and they will therefore stand in need of assistance.'[23] And in 1966 another WHO Expert Committee referred to the conversion from malaria control to malaria eradication: 'in the early days [of malaria eradication], some malaria control programmes were renamed malaria eradication programmes without any significant change being made in the plan of operations.'[24]

Thus the influence of the United States and its monetary contributions played a great role in propelling many national malaria programmes towards eradication campaigns. The arguments against control, and those in favour of eradication, were now sponsored by the United States, the WHO, UNICEF and also, understandably, by the developing countries which would be the main beneficiaries if malaria were indeed eradicated:

> The response to the [malaria] alarm rung by WHO has been astonishing. All the international agencies are telling the same story with a unanimity that is almost as novel as it is pleasing. The governments of most of the people . . . still unprotected agree on eradication, at least in principle, and many of them are attempting it.[25]

Because of these factors, the WHO turned down the narrow path towards eradication, leaving itself very little room for manoeuvre, save for a U-turn.

21. See M. J. Andray, 'Progress of the Malaria Control Programme, Administrative Patterns, Advisability and Practicability of Eradication', Working Paper 22, Interregional Conference on Malaria, 27 Apr. 1956, pp. 1–5.
22. See Keeny, *op. cit.*, p. 2.
23. See TRS 205, 1961, p. x.
24. See TRS 357. 1967, p. 24.
25. Keeny, *op. cit.*, pp. 1–2.

23

JUSTIFICATIONS FOR THE M.E.P.

The period under discussion here not only witnessed a dramatic new role for the WHO's advisory services, it also brought to light the strong connection between health and economics. The fact that the WHO was encouraging the conversion of malaria control programmes into MEPs meant that affected countries became (or remained) eligible for funds from health aid donors. For the first time, the WHO needed to justify the projected expenditure of aid dollars on malaria; it had to justify the relevance of malaria eradication in general. Moreover, the high short-term cost of the eradication programme made the economic arguments seem even more attractive and relevant.[1]

For countries such as the United States, this justification was of immense importance because it offered a final solution to malaria which would also free aid dollars for other projects. Also, as discussed earlier, malaria provided an ideal aid project that could serve the purposes of propaganda, both for the national government and for the foreign donor. It was a good foreign aid tool.

In the overall justification for a MEP, the direct human suffering was only one of the components that was considered relevant. The economic and social importance of malaria eradication was also considered of considerable importance; this importance was said to derive from the many insidious effects of malaria. One WHO publication painted the picture thus: 'Malaria is the world's greatest single cause of disablement; it stunts physical and mental development; it hampers the exploitation of natural resources, reduces agricultural production, and impairs industry and commerce.'[2]

The amount of information relating to the economic importance of malaria was quite small in the early 1950s. This lack of basic data was the main reason for a lack of consensus regarding the effect of malaria on the distribution of population, on population movements, on demographic trends, on agriculture, industry, transportation, education and social welfare.[3]

1. See TRS 123, 1957, p. 9.
2. WHO, *Malaria Eradication: a Plea for Health*, Geneva, 1958, p. 5.
3. A case study was conducted by Gladys Conly, in 1975 on '*The Impact of Malaria on Economic Development*', which was produced as a PAHO publication (PAHO, Washington, DC, 1975). This was one of the first in-depth studies showing an inverse correlation between the extent of malaria and development.

Despite these differences, it was suggested by the WHO that in at least 120 countries and territories of the world, out of a total of 210 (in 1955), malaria hindered economic development.[4] The WHO did admit, however, that it was not possible at the time to assess statistically the full economic effects in all the areas where the disease was rife: 'The relationship between health and economic development has long been recognized, but computation of health factors in economic terms is a relatively new technique.'[5]

Various claims were made about estimates of the loss to the economy due to malaria and, though these were described as 'partial and incomplete' by the WHO itself, the Organization suggested that they 'do show for the areas concerned serious losses in human capital, in man-hours and in agricultural and industrial output'.[6] The benefit to sugar plantation and production that would result from malaria eradication in the Hawash Valley in Ethiopia was cited as an example of the economic impact of malaria. It was estimated that in the space of thirty-five years, the development of the entire valley could raise family income from about 200 Ethiopian dollars per year to 736 dollars.[7] Although this sort of argument was never made explicitly in the early days of international public health when cholera was a major scourge, it had now gained legitimacy. It was very difficult, at the time, to disagree intuitively with these claims.

The effect of malaria on the economy was illustrated by arguments concerning cost/benefit analyses, labour and land utilization, and industrial development. These original arguments were not scrutinized rigorously for several reasons, one of which was the lack of adequate data, another the haste with which the MEP was undertaken. According to the WHO, part of the reason for this haste was the fear that the anophelines would develop resistance to DDT if an attack was not immediately mounted. As of 1958, of the sixty species of mosquitoes known to be malaria vectors, four had developed resistance against insecticide and the WHO suggested that 'there are indications that the insecticides now available could become ineffective within five to ten years. This would deprive us of the only practical means of eradicating malaria at present available.'[8]

4. See 'Proposed Study for the Socio-economic Evaluation of Malaria Eradication Programmes', WHO document ME/68.6, 1966, pp. 1–12.
5. See Conly, *op. cit.*, p. v.
6. At the time there were no concrete data to prove even these claims, although they are now considered valid. See *Malaria Eradication: a Plea for Health, op. cit.*
7. See 'Report on the Second Regional Conference on Malaria Eradication', WHO/Mal/265, 20 May 1959, p. 25.
8. *Malaria Eradication: a Plea for Health, op. cit.*, p. 10.

'The prevention of malaria on a large scale is a great economical as well as a great humanitarian undertaking', wrote Ronald Ross in 1911.[9] In 1955 too, both economic and humanitarian arguments were used. As Bruce-Chwatt has noted: 'Of all the human diseases malaria is the one that gave rise to the greatest number of attempts to quantify its direct and indirect adverse effects on socio-economic conditions.'[10]

Cost of Medical Care vs. that of Eradication

Expenditure on medical care, drugs and hospitalization for malaria cases varies from country to country, according to the availability of local medical services and their degree of development. One feature, however, is common to such expenditure in all affected countries: it is a recurrent and thus continual drain on the national economy. It has been suggested that 'the total amount of this expenditure over a five-year period may be as much as the estimated cost of malaria eradication, for which the capital outlay is limited to a period of about five years.'[11] The WHO estimated that it would cost about US$600 million for the first five years of the eradication programme:

> An eradication programme in an area where transmission had not previously been interrupted might require 4 or even 5 years of spraying. If, in this area, malaria control had already interrupted transmission, eradication might then require only 3 or 4 years of spraying.[12]

Moreover, the WHO claimed that after 1962 the budgetary requirements for malaria eradication would diminish yearly and from then on the financial burden would be shared among a much greater number of nations, as it would be in the interest of countries freed from malaria to help others to achieve eradication.

It was expected that in the early stages of the MEP the expenses would be equally divided between insecticides, transport and salaries; in later stages, salaries were to take up the greatest part. Of the various estimates of malaria control by residual spraying, per person protected, figures as low as US$0.11 (in Southeast Asia) and $0.455 (in the Americas), and as high as $0.80 (in Africa), were given as the expected expenses. The cost of eradication would, the WHO

9. Ronald Ross, *The Prevention of Malaria*, John Murray, London, 1911, p. 7.
10. L. J. Bruce-Chwatt, 'The Challenge of Malaria: Crossroads or Impasse?', in Clive Wood (ed), *Tropical Medicine: from Romance to Reality*, Academic Press, London, 1978, p. 39.
11. *Ibid*., pp. 10–12.
12. TRS 123, 1957, p. 16.

argued, be 10 per cent higher.[13] This 1957 estimate gave the total cost of eradicating malaria from the world over the subsequent eight to ten years as $1,691 million.[14]

In 1959, the WHO estimated the cost of eradicating malaria to be $1,657.5 million, of which $57.5 million was the cost of its advisory services.[15] Later, in the mid-1960s, the International Cooperation Administration of the United States requested a group of American scientists to calculate the cost of global eradication from 1960 until completion of the task. This panel estimated the cost at $1,342.5 million.[16]

By 1963 the WHO had come up with a further calculation of the cost of malaria eradication from 1963 until completion of the task, on a country-by-country basis – these cost forecasts were 'prepared for every malarious country of the world, regardless of whether or not an eradication programme is planned'.[17] Despite the claim, not 'every malarious country' was included in the forecasts, which did not take into account malaria eradication costs for countries in sub-Saharan Africa for the period 1968 onwards; moreover, the 750 million inhabitants of the PRC, North Vietnam and North Korea were totally excluded from the forecasts since they were not members of the WHO.

The total estimate from 1963 to the end of the project was calculated as $1,806 million, of which $84 million was the estimated expense of WHO advisory services. The increase in cost from the 1959 estimates was blamed on: (i) influx of populations into malarious areas, thus increasing the population at risk and the challenge of eradication; (ii) increase in prices of labour and materials of approximately 4 per cent annually; (iii) increased use of pesticides; and (iv) use of more expensive insecticides due to vector resistance to cheaper ones.[18] Despite the change in estimates, the overall price of malaria eradication was not considered high.

13. *Ibid.*, p. 6. Also see Wood, *op. cit.*, p. 40.

14. See E. J. Pampana, 'Unexpected Cost Increases of Malaria Eradication Programme', WHO/Mal/208, 26 Aug. 1958, for details.

15. See 'Forecast of Global Cost and Financing of Malaria Eradication', EB33/4 Add. 1., 18 Dec. 1963, p. 1.

16. See International Cooperation Administration Expert Panel on Malaria, 'Report and Recommendations on Malaria: a Summary', *Am. J. Trop. Med. and Hyg.*, vol. 10 (1961), pp. 451–502.

17. See EB33/4 Add. 1, 18 Dec. 1963, p. 1; also see EB33/4, Annex, 1964.

18. See EB33/4 Add. 1, 18 Dec. 1963, p. 2; also see Pampana, *op. cit.*, pp. 1–4.

Manpower Losses

Premature death caused by malaria was the major concern regarding losses in manpower. The high mortality rates among infants and children in many parts of the world due to the direct effects of malaria added justification to calls for eradication of the disease. In Africa, for example, it was estimated that 10–15 per cent of children below the ages of three or four died of the direct effects of the disease. The indirect effects (when malaria increased the mortality from other diseases) were not assessed, but were also presumed to be substantial.

Malaria raised morbidity rates too. It was shown that each infected adult suffered from at least one recurrence of malaria annually which incapacitated him or her for an average of six days. Computation of the total number of malaria cases and the percentage of the economically active population showed that in 1955 the annual loss of working time due to the average six-day attack was some 130 million working days in India, 4 million in Mexico and between 9 million and 9.5 million in Thailand.[19]

In addition to causing the loss of life-capital through premature death and the loss of working time through the annual six-day attack, malaria decreases working capacity throughout the year. The money value of these losses caused by the decrease in production could not be calculated in 1955 because this required the determination of the exact extent of disablement. These data were not available at the time, but in India the annual loss on this account was estimated at US$400 million.[20]

Population Movements and Land Utilization

In 1955, the relationship between the distribution of malaria and the distribution of populations was difficult to gauge with any degree of certainty. What was clear is that malaria had been introduced into certain regions by massive population movements, as in the case of the highlands of Rwanda-Urundi, where the disease was brought by Belgian troops during the First World War. To take another example, malaria was unknown on the high plateaus of Madagascar until the end of the nineteenth century, when migration from the coastal areas imported the disease. The development of rice cultivation by

19. See *Malaria Eradication: a Plea for Health, op. cit.*, p. 6.
20. See A. J. Sinton, 'What Malaria Costs India', *Record of the Malaria Survey, India*, no. 6, Delhi, 1936; also see *Malaria Eradication: a Plea for Health, op. cit.*, p. 6.

the transplanted population in the higher regions also served to increase breeding sites for malaria vectors.

Malaria experts suggested that the movement of populations was closely linked with economic progress and was one of the essential requirements for this progress. Malaria, by impeding the movement of populations, or by invading new territories because of better transportation facilities, was considered to exert a prejudicial effect on the development of the area involved.[21]

In the densely populated monsoon areas of Asia, Central America and equatorial Africa, great tracts of fertile land lay uncultivated or abandoned as a direct consequence of endemic malaria. Some of these lands were beginning to be cultivated in Ceylon, India, Java and Mexico as a result of malaria control measures. The positive influence that malaria eradication would have on farming was self-evident to every agriculture-based economy.

The areas described here were considered the main, though not the only, ones in which the effect of malaria was calculable in economic terms. The MEP recognized the need to express these arguments in more concrete terms with reliable data, and aimed to do so while the programme progressed: 'the techniques designed to express the effects of the disease in economic terms can and will be improved.'[22] Obviously, strong associations between malaria and economics would serve to confirm the importance of the MEP.

21. *The Report on the Malaria Conference in Equatorial Africa*, TRS 38, WHO, 1951, suggested that the mass movements of non-immune or semi-immune populations to malarious areas should be supervised in order to prevent consequences due to their exposure to a new infection. See pp. 24–5.
22. See *Malaria Eradication: a Plea for Health, op. cit.*, p. 7.

24

EARLY RESULTS

Early Successes of the MEP

The sixth WHO Expert Committee on malaria, convened in 1956, worked out the global strategy of malaria eradication. In view of the absence of any previous precedent of an international health programme of similar magnitude, the following decade was certainly the best of times for public health in general and malaria eradication in particular.

The early results of the global campaign, thanks to the high effectiveness of DDT and the WHO methodology of eradication that had been developed over the years by WHO Expert Committees on malaria, were spectacular. As early as March 1957, the WHO had declared that in ten countries or territories[1] malaria eradication was 'practically or totally achieved'.[2] However, the WHO declaration proved to be over-confident. It was not until 1961 that Venezuela became the first country to claim successful eradication. In 1962 two Caribbean island groups, St Lucia, and Grenada and Carriacou, were certified[3] by the WHO as having eradicated malaria.[4] Overall, by 1966 ten countries had achieved malaria eradication: Venezuela, Grenada and Carricou, St Lucia, Trinidad and Tobago, Dominica, Jamaica, Hungary, Spain, Bulgaria and China (Taiwan). Of these ten, five were from the Americas Region of the WHO, where most (approximately 43 per cent) of the international financial assistance for malaria eradication had been spent.[5]

The euphoria engendered by the early successes led many African colonies, for which the colonial powers had not established malaria eradication programmes, to declare malaria eradication a national goal immediately upon receiving independence and applying for

1. French overseas departments were here counted as units.
2. See OR 79, 1957, annex 11.
3. The criteria for the determination of eradication of malaria were established in the seventh report of the WHO Expert Committee on Malaria, 1959. The criteria are also discussed in 'Registration of Areas in which Malaria has been Eradicated,' Mal/Exp.Com.8/WP/23, 15 June 1960, pp. 1–5.
4. See OR 143, 1965, p. 98; also see EB33/4, 'Report on Development of Malaria Eradication Programme', 18 Nov. 1963.
5. See OR 160, annex 6, p. 56; and OR 135, annex 6, p. 77.

WHO and UN membership.[6] In countries such as Iran, the rush to launch an eradication programme meant that geographical reconnaissance of the malaria situation was not completed, 'since the conversion of . . . control measures into an eradication programme did not at once allow time'.[7]

Other countries, for instance Ethiopia, were persuaded to embark on malaria eradication by senior WHO officials such as Dr Pampana and Mr Roy Fritz, chief of the USAID malaria division.[8] The fact that a malaria epidemic had ravaged Ethiopia in 1958, causing the loss of 100,000 lives (mostly among children and the aged), was pointed to as a lesson for those still sceptical of malaria eradication:[9] 'such catastrophic outbreaks could be avoided only by adopting and implementing the policy of malaria eradication.'[10] Ethiopia started a malaria eradication programme soon after.

From the declaration of the eradication policy in 1955 onwards, an immense effort was deployed by some sixty countries, guided and coordinated by the WHO, and supported by multilateral or bilateral funds. The enormity of the task can be appreciated by the size of the workforce and the volume of insecticide: at its peak in 1961, a total of 65,000 tons of DDT and 5,000 tons of other insecticides (dieldrin, HCH) were applied annually by 130,000 spraymen.[11] In addition, some 3,000 microscopists throughout the world were fully employed by national eradication services.[12] In India alone, 60

6. Many of these countries were associate members of the WHO before independence, but the colonial powers did not request assistance for them, presumably because they felt responsible for the health of their colonies. Before the WHO's malaria eradication programme, developing countries had not attempted eradication independently. Certainly, the colonies did not have eradication programmes before independence.

7. See 'Appraisal of Typical Malaria Eradication Programmes in the Eastern Mediterranean Region: Iran', Mal/Exp.Com.8/WP/20, 15 June 1960, p. 3.

8. In the period August 1956 to December 1959, the International Cooperation Administration and the Ethiopian government had spent US$104,351 on pilot projects. See 'Final Report of Malaria Pilot Project: 1956–1959', by M.A. Zaphiropoulos, Senior WHO Advisor, Em/Mal/42, p. 12. Also see M.A. Farid, 'The Malaria Programme – from Euphoria to Anarchy', *World Health Forum*, vol. 1, nos 1 and 2, WHO, Geneva, 1980, p. 13.

9. See 'Report on the Second Regional Conference on Malaria Eradication', WHO/Mal/265, 16 Nov. 1959, p. 6.

10. *Ibid.*, p. 7.

11. L.J. Bruce-Chwatt, 'The Challenge of Malaria: Crossroads or Impasse?' in Clive Wood (ed), *Tropical Medicine: from Romance to Reality*, Academic Press, London, 1978, p. 28. Also see P. Bertagna, 'New Insecticides in Malaria Eradication Programmes', Mal/Exp.Com.9/WP/18, 23 Mar. 1962, p. 11.

12. See Wood, *op. cit.*, pp. 28–9.

million pounds of DDT powder were needed in 1960.[13] Even in the final stages of the MEP, approximately 100 million houses a year would need to be sprayed with insecticide.

Early results justified the immensity of the MEP. Spectacular successes were evident in the European countries, in the Middle East, in India, Ceylon, Taiwan and other countries of the Western Pacific, Venezuela and Mexico.[14] In places where the results were unclear, the WHO urged acceleration of eradication programmes and offered financial assistance for this to be achieved.[15]

By 1963, out of the 147 countries or other political units originally recorded as having malarious areas, the WHO claimed that '45 have wholly or partially eradicated malaria and a further 37 have Malaria Eradication Programmes in the attack and consolidation phases.'[16] In terms of population figures, this meant that, of the people originally inhabiting malarious areas (not including the PRC, North Korea and North Vietnam), 339 million (22.6 per cent) were said by the WHO to live in areas where malaria had been eradicated. A further 728 million (48.6 per cent) were covered by eradication programmes.[17] Only 125 million (8.3 per cent) were said to be still living in countries which had no plans for eventual eradication programmes.[18]

It has been estimated that by 1968 the number of people living in endemic malarious areas of the world and virtually freed from the danger of transmission of the disease increased from 316 million to 997 million.[19] Moreover, the direct mortality attributed to malaria decreased from an annual figure of some 2.5 million to less than 1 million. In India alone the annual malaria mortality figure was stated to have fallen from 750,000 in the 1950s to about 1,500 in the late 1960s.[20]

Thus the success of the world malaria eradication campaign, which in fact continued unmodified for a decade, can be judged from figures covering the period 1959 and to 1968.[21] The campaign was mainly based on covering all dwellings in malarious areas with a residual insecticide, and aimed at synchronization so that neigh-

13. See 'Dosages and Frequency of Application of Insecticides for Malaria Eradication', Mal/Exp.Com.8/WP/8, 31 May 1960, p. 1.
14. See OR 181, 1962, annex 19, pp. 186–8.
15. OR 118, 1962, annex 13, pp. 116–18.
16. 'Report on Development of Malaria Eradication Programmes', EB33/4, 18 Nov. 1963, p. 5.
17. *Ibid.*, p. 18.
18. *Ibid.*, pp. 6–7.
19. See OR 176, annex 13, p. 108.
20. *Ibid.*, p. 29.
21. The changed strategy is discussed later in this section. Also see 'Re-examination of the Global Strategy of Malaria Eradication', OR 176, annex 13, 1969, pp. 106–26.

bouring national campaigns would protect each other against re-introduction of the infection. It was estimated that each national campaign (in the absence of previous operations) would take at least eight years, according to the four-phase scheme mentioned earlier.[22]

A recapitulation of the programme's progress, as it developed from one year to the next, showed that the attack phase reached its peak in 1961,[23] and subsequently the population protected had passed into the maintenance phase at the rate of 100 million a year in 1964, 1965 and 1966.[24] By 1968 eradication had been claimed in thirty-six countries,[25] and the population of 651 million in this maintenance phase constituted well over one-third of the total population of the 147 countries (excluding the PRC, North Korea and North Vietnam) at risk from malaria.[26]

Despite the early successes, there were also remarkable failures. As early as 1956, S. M. Keeny had warned that while eradication was possible, it was not certain:

> The prophets of WHO have shown us the Promised Land, which, of course, has eradicated malaria. The vision is so dazzling that many people seem not to have heard clearly the stern words about how hard it is going to be to get there.[27]

Some early set-backs to the eradication efforts are discussed below.

Early Setbacks to the MEP

Up until 1962, most writers on malaria were optimistic about the efforts against malaria. Colbourne, for instance, wrote: 'In no country has eradication been shown to be impracticable.'[28]

22. As will be obvious from different figures given earlier, these timings were not always constant. See A. Gabaldon, 'The Time Required to Reach Eradication in Relation to Malaria Constitution', *Am. J. Trop. Med. and Hyg.*, vol. 5 (1956), pp. 966–76.
23. The other phases peaked at the following times: preparatory phase, 1964; consolidation phase, 1965; maintenance phase, 1966. See TRS 357, 1967, p. 21.
24. See TRS 357, 1967, p. 21.
25. Sixteen of these countries received assistance from the WHO; the rest from other sources. See OR 176, annex, 1969, p. 110.
26. The 651 million figure represented 37.6 of the total population (1,733 million) of the originally malarious areas, as compared with 21.5 in 1959. See OR 176, annex 13, p. 110.
27. See S. Keeny, 'Organizing for the Last Battle against Malaria', Inter-regional Conference on Malaria, Working Paper 25, 11 May 1956, p. 1.
28. This was a corollary to Dr Soper's dictum that 'malaria eradication is possible but difficult'. See M. J. Colbourne, 'A Review of Malaria Eradication Campaigns in the Western Pacific', *Annals of Tropical Medicine and Parasitology*, vol. 56 (1962), pp. 42–3.

Although WHO reports from the period 1955–68 are rife with examples of early success of the kind mentioned above, many problems and set-backs were overlooked at the time as the Organization was overcome by a tide of euphoria following these successes. An informal review of journal articles on malaria during this period indicates the striking scarcity of articles on failed attempts. These set-backs only came to be noticed when it was realized that the great emphasis on successes had overlooked a great backlog of failures, which were, by 1968, seen as serious challenges to the eradication of malaria.

The recrudescence of malaria was evident in many areas, euphemistically referred to by the WHO as 'problem areas',[29] where 'interruption of malaria transmission has not been achieved after several years of spraying.'[30] It was realized that the implementation of the programme thus far had not been without fault, and that a whole new strategy was required to combat these problems which had only recently been perceived, although they had apparently existed from the early stages of the programme.

The new realization did not deter the WHO from minimizing the extent of the 'problem areas'. In each country the 'problem area' represented only a part of the territory involved in the national eradication programme. Countries where no full-scale malaria eradication programmes had been attempted were not included in the definition of problem areas. This administratively justified classification underestimated the effective extent of problem areas even though the factors responsible for difficulties in anti-malarial programmes, eradication or not, were the same or similar.[31]

New problems also appeared as the MEP progressed. In the Americas Region, the widespread use of insecticides for agricultural purposes in a number of countries had led to the vector mosquitoes building up resistance to these insecticides. In parts of Mexico and Central America, this, together with other ecological factors, was blamed for the development of 'problem areas'.[32] This situation

29. Funding problems were blamed for the existence of these 'problem areas'. See OR 176, annex 13, 1969, p. 113.

30. See E. Pampana, 'Problem Areas', Mal/Exp.Com.14/67.10, 27 June 1967, p. 1; I. Vincke, 'Practical Methods for the Study of Factors Causing Difficulties in Malaria Eradication', Mal/Exp.Com.10/WP/36, 9 Aug. 1963, p. 1.

31. See L. J. Bruce-Chwatt, 'Global Review of Malaria Control and Eradication by Attack on the Vector', *Misc. Publications of the Entomol. Soc. of America*, vol. 7, no. 1 (1970), p. 17.

32. For different aspects of problem areas, see J. Kerr, 'Problem Areas in Malaria Eradication Programmes', Mal/Exp.Com. 10/WP20, 24 June 1963, pp. 1–4; and M.A. Farid, 'Problem Areas in Malaria Eradication Programmes', Mal/Exp. Com.10/WP/15, 14 June 1963, pp. 1–3.

was aggravated by steadily diminishing funds, caused by a show of non-confidence by the major donor agencies.

In the Southeast Asia Region, the progress in the programme had been marked, notably in India, which accounted for one-third of the world population living in malarious areas. However, by 1969 there had been a noticeable increase in the number of cases in some areas in the consolidation and maintenance phases, due to the non-availability of adequate quantities of insecticides to deal promptly with foci, and to the inadequacy in some areas of health service coverage; 'as a precautionary measure', it had been deemed advisable to reinstitute spraying in parts of the country.[33] Despite the recrudescence since 1965, by 1969 the number of malaria cases in India was not rising as dramatically as it was in the rest of the region.

The results in India were obtained by an effort involving the cooperation of large segments of the population in one way or another, at a total cost of US$380 million to the country and its external supporters. Although some populations living in areas with MEPs did gain some health benefits, application of a reasonable 12 per cent to the discount rate employed in the calculations indicated that time-limited malaria eradication was not more economical than time-unlimited malaria control. For the first time, one of the major economics-based arguments in favour of the original eradication programme was nullified. It now appeared that malaria control programmes were at least as useful (if not more so) as those aimed at eradication.[34]

By the late 1960s, various factors slowed the hitherto impressive progress of this campaign. In the Southeast Asia Region, the DDT resistance of *A. culicifacies*, first reported from Baroda by Giles in 1960, had expanded to several Indian states and parts of West Pakistan. Over-optimistic malariologists, however, did not see this as a threat; one said that the situation 'did not seem to constitute a major problem'.[35] This was one example of the great miscalculations of the public health leaders of the time. India and Pakistan have seen by far the most dramatic increase in malaria. In India, the incidence of the disease rose steadily between 1962 (62,000 cases) and 1969 (349,000 cases), and thereafter exploded to an appalling 4.2 million in 1975. In Pakistan, USAID reported an increase in

33. See A. W. Brown, J. Haworth and A. Zahar, 'Malaria Eradication and Control from a Global Standpoint', *J. of Medical Entomology*, vol. 13, no. 1 (1976). p. 10.
34. *Ibid.*, p. 11.
35. See H. Cleaver, 'Malaria and the Political Economy of Public Health', *International J. of Health Services*, vol. 7, no. 4 (1977), p. 559.

malaria cases from 9,500 in 1968 to 10 million in 1974. The increase of malaria incidence in the Indian subcontinent has not been attributed to any great extent to insecticide resistance in the mosquitoes, the most frequently cited WHO technical problem.[36]

The warnings had come as early as 1948. Viswanathan and Ramachandra Rao had recorded reduction in sensitivity in the second year of spraying (as compared to the first) in the case of both *A. fluviatilis* and *A. culcifacies*. This led them to conclude that: 'as long as DDT is sprayed at the dosage and with the intervals that are at present generally adopted in this country [India], eradication of vector species could not be possible even after continued spraying over a number of years.'[37] They also pointed out that eradication schemes have undoubted utility only under restricted and specialized conditions and that this indicated their unsuitability for vast countries like India. This specific warning went unheeded.

In 1963, Ceylon had reported only seventeen cases of malaria; however, between 1965 and 1968 several pockets of malarious areas appeared which were not dealt with in a timely or adequate manner. In the widespread epidemic that ensued in 1968, over 1 million malaria cases were reported. In Indonesia, too, the initial progress was not maintained because of local administrative and economic difficulties, lack of essential imported commodities, and political unrest after 1965.[38]

In the Eastern Mediterranean Region, technical problems in the southern parts of Iran and Iraq, including the double insecticide resistance of the principal vector as well as the large-scale movements of nomadic populations, endangered the progress made in other parts of these countries.[39]

Sub-Saharan Africa had been excluded from the MEP of the WHO right from 1955, because of the area's extremely high intensity of malaria transmission, almost complete lack of health infrastructure and lack of national resources.[40] Moreover, in the African

36. *Ibid.*
37. See V. Venkat Rao, 'A Critical Review of Malaria Control Measures in India', *Indian J. of Malariology*, vol. 3 (Dec. 1949), p. 319. Also, for general discussion of the Indian malaria eradication programme, see D.J. Pletsch, F.E. Gartrell and E. Harold Hinman, *A Critical Review of the National Malaria Eradication Programme of India*, US Technical Cooperation Mission to India, New Delhi, 1960.
38. See L.J. Bruce-Chwatt, 'Resurgence of Malaria and Its Control', *J. of Tropical Medicine and Hygiene.*, vol. 77, no. 4 (supplement), 1974, p. 62.
39. See TRS 357, 1967, p. 36; and TRS 291, 1964, p. 24.
40. For general references regarding anti-malaria activities in Africa, see L. Molineaux and G. Gramiccia, *The Garki Project*, WHO, Geneva, 1980; 'Approach to Malaria Eradication in the African Region', Mal/Exp. Com. 13/66.2, 1966, pp. 1–5; and TRS 38, 1951.

Region very little progress had been made against malaria although pilot projects and field research projects assisted by the WHO had been undertaken. No practical method of interrupting transmission had been found.

Apologists of the eradication programme's failure, such as Gramiccia and Hempel, claimed that in general the countries making unsatisfactory progress in malaria eradication were those that had originally had the highest mortality rates for malaria; that is, those in which the malaria problem was originally most severe.[41] While this may have been partly true, it certainly did not explain the exaggerated expectations which the original euphoria had created, and because of which the disappointment of the failure was so great.

Gramiccia and Hempel also went on to say that the high cost of running a MEP demands considerable allocations from a government's budget and, in most instances, external support for its proper conduct and financing. They observed that in those countries where programmes did not show satisfactory progress for a number of years, and in which the hope of achieving eradication within a definite time-limit appeared unrealistic, a tendency had developed to use funds, which previously had been devoted to the eradication of malaria, for other purposes of national interest not necessarily connected with health.[42]

Even though doubts about the success of eradication were being expressed in large numbers by 1966 in restricted WHO documents,[43] the metaphorical crossroads in the history of malaria eradication, which had been originally crossed in 1955, was crossed back in 1969, when the possibility of the global and rapid eradication of human malaria was officially questioned for the first time and the desirability of malaria control as an alternative target was endorsed by the WHA. This drastic change in the MEP's orientation was largely due to a steady decline in the successful anti-malaria activities seen in the first ten years of the eradication programme.

The apparent need to return to malaria control had more than a psychological impact on the individuals, organizations and governments involved in malaria eradication. The WHO and all the donor agencies were now confronted with the task of replacing the strict

41. See G. Gramiccia and J. Hempel, 'Mortality and Morbidity from Malaria in Countries where Malaria Eradication is Not Making Satisfactory Progress', *Am. J. Trop. Med. and Hyg.*, vol. 75, no. 105 (1972), p. 189.

42. *Ibid.*, p. 191.

43. For instance, see 'Assessment of Present Status of Malaria Eradication Programmes', Mal/Exp.Com.13/66.3, 13 Sept. 1966, p. 5; 'Review of Major Factors Affecting the Progress of Malaria Eradication Programmes; Planning', Mal/Exp. Com.13/66, Sept. 1966, p. 7.

and fairly dogmatic creed of malaria eradication with the amorphous generalities of the more flexible, less ambitious, unending and previously abandoned desiderata of malaria control.[44] The main issue was (and still is) how to adapt malaria eradication operations to the new situation.[45] A number of essential differences between malaria eradication and malaria control, which previously were only of academic interest, had to be taken into account in establishing operational criteria.

The objective of malaria eradication was abandoned in 1969 by the WHO, and the Organization again started recommending malaria control to its member states. Malaria eradication advances only continued to be retained in Europe and in parts of the Americas Region.

44. For a discussion of this after the change in strategy in 1969, see TRS 549, 1974.
45. OR 176, annex, 1969, p. 107.

25

LIMITATIONS OF THE M.E.P.

Before embarking on any discussion of the specific factors inhibiting progress in national MEPs, it is important to summarize the exact role of the WHO in such programmes.

The administration and coordination of MEPs at the national level were organized around three levels of command: central, intermediate and peripheral. The central level was the locus of power and coordination in the national MEPs and included the following functions: formulation of policy, feasibility studies, definition of objectives and targets, preparation of budgets, staff training and programme evaluation. The intermediate level was centred around the local medical officer, whose main role was to supervise the insecticide-spraying teams that made up the peripheral level.

The WHO's interaction with national MEPs was largely at the central level, where international health consultants from Geneva and the regional offices advised national Health Ministries on the practicability of MEPs. Sometimes WHO assistance in starting national malaria eradication programmes was limited to the provision of one short-term consultant to the national Health Ministry to assist with the preparation of a plan of operation for malaria eradication.[1] By 1965, there were 381 WHO malaria advisory staff involved in country, inter-country and inter-regional projects – significantly greater than the 244 advisors in 1958.[2]

More specifically, WHO advisors played a role in: (1) overall guidance in the planning, execution and evaluation of MEPs by developing concepts, methodologies, operational standards or criteria, and evaluation procedures; (2) providing technical expertise in defining national MEPs, and assisting governments in preparing their national staff for anti-malaria campaigns; and (3) assisting member states with supplies and equipment, when possible.[3]

By 1966, thirty-seven of the forty-one WHO-supported national eradication programmes had postponed their anticipated dates of completion by between one and ten years.[4] Failure seemed

1. See OR 90, 1958, pp. 3–4.
2. OR 151, 1966, p. 85.
3. TRS 537, 1974, pp. 48–9.
4. See 'Assessment of Present Status of Malaria Eradication Programmes', Mal/Exp. Com.13/66.3, Sept. 1966, pp. 1–10. Also see TRS 357, 1967, p. 28.

pervasive, and there remained little question by this stage that malaria was not eradicable in the foreseeable future.

In examining the factors which played an important role in the ultimate failure of malaria eradication, the review of forty-one WHO-assisted MEPs carried out in September 1966 by a WHO Expert Committee on malaria, as well as the findings of subsequent studies, are considered here.[5] In recent studies particular attention has been paid to the economic, social and human ecological factors in addition to the administrative and technical factors. Many of these are of course closely inter-related. For instance, administrative shortcomings delaying the provision of insecticides or the recruitment and training of staff may lead to technical problems; conversely, where technical difficulties develop, the supplementary or corrective measures may present administrative and financial problems.

The WHO acknowledged that the major factors favouring malaria eradication included a malaria situation responsive to residual insecticides, the presence of national health infrastructure, previous extensive experience with malaria control operations and, above all, the political will on the part of the national government to prioritize malaria above most other health concerns. Constraints on the success of MEPs are discussed below.

Inadequate Planning

It is now recognized by public health specialists that the planning and execution of malaria eradication operations do not lie totally within the sphere of expertise of the malariologist who is responsible for demonstrating the technical feasibility of the operations. It has become very clear that careful planning from the start is essential, and that a campaign should not begin until everything is ready – this was not self-evident to many during the MEP. In 1960, a WHO document recognized the failure of some eradication programmes due to inadequacies in planning and warned that 'planning should not be too optimistic'.[6] Problems, however, continued. For instance, the main difficulty in the Western Pacific Region of the WHO was the conversion of control programmes already in operation into efficient eradication campaigns.[7] With regard to planning

5. See TRS 357, 1967, pp. 23–56.
6. See A. P. Ray, 'Review of the Present Status of Malaria Eradication and Prospects for the Future', Mal/Exp.Com.8/WP/15, 15 June 1960, p. 3.
7. M. Colbourne, 'A Review of Malaria Eradication Campaigns in the Western Pacific', *Annals of Tropical Medicine and Parasitology*, vol. 56 (1962), p. 41.

in these and other eradication programmes reviewed by the WHO in 1966, the Organization suggested that 'corrective actions have either been too slow and ineffective or have not taken place at all, resulting in a breakdown in operations.'[8]

Although planning was considered one of the strong points of the MEP at its outset, and it was presented as one of the major reasons why the disease was eradicable, by 1969 the WHO was placing part of the blame for the set-backs in the eradication programme on the inadequacy of planning. Basic mistakes were made; for instance, the Indian malaria eradication programme did not take into consideration the county's annual 8 million increase in population.[9] In one restricted WHO document dated 1966, there was an admission of 'inadequacies and gaps' in all the original plans of operations.[10]

In the heyday of malaria eradication, health had been considered the monopoly of the WHO at the international level, and other specialized agencies were not asked to contribute to the planning of MEPs. In 1969, however, it was suggested that pre-eradication planning teams did not always receive the necessary expert advice on economic, sociological and administrative aspects:

> Pre-planning studies for malaria eradication programmes are too often confined to the malariological aspects and do not adequately take into account economic and social factors including rural community development programmes, the nature and location of economic development projects, the habits of the population, migration and transhumance into and out of malarious areas, the attitude of the people to sickness, their ability to understand the advantages of disease eradication, their level of education and their priority needs.[11]

The inference was that much of the failure of MEPs was due to non-medical (and thus non-technical) aspects that other international organizations were more capable of dealing with than the WHO was.

Just as economic arguments were used to justify the commencement and existence of the MEP, they were also given as the reason for its demise. While the WHO suggestion that many of the MEPs were developed prior to the formulation of long-term national health and socio-economic development plans was valid, this did not excuse the Organization for itself paying so little heed to such factors at the start of the MEP when it was encouraging countries

8. See Mal/Exp.Com.13/66.6, *op. cit.*, p. 1.
9. Ray, *op. cit.*, p. 2.
10. See 'Review of Major Factors Affecting the Progress of Malaria Eradication Programmes: Planning', Mal/Exp.Com.13/66.6, 13 Sept. 1966, p. 1.
11. OR 176, annex 13, 1969, p. 114.

to start eradication programmes. The WHO also suggested that another reason for the failure of MEPs had been the lack of sustained government support and active international cooperation from relevant government agencies.[12] Johnson has reported otherwise – he thought that the MEP

> has made tremendous progress in its less than a decade of concerted activity. Cooperation in border areas between many countries has been established where such cooperation previously had not existed. Countries politically antagonistic toward each other usually cooperate in a splendid manner when it comes to matters of malaria eradication, since malaria is a common enemy.[13]

Colbourne gives some examples of international cooperation for malaria. In the Western Pacific, the governments of Laos, Cambodia, Vietnam, Thailand, Malaya and Burma sent representatives to a meeting once a year. Similar meetings were attended by malariologists and medical administrators from the governmental authorities of Borneo, New Guinea and the islands of the Southwest Pacific. These meetings proved invaluable as a stimulus to antimalarial operations, technical discussion and, especially, the development of the personal relationships that facilitate the exchange of information and the avoidance of bureaucratic delay. They could not, however, produce satisfactory operations in a frontier area unless each of the national malaria services had itself overcome the difficulties described above. For instance, there were extensive difficulties with the Indian MEP in areas bordering Pakistan and Burma.[14]

Not only were there some problems with inter-state cooperation in malaria programmes, but difficulties were also experienced within states. For instance, the Indian MEP was implemented by the country's individual states, which were autonomous in health matters. Thus different parts of the country had different levels of priority and motivation for malaria eradication.[15]

It was clear by 1969 that many countries had embarked on MEPs and agreed to their commitments in good faith, 'without actually realizing how demanding these commitments would be until later they found themselves unable to meet their responsibilities'.[16]

12. See WHO OR 176, annex 13, 1969.
13. D.R. Johnson, 'Development of the Worldwide Malaria Eradication Programme', *Mosquito News*, June 1966, p. 115.
14. Ray, *op. cit.*, p. 5.
15. *Ibid.*
16. See Mal/Exp.Com.13/66.6, *op. cit.*, p. 6.

Many MEPs were undertaken with the help of bilateral and multilateral aid. Expectations that such aid would continue to be available right up to the end of the eradication programme led to optimism at the national Health Ministries in spite of the limited national facilities and finances available to perpetuate the work that was begun with foreign aid. Unsurprisingly, as soon as an effort required extension beyond what the early plans (funded by foreign aid) had envisioned, the whole operation broke down: 'Deficiencies in planning . . . [gave] rise to inadequate definition of the task and to insufficient preparation, resulting in ineffective operations.'[17]

Difficulties were also experienced 'in bringing the national eradication programme and other health projects into the broader economic context, due to public health administrators' and malariologists' lack of familiarity with economic project planning'.[18] The fact that WHO country representatives interacted almost exclusively with, and worked at, the Ministries of Health concerned added to a lack of familiarity with other sectors.[19]

While at the beginning of the MEP the WHO projected completion within five to eight years, by 1969 it was argued that 'a Malaria Eradication Programme covering an entire country may extend when planned on a staged basis over fifteen or more years, and the necessity of revision is bound to occur.'[20] The new time-frame was justified on the grounds that in the past inadequate provision had been made for continuous review and evaluation of the operation, with the result that plans could not be quickly modified where necessary, nor rapid action taken to remedy the deficiencies.

There was also the time factor. The atmosphere during the 1950s and early 1960s was suitable for international and bilateral assistance and plans for operations had to be produced quickly if programmes were to receive financial aid. Since help was often restricted to eradication programmes only, 75 per cent of the MEPs were embarked upon soon after the 1955 WHA resolution, when UNICEF help became available. Thus there was often no preparation phase or interval between the end of malaria control and the beginning of malaria eradication activities. Since planning presupposes knowledge of the present situation and a study of the future evolution of the factors involved in the eradication efforts, the

17. See 'Assessment of the Present Status of Malaria Eradication Programmes', Mal/Exp.Com.13/66.3, 13 Sept. 1966, p. 10.
18. See 'Malaria Eradication throughout the World', *WHO Chronicle*, vol. 13, 1959, p. 348; and OR 176, annex 13, 1969, p. 114.
19. Personal communication with senior WHO administrators.
20. OR 176, annex 13, 1969, p. 114.

rush towards eradication was conducive to bad or inadequate planning.[21]

The original WHO suggestion that a one-time malaria eradication expense would bypass the continual expenditure required in malaria control also appeared inaccurate. By 1969 the WHO claimed that the maintenance phase of the programme was not usually included in the original malaria eradication and national health plans, and that there was frequently no provision for the future integration of the functions and the personnel of the malaria service into the general health service:

> Experience has shown that once the maintenance phase has been reached, although the expenditure required specifically for malaria is greatly reduced, the *total budget for public health* has to be maintained at the same total general level, or even increased.[22]

Had this been known by the international aid agencies in 1955, it is doubtful that they would have expressed interest in financing an eradication effort. Indeed, the promise that malaria eradication would not be a recurring expense rendered the venture attractive at the start.

The MEP was now no longer considered as a separate, specialist entity – as it had traditionally been for the last fourteen years of the programme – but was seen to be inextricably linked with public health services in general. Furthermore, for the first time, a role for non-medical experts such as economists, sociologists, public administrators and expert planners was seen as important for malaria eradication. All these elements were not part of the malaria eradication effort in the first ten or fifteen years of the MEP; they were now seen as essential components of national socio-economic development plans, which were in turn considered crucial for successful eradication. The new approach visualized an inter-sectoral, or 'horizontal', attack on malaria, although no such generalized approach had been preached previously by the WHO (or implemented by its 'demonstration teams') as it had encouraged a centralized malaria service to run the eradication programme.[23]

Administrative Problems

Administrative and financial difficulties were perceived as pervasive obstacles to the progress of malaria eradication. Experience had

21. See Mal/Exp.Com.13/66.6, *op. cit.*, pp. 2–3.
22. *Ibid*. Author's emphasis.
23. *Ibid*., p. 8.

shown that these administrative difficulties were more serious than the technical ones, and that no eradication campaign should be started until an efficient organization could be guaranteed. It was noted that in some eradication programmes the existence of suspected epidemiological problems could 'neither be confirmed nor denied because the programme administration and organization was too poor'.[24] However, governments were so impressed by the great and immediate advantages to the public health to be gained by even imperfect operations, and by the need to speed up their own anti-malarial operations in order not to fall behind those of their neighbours, that some operations were launched without proper preparation.[25] As is admitted in one restricted WHO document: 'some malaria eradication programmes started without adequate preparation and later it was necessary to proceed to a re-definition, to a new plan of operations, to the provision of adequate facilities and then to start again.'[26]

A sound administrative backing is of the utmost importance for the successful implementation of a MEP, as the operations have to be carried out not only efficiently but also on a definite time schedule which is determined by epidemiological considerations. Where the general administrative services of a country and its public health organization were well organized and stable, MEPs were said to have progressed rapidly:

> Even when the health services are not fully developed, provided the general administrative organization of the country is sound, the programmes have tended to progress well. But where the general administrative methods and practices of a country have been inadequate, these deficiencies have been reflected in the health services and have thus led frequently to setbacks in malaria eradication.[27]

As far as most developing countries were concerned, however, mismanagement was fairly common.[28]

The 'pessimistic outlook' for many MEPs in 1966 was attributed to the fact that 'the [national] administrative structure[s] and the

24. See Tito Lopes da Silva, 'Criteria for Assessing the Prospects of Success of Malaria Eradication Programmes', Mal/Exp.Com.9/WP/4, 21 Mar. 1962, p. 4.
25. Colbourne, *op. cit.*, p. 33.
26. See 'Assessment of Present Status of Malaria Eradication Programmes', Mal/Exp.Com.13/66.3, 13 Sept. 1966, p. 4.
27. OR 176, annex 13, 1969, p. 114.
28. Personal communication with Dr M. A. Farid, Geneva, 3 Aug. 1989.

[public health services] are very defective.'[29] As one WHO document said:

> In the Americas, as in other malarious regions of the world, administrative and operational problems are the most frequent causes of failure or set-backs in the effort towards eradication, and they have affected all the programs to some extent at one period or another of their development.[30]

WHO experts suggested that if these aspects had been 'more realistically evaluated in the planning stage, it is possible that these MEPs would not have started until such time as the minimum requirements for launching an eradication programme were attained'.[31]

Intentional mismanagement was also evident in places. As one WHO document states, directors of the national health services 'can make or break a MEP'.[32] 'Personalities and [their] interests' became an important factor.[33] Certain directors of national health services had their own priorities, and delayed implementation of anti-malaria activities as much as possible. The Director of Health Services of Pakistan was one such individual. The WHO advisor to Pakistan, Dr Farid, only overcame the two-year delay in anti-malaria activities in Pakistan by a direct appeal to Ayub Khan, the country's President.[34]

In so far as it was considered at all, by 1969 it was evident that in 1955 administrative mismanagement had been seriously under-estimated as a possible source of major set-backs for malaria eradication efforts. Successful MEPs had shown that good management was necessarily predicated on clear and open lines of communication between the centre and the periphery of malaria operations. Dedicated and competent staff with a realistic and precise understanding of their role in the overall eradication picture were crucial. The WHO admitted that 'insufficient attention appears to have been given to techniques of modern management which may be of

29. See 'Administration and Finance', Mal/Exp.Com.13/66.5, *op. cit.*, p. 2.
30. While these problems were present, in some of their many aspects, it is impossible to determine the exact extent to which technical problems also contributed to the persistence of transmission. The main problems of a technical nature have do with the resistance of the vector and it was 'not felt that problems inherent in the parasite will seriously hold back eradication'. Ironically, the level of the parasite is where the latest research is concentrated. See Guzman Garcia-Martin, 'Status of Malaria Eradication in the Americas', *Am. J. Trop. Med. and Hyg.*, vol. 21 (1972), p. 627.
31. *Ibid.*
32. See 'Administration and Finance', *op. cit.*, p. 3.
33. *Ibid.*, p. 6.
34. Personal communication with Dr M.A. Farid, Geneva, 11 Aug. 1987.

great assistance in simplifying methods, improving efficiency and reducing the costs of eradication.'[35] This criticism was directed against the WHO itself, because it had a major role in the education of personnel to be involved in the MEP.

The fact that malaria eradication was run separately as a vertical programme also caused problems. In 1955 it had appeared to planners and even to governments that a time-limited programme with the features of a MEP could not succeed if it were constrained to operate under standard government administrative procedures. Therefore, the programmes were placed closer to the Minister of Health and given higher priority than other health issues. For instance, in Morocco the anti-malaria activities were given priority over all other public health activities for the expected duration of the eradication programme – that is, till 1963.[36]

The MEPs were also accorded a great deal of autonomy within national Health Ministries.[37] However, such autonomy tended to isolate the malaria service from the general health services: it essentially 'cut the malaria organization away from the health service'.[38]

Close coordination of the malaria and general public health services, if preferable in the initial phases, was incrementally critical in the later stages of the eradication programme.[39] In fact, during the final or maintenance phase of malaria eradication, 'the entire task [of eradication] is the responsibility of the general public health organization.'[40] Since the general public health service was often excluded from the early malaria eradication efforts, it was not keen on cooperating during the later stages. Moreover, the high priority given to MEPs (at the expense of other public health ventures) 'created jealousy at all levels within and outside the health department, so that cooperation has not been forthcoming and every effort has been made to withdraw, at the most suitable opportunity, these facilities from the MEP'.[41]

By 1969, the WHO reported that in MEPs it had often not been possible to secure the necessary cooperation from other government

35. OR 176, annex 13, 1969, p. 114.
36. See G. Gramiccia, 'The Organization of Malaria Eradication within the Framework of General Public Health Administration', Working Paper 29, Expert Committee, 26 Aug. 1958, p. 6.
37. TRS 357, 1967, p. 30.
38. See 'Administration and Finance', *op. cit.*, p. 5.
39. See TRS 132, 1956, p. 31.
40. See Ray, 'Review of the Present Status of Malaria Eradication', *op. cit.*, p. 4; TRS 294, 1965, p. 12; and A. Ray, 'Maintenance of Achieved Eradication', Mal/Exp.Com.12/WP/2.65, 21 Aug. 1965, p. 2.
41. See 'Administration and Finance', *op. cit.*, p. 5.

sectors, such as education, agriculture, land settlement, or from private agencies and local bodies in close contact with communities.[42] Thus even the technical experts were exhibiting behaviour that functionalists only expected from politicians.

With regard to administrative problems in the MEP, it seems clear that the national and international medical personnel in charge essentially lacked the administrative skills required to coordinate the operations in the field, such as spraying and epidemiological surveys.[43] The WHO did not emphasize the importance of administrative skills in its seemingly cook-book approach to malaria eradication. As early as 1956, WHO documents described the ideal national MEP director as an individual with some technical knowledge of malaria, fortified with 'courage, persistence, and above all faith'. Administrative ability or training was not mentioned.[44] As MEPs started to fail, the Organization refused to accept responsibility for administrative problems by claiming that 'it is not for the physician to study population movements; this is the task of geographers and of the administration.'[45] However, since non-medical experts such as geographers were seldom, if ever, invited to help in the original plans for malaria eradication, the WHO's denial of responsibility was not entirely valid.

Not only were non-medical experts not invited to help plan the MEP at the outset, but the level of future administrative difficulties was vastly underestimated by WHO experts. For instance, one WHO Expert Committee considered administrative difficulties a not unmanageable challenge for the physicians who were to run MEPs: 'The administrative difficulties must not be exaggerated; they can usually be overcome by taking the appropriate steps in each locality.'[46] The WHO experts were so confident about their ability to deal with administrative problems that they suggested:

> In countries where the public health service is not well developed, the development of an eradication service will be a pattern of an efficient [administrative] service and will serve as a nucleus around which the public health service can be built. In many cases, the malaria eradication programme will represent the first fully efficient public health service given to the public.[47]

42. *Ibid*. Also see I. Vincke, 'Practical Methods for the Study of Factors Causing Difficulties in Malaria Eradication', Mal/Exp.Com.10/ WP/36, 9 Aug. 1963, p. 4.
43. TRS 132, 1956, p. 21.
44. *Ibid*., p. 17.
45. See Vincke, *op. cit.*, p. 4.
46. TRS 132, 1956, p. 13.
47. *Ibid*., p. 31.

Needless to say, the confidence about handling the administrative difficulties with ease has diminished considerably since the failure of the MEP. For instance, the WHO's 1982 seventh Asian Malaria Conference regarded the development of management skills as its top priority for subsequent anti-malaria activities.[48]

Financial Constraints

Financial difficulties were numerous, frequently mirroring the hostile economic environment in which many countries found themselves. The persistence of so many MEPs well past their originally predicted date of completion also stressed the limited and diminishing budgets of the anti-malaria campaigns. Funds committed to other health and development priorities were not easily diverted to meet unforeseen demands for additional finance for the MEP. In many instances the financial difficulties were exacerbated by inadequate estimates of the cost of the programme, due to lack of adequate prior studies and detailed costing:

> Though most malarious countries have accepted the objective of malaria eradication and many have progressed a long way toward this goal, relatively few have carefully assessed at the outset the size of the problem and what additional efforts and resources would be needed.[49]

The possibility of technical or operational difficulties was often not anticipated in the original project plans, rendering the absence of contingency plans unsurprising. Central planning boards were frequently not forewarned that additional funds might be required if the disease proved more intractable than expected. In a number of instances, national governments were their own worst enemies. By taking short-cuts and prematurely curtailing essential operations, serious set-backs were incurred that in the long term would create a considerably greater financial burden for the countries concerned. The situation was summarized by the sixth report of WHO's Expert Committee on malaria as follows: 'the chief obstacle to malaria is the lack of men, money and materials, and [the fact] that these essentials are required in those parts of the world where financial resources are in demand for every kind of development.'[50]

For as long as it was available, multilateral and bilateral financial assistance was fairly well coordinated at the country level. Most

48. See TRS 680, 1982, p. 54.
49. See 'Criteria for Assessing the Prospects of Success of Malaria Eradication Programmes', *op. cit.*, p. 3; and TRS 357, 1967, pp. 26–7.
50. See TRS 123, 1959. Also see Colbourne, *op. cit.*, p. 40.

of the American funding was distributed on a bilateral basis by USAID. But by the early to mid-1960s financial constraints had become a major factor inhibiting the progress of the MEP. The contribution from UNICEF, which had ranged from US$4.1 million to $8.8 million annually, was being phased out by 1964. UNICEF argued that 'no country where eradication has been shown to be technically and practically feasible is still waiting for financial assistance.'[51] USAID, which had over the past twenty years contributed $375 million to twenty-eight national programmes, changed its priorities and terminated its support for all MEPs except those of Nepal and Haiti. The decentralization of malaria assistance and the placing of its control in the hands of local directors of USAID missions was a harbinger for the precipitous decrease in MEP funding. Many USAID mission directors were more interested in endorsing family-planning programmes, which they felt would address the growing problem of over-population.[52]

By 1976 the international funds allocated to anti-malaria activities represented only 42 per cent of those available ten years earlier; if the monetary depreciation over that period is taken into account, the 1976 funds amounted to less than 20 per cent of the former financial assistance.[53]

Over the years 1957–67 the WHO had spent some US$87 million on the MEP (including the funds available under the technical assistance component of the UN Development Programme).[54] During the same period UNICEF provided supplies to the value of $70 million. Assistance provided by USAID during this decade amounted to $225 million in dollar grants, $218 million in grants from US-owned local currency and $88 million in low-interest loans. The expenses of national governments (considered to be approximately four times as much as those of the WHO and UNICEF) were

51. See 'Malaria Eradication: a Report to the Unicef Executive Board', E/ICEF/417, 3 May 1961, p. 127. Also see 'Report on Development of Malaria Eradication Programmes', EB33/4, 18 Nov. 1963, p. 41; OR 79, 1957, annex 11; and T. Lepes, 'Present Status of the Global Malaria Eradication Programme and Prospects for the Future', *Am. J. Trop. Med. and Hyg.*, vol. 77, supp. 4 (1974), pp. 47–53.
52. See E. A. Smith, 'AID Policy on Malaria', vol. 42 (1974), pp. 19–20. See Farid, 1980, *op. cit.*, p. 16, and T. Weller, 'World Health in a Changing World', *Am. J. Trop Med. and Hyg.*, vol. 77, supp. (1974), p. 56. Also consult 'The Participation of Federal Agencies in International Scientific Programs', 90th Congress, first session, US Government Printing Office, Washington, DC, 1967, p. 138.
53. See L. J. Bruce-Chwatt, 'The Challenge of Malaria: Crossroads or Impasse?' in Clive Wood (ed.), *Tropical Medicine: from Romance to Reality*, Academic Press, London, 1978, p. 35.
54. See 'Report on Development of Malaria Eradication Programmes', EB33/4, 18 Nov. 1963, p. 41; OR 135, annex 6, 1964, p. 77; and OR 79, annex 11, 1957, p. 119.

estimated at $650 million. The national expenditure was most likely higher. Estimates suggest that the total cost of these ten years of malaria eradication was approximately $1,339 million; at least 40 per cent of this was contributed by the United States.[55] Moreover, it was clear that in areas where malaria eradication had been claimed, this had cost up to $2 per person protected, and not the 11 cents per person that had been the projected expense by the WHO at the start of the MEP.[56]

Operational Setbacks

Among operational factors are included: preparatory arrangements, coverage of all endemic areas, supervision of the MEP teams, evaluation of progress and public cooperation. In the early stages of MEPs three crucial mandatory operational factors were: (1) painstakingly exact organization; (2) thorough geographical reconnaisance of malarious areas; and (3) deliberate supervision at all levels of the programme. Where these three prerequisites were fulfilled, adequate logistical support, including the maintenance of transport and equipment, was ensured.[57]

Many of the obstacles to total coverage were due to administrative deficiencies. There were, however, circumstances in which such coverage could be considered technically difficult. The spraying of DDT or some other insecticide on the walls of houses was easier said than done. The difficulties faced included anophelines that bit outside the sprayed houses, nomadism[58] and the use of temporary farm huts which often had nominal walls at best. In the mountainous areas of Cambodia, where huts seldom, if ever, had walls, the problem seemed insoluble.[59]

55. See Wood, *op. cit.*, p. 40; and G.M. Jeffery, 'Malaria Control in the 20th Century', *Am. J. Trop. Med. and Hyg.* vol. 25, no. 3 (1976), p. 364.
56. See Bruce-Chwatt in Clive Wood, *op cit.*, p. 41.
57. See 'Review of Major Factors Affecting the Progress of Malaria Eradication Programmes: Operations', Mal/Exp.Com.13/66.8, Sept. 1966, p. 1.
58. Nomadism was considered the most serious obstacle to successful eradication in countries such as Vietnam, Thailand, the Philippines and Iran, where seasonal nomadism is a part of many peoples's normal lives. See M.E. Farinaud, 'Thoughts on Problems of Malaria Eradication and Their Solution', Mal/Exp.Com.10/WP/27, 9 July 1963, p. 2. Also see 'Appraisal of Typical Malaria Eradication Programmes in the Eastern Mediterranean Region', Mal/Exp.Com.8/WP/20, 15 June 1960, p. 6; and C. Mofidi, A. Mohtadi, K. Moradpour and G. Djalali, 'Present Aspect of Malaria and its Control among Nomadic Tribes in Iran', Working Paper 34, Expert Committee, 28 Aug. 1958, pp. 1–7.
59. See Colbourne, *op. cit.*, p. 39. For a general discussion of sociological factors affecting malaria eradication, see Albert Wessen, 'Human Ecology and Malaria', *Am. J. Trop. Med. and Hyg.* vol. 21, no. 5 (1972), pp. 658–62.

Logistical problems of access arose in various countries, owing to the difficult terrain,[60] low population densities dispersed over large land masses, and the national government's inadequate political control of areas where it was in dispute with separatist movements or neighbouring states.[61] Operational efficiency was also limited by native populations, some of whom had special habits, taboos or superstitions that were not conducive to malaria eradication measures.

Failure to achieve adequate and timely spraying coverage was often attributable to a shortage of motivation and leadership, and to the inability of the administrations concerned to adhere closely to what little planning that existed. Not surprisingly, reverses frequently occurred as the progression of areas from attack to consolidation phase was not infrequently decided arbitrarily on the basis of a pre-established time schedule and financial considerations, rather than on the basis of epidemiological criteria.[62]

In some instances during the MEP and later, violent opposition to spraying had distasteful political origins, and in such cases only a miracle could have controlled malaria. One example of the political use of malaria was evident in the Philippines: in response to the failure of a development programme offered to satisfy the demands of the Muslim insurgents in Mindanao and the Sulu Archipelago, the government decided in 1973 to stop malaria control spraying on at least one important island in order to allow malaria to spread unchecked among the insurgent population. 'There is a lot of malaria down there,' the Filipino military commander of the region is reported to have said, 'so we have stopped spraying. Sooner or later the rebels will be too weak to fight.'[63]

Numerous other operations problems arose as the MEPs progressed. The provision of insecticide according to precise schedules sometimes proved too demanding for some programmes. Cooperation from householders was not always forthcoming, as they resented the invasion of their privacy and objected, for various reasons, to the spraying routine. All this coincided with (or was perhaps caused by) a gradual decrease in financial support from

60. See 'Review of Major Factors Affecting the Progress of Malaria Eradication Programmes; Operations', *op. cit.*, p. 7.

61. As one WHO document points out, 'Area of insecurity disrupt the essential continuity of both attack and surveillance operations and may even render areas heavily infested with malaria temporarily inaccessible to eradication personnel.' See 'Report in Development of Malaria Eradication Programmes', EB33/4, 18 Nov. 1963, p. 29.

62. See Arnoldo Gabaldon, 'Difficulties Confronting Malaria Eradication', *Am. J. Trop. Med. and Hyg.*, vol. 21, no. 5 (1972) p. 637.

63. See *New York Times*, 'Drive to Pacify Southern Philippine Moslems is Begun', 11 Dec. 1972, and 'Manila is Using Malaria Mosquitoes to Fight Rebels', 29 Mar. 1973.

multilateral and bilateral agencies. Moreover, a seemingly unending inflationary rise in the cost of insecticides and labour affected some of the largest MEPs in Afghanistan, India, Pakistan, Thailand, Ceylon and Indonesia.[64]

A number of countries were dependent to a very large extent on external aid in order to implement their MEPs. The uncertainties surrounding the provision of these funds, which were subject to changes in the donors' priorities, and to the developing countries' inability to forecast the availability of their own funds, was an additional factor to be reckoned with. Insecticides, normally an imported commodity, were frequently supplied through this form of assistance. Hence countries unable to complete the earlier stages of the programme on the planned dates were liable to encounter serious operational difficulties if international and bilateral aid was not maintained at the level foreseen.

The maintenance of eradication, once it had been achieved, had initially been assumed to be a responsibility of a country's general health services when the consolidation phase ended. This proved to be a grave error in the original strategy. With few exceptions, when programmes were launched health services were not provided at the level of total coverage required, and it was unrealistic to expect the development of these services to keep pace with the progress of a 'crash' programme like malaria eradication.[65]

The intensity of vigilance at the end of the MEP was dictated by the level of malariogenic potential, which in turn depended on factors related to the vector, people and the environment. With low malariogenic potential, preventing the re-establishment of endemicity was a manageable task compared with the situation in high malariogenic areas where the speed and quality of epidemiological surveys, sound functioning of laboratories and effectiveness of remedial measures were essential. In countries with well-developed health services which had access to good epidemiological intelligence, there was in general no difficulty in sustaining malaria eradication. In the long term, the maintenance of achieved eradication depended on the existence of an adequate organization to carry out the necessary remedial measures as infection pockets resurfaced. This was another major area of underestimation by the WHO in 1955: in some countries there was a tendency to integrate the malaria service into the health service too soon,

64. See E. S. Pampana, 'Unexpected Cost Increases of Malaria Eradication', WHO/Mal/208, 26 Aug. 1958. Also see L. J. Bruce-Chwatt, 'Resurgence of Malaria and Its Control', *Am. J. Trop. Med. and Hyg.*, vol. 77, no. 4, supp. (1974), for discussion.
65. A. Ray, 'Maintenance of Achieved Eradication', Mal/Exp.Com. 12/WP/2.65, Sept. 1965, p. 1.

'particularly where the resources of the malaria service are better than those of rural health services', thus utilizing funds provided to combat malaria for other public health projects.[66]

Personnel and Training

While it was recognized that good training for the malaria service staff constituted one of the most important factors in achieving successful results, more attention also needed to be paid to training the staff of the general health services in the principles of malaria control from the maintenance phase onwards, which was the responsibility of the entire health service.

Of the twenty-eight eradication programmes which the WHO declared to be behind schedule in 1966, seventeen faced 'serious deficiencies in personnel'.[67] Programmes without long-term personnel policies started flagging as their staff's *esprit de corps* was progressively eroded, and the sense of belonging to a health service engaged in the important task of malaria eradication was 'usually missing'.[68] Job security was limited in the time-limited eradication efforts, and no assurances were given to personnel about their future. There were incidents when personnel were not paid for months or were dismissed suddenly.[69] As pointed out in one WHO document, 'in general, malaria eradication services have not attracted the best available human resources and frequently there has been a high staff turn-over.'[70]

In areas where the staff knew that there would be continuity of public health work, enthusiasm was maintained; where this was not clear, it often became a cause of deterioration in MEPs during the final stages, precisely when exacting and careful commitment to detail was absolutely crucial. The premature transfer of malaria personnel, particularly at the professional level, to the general health service before the maintenance phase was fully organized caused difficulties in some programmes.

Charges of incompetence have also been made against those involved in malaria eradication activities:

> I would put the higher health authorities to blame. Very frequently the chief official, the one who makes the decisions, is ill-advised by the regular public

66. See 'Review of Major Factors Affecting the Progress . . . Operations', *op. cit.*, p. 4.
67. See 'Review of Major Factors Affecting the Progress of Malaria Eradication Programmes: Personnel and Training', Mal/Exp.Com.13.66.7, Sept. 1966, p. 1.
68. *Ibid.*, p. 5; and TRS 357, 1967, p. 30.
69. See 'Personnel and Training', *op. cit.*, p. 4.
70. *Ibid.*

health administrators and health planners, who often lack knowledge of malaria epidemiology and of the methods to interrupt transmission, and are, therefore, not appropriate consultants in this field. On several occasions I have found that these specialists misinterpret the facts, forget the true meaning of malaria as an important public health problem, and do not give the necessary priority to the program. The recent resurgence in Venezuela can be attributed mainly to this factor.[71]

Such charges of incompetence are understandable in view of the training of malaria eradication staff.

Training senior malaria eradication staff posed various problems. For instance, there was the difficulty of sparing national malaria experts from their duties for long periods of time in order to carry out the training. This problem was especially important in view of the fact that each malaria eradication official often needed to be trained at different stages of the eradication programme about the changing tactics and priorities.[72]

Most of the training of senior staff took place at one of six WHO malaria eradication training centres: in Belgrade (Yugoslavia), Kingston (Jamaica), Lagos (Nigeria), Lomé (Togo), Manila (Philippines) and Maracaibo (Venezuela).[73] Between 1959 and 1969, over 100 courses (between three and fourteen weeks in length) in malaria eradication were attended by 2,000 senior national and international anti-malaria staff.[74] These courses were meant to offer 'special indoctrination as to the [malaria eradication] programme and its requirements'[75] and were strictly on medically related topics such as the parasitology and entomology of malaria.[76] The courses did not offer any training in administrative aspects of malaria eradication.

While the 'indoctrination' aspect of the malaria courses was meant to aid in the uniform attack on malaria worldwide, the strictly medical emphasis of the training was probably partly to blame for the inability of these same medical experts to be effective administrators. Sometimes training centres did not coordinate their efforts with those of the individual MEPs so as to ensure that training met even the medical needs of the programme.[77] Moreover, when MEPs reverted to malaria control programmes in 1969, the 'indoctrination' had to be modified dramatically.[78]

71. Gabaldon, *op. cit.*, p. 638.
72. See 'Personnel and Training', *op. cit.*, p. 3.
73. TRS 467, 1971, p. 34.
74. *WHO Chronicle*, 1969, vol. 23, pp. 233–56.
75. TRS 132, 1956, p. 18.
76. See TRS 537, 1974, p. 27.
77. See 'Personnel and Training', *op. cit.*, p. 2.
78. For instance, the *WHO Handbook on Malaria Training*, WHO, Geneva, 1966, had to be revised in the light of the changed strategy.

Technical Problems

Among the causes of technical difficulties encountered in malaria eradication were the physiological resistance of the vector mosquito to insecticides, the behaviour characteristics of the vector (such as excito-repellency, outdoor resting and biting), the resistance of malaria parasites to drugs[79] and, as mentioned above, factors related to human ecology. By 1968 fifty-six species of anopheles mosquitoes were resistant to DDT.[80] The WHO 'Re-examination of the Global Strategy' in 1969 claimed that: 'The extent of areas with strictly technical problems is essentially limited to about one percent of the total population under the eradication programme.'[81] Essentially, the Organization was suggesting that, since its role was purely technical, the other 99 per cent was beyond its mandate and thus not its responsibility. This belief in technical competence was evident throughout the eradication period. For instance, while discussing the causes of failure in the Indian MEP, one senior malariologist claimed that 'there was no technical problem which has affected the course of the Indian programme.'[82]

The main technical constraints involved the development of mosquitoes' resistance to DDT and other insecticides. In some places, 'insecticides alone have not succeeded in interrupting transmission'; in others, where the promised ancillary benefits of DDT spraying were not realized, insecticides were even blamed for the transmission. In parts of India, various rural populations refused to have their houses sprayed with DDT, having experienced no decrease in the bed-bug population as promised by the MEP teams. Indeed, the bed-bugs quickly developed resistance to DDT and actually showed an increase in numbers after spraying.[83]

79. As of 1963, however, there were 'no clearly proven cases where the . . . [parasite] compromises the eradication programme of malaria'. See Vincke, *op. cit.*, p. 3.
80. See TRS 443, 1970, p. 3. Also consult 'Report on Development of Malaria Eradication Programmes', *op. cit.*, p. 30.
81. TRS 176, annex 13, 1969, p. 117. Later this was not the official line. In fact, if articles in WHO publications such as the *WHO Chronicle* and the *Bulletin of WHO* are any indication of the WHO's policy, the arguments dealing with technical failure due to the inescapable resistance of the vector to insecticide were more popular.
82. See Ray, 'Review of the Present Status of Malaria Eradication', *op. cit.*, p. 1.
83. *Ibid.*, p. 2. Also consult Wood, *op. cit.*, p. 33; and A. W. Brown, J. Haworth and A. Zahar, 'Malaria Eradication and Control from a Global Standpoint', *J. of Medical Entomology*, vol. 13, no. 1 (1976), p. 19.

26

THE RETURN OF MALARIA CONTROL

By 1969, all the problems discussed above were considered overwhelming; the malaria eradicators were in retreat, so that the years after 1969 were referred to as the death years of the global strategy. The majority of continental countries in the tropics were still engaged in the attack phase over large areas, and the eradication programme had not succeeded in outstripping the development of insecticide-resistance in the vectors, among other problems. In some parts of the world, particularly Central America, much of the anopheline resistance was attributed to the contamination of the larval breeding areas with insecticides applied to agricultural crops.

Following these developments, an alternative insecticide, malathion, costing seven times as much,[1] was substituted for DDT in treating malaria foci that were reappearing in consolidation areas in India and Turkey,[2] and in attack phase areas in Iraq, southern Iran and southern Afghanistan. A total of 1,200 tonnes were used by 1971.[3] In Central America, where malathion-resistance had already appeared in *A. albimanus* in El Salvador, the insecticide propoxur was substituted;[4] by the following year 800 tonnes of this insecticide, at twenty times the price of DDT, were used in Iraq.[5]

The failure of the original insecticides in this way led to the final realization that very little of the MEP could be salvaged. Accusations were aimed in all directions, from national governments to donor agencies, to international organizations. In view of the fact that the international MEP was largely directed from the WHO headquarters in Geneva, it is not surprising that the Organization was also considered culpable for the failure of the eradication efforts. Critics of the WHO claimed that:

1. See P. Bertagna, 'New Insecticides in Malaria Eradication Programmes', Geneva, Mal/Exp.Com.9/WP/18, 23 Mar. 1962, p. 5; and 'New Insecticides to be Used in Malaria Eradication – Definition of Criteria and Standards', Mal/Exp.Com.11/WP/19, 10 Apr. 1964, pp. 1–5.
2. See OR 90, 1958, p. 5.
3. Resistance was evident even as early as 1962 in some of these countries. See Bertagna, *op. cit.*, p. 10.
4. See Bertagna, *op. cit.*, p. 10.
5. Some propoxur-resistance was also reported by 1971. See G.P. Georghiou, 'Studies on Resistance to Carbamate and Organophosphorus Insecticides in *Anopheles albimanus*', *Am. J. Trop. Med. and Hyg.*, vol. 77 supp. 4 (1974), pp. 47–53.

Experts sitting in WHO Headquarters in Geneva, whose job was to coordinate the global programme, began to interfere, advising when to stop spraying and how to utilize the malaria funds, failing to leave the matter in the hands of those on the spot who knew about the local malaria situation.[6]

In fact, the role of the WHO during the later stages was not significantly different from that which it had played in the earlier, happier days of the MEP. However, the perception of national governments and Health Ministries had changed dramatically: they felt betrayed by the WHO and lost faith in the Organization, viewing its expert advice as interference. The World Health Organization which had encouraged countries to start MEPs now found itself the messenger of ill tidings regarding the future of those programmes.

Along with the technical problems of resistance and the administrative bungles, several operational problems also arose, mainly as a result of the contraction of financial support from multilateral and bilateral sources. Because of the diminishing funding, the WHO found it increasingly necessary to fund eradication programmes through its regular budgetary mechanism, resulting in an overall reduction in expenditure.[7] The WHO had budgeted US$84 million in 1963 for advisory services alone; by 1969 the figure had fallen by more than half.[8]

Several authors have suggested that USAID's decreased funding of malaria eradication was due to a concomitant increase in funding for family planning programmes.[9] Indeed, as early as 1954 the issue of increased population due to anti-malaria activities had arisen: a WHO Expert Committee on malaria at the time said that it 'did not concur with the widely expressed opinion that the application of public health techniques such as malaria control should be delayed for fear of increasing the population'.[10] In 1969 Dr John Bryant of the Rockefeller Foundation warned against the use of ill-health, under-nourishment and the misery of poverty as a means of solving the problem of the population explosion. He said: 'Complacency about or even tolerance of a high level of

6. M.A. Farid 'The Malaria Programme – from Euphoria to Anarchy', *World Health Forum*, vol. I, nos 1 and 2, WHO, Geneva, 1980, p. 15.
7. See TRS 176, annex 13, 1969, p. 119.
8. *Ibid.*
9. See E.A. Smith, 'Present Status of the Global Malaria Eradication Programme and Prospects for the Future', Geneva, Mal/Exp.Com.14/67.4, 12 Sept. 1967, p. 19. Also consult Farid, *op. cit.*, p. 16; and T.H. Weller, 'World Health in a Changing World', *Am. J. Trop. Med. and Hyg.*, vol. 77, supp., pp. 74, 56.
10. See TRS 80, 1954, p. 6.

mortality because it slows population growth is simply not permissable.'[11] The lack of sustained funding was blamed on the great expectations created at the outset of the MEP: 'For who is willing to respond as wholeheartedly to an appeal for additional support if the results originally promised are not delivered on schedule?'[12]

Major cutbacks in international funding, together with an inflationary rise in the cost of materials and labour, and significant shortages in DDT supply, did irreparable damage to many eradication programmes. Some of the programmes strongly affected included those of India, Pakistan, Ceylon and Thailand.

The international shortage of DDT was largely a result of falling production in the United States, following vociferous protests by environmental groups about the hazardous effects of the insecticide. Bruce-Chwatt has observed that DDT toxicity in people was known to be very low and there was no evidence that those whose houses were sprayed with it were at any risk. However, DDT had been shown to have adverse effects on certain animals such as cats, chickens, predatory birds and fish.[13] These effects on animals motivated the environmentalist groups to lobby successfully against US production and use of DDT. Once developed countries banned DDT use within their own borders, its use in developing countries became more difficult to justify. National leaders became suspicious of the goodwill of developed countries which were reluctant to use DDT at home but ready to sell it abroad.

By 1972, malaria control efforts had been launched or strengthened in nineteen African countries. The malaria situation in sub-Saharan Africa had not improved since the MEP was launched. It was now argued that the situation in Africa, which was originally left out of the eradication effort, was one of the main reasons that the global anti-malaria campaign was revised to include organized control activities as well as eradication programmes.[14] Some years

11. John Bryant, *Health and the Developing World*, Cornell University Press, Ithaca, NY, for Rockefeller Foundation, 1969, p. 100.
12. Clay Huff, 'Unfinished Business', *Am. J. Trop. Med. and Hyg.*, vol. 13 (1964), p. 245.
13. L.J. Bruce-Chwatt, *Essential Malariology*, John Wiley, New York, 1985, p. 301. Also consult WHO TRS 475, 1971, p. 5.
14. See A.W. Brown, J. Haworth and A. Zahar, 'Malaria Eradication and Control from a Global Standpoint', *Medical Entomology*, vol. 13, no. I (1976), p. 15. Also see 'Approach to Malaria Eradication in the African Region', Mal/Exp.Com.13/66.2, 13 Sept. 1966, p. 4.

later, economic justifications were offered in favour of malaria control, as they had been earlier for malaria eradication.[15]

However, a more realistic interpretation is that this departure from absolute eradication represented a dilution of the original plan, allowing for a gradual shift towards malaria control. Indeed, the MEPs in Burma, Cambodia and South Vietnam were converted to control programmes in 1971.

With global eradication remaining an alleged long-term goal, the 22nd WHA (1969) decided that those MEPs judged to have a good prospect of success should be pressed to their ultimate conclusion, but that otherwise the nature of the anti-malaria operations undertaken by a country should be fitted to its public health resources. The re-examination also 'brought out the clear recognition of the need for the future strategy to retain a large measure of adaptability' and suggested a diversification of means of attack on the vector. 'The present methods of eradication, based mainly on the interruption of transmission by insecticide spraying, are essentially suited to stable communities living permanently in fixed habitations.'[16] Thus the programmes instituted in Saudi Arabia, Somalia, Egypt and Sudan were control programmes, based on larvicides and larvivorous fish as well as house spraying.[17]

The revised strategy of the WHO was basically intended to tell Third World countries which had failed to attain the goal of malaria eradication within the prescribed period of one decade that, from then on, they had to develop their long-term plans within their overall health and socio-economic development objectives and within their own system of priorities. Thus the de-prioritization of malaria funding by agencies such as UNICEF and USAID had forced the WHO to take similar action. The new strategy also emphasized that complete eradication of malaria from the world remained primarily a task of national public health organizations. This accentuated the feeling of pessimism that the goal of malaria eradication in developing countries was beyond reach for the foreseeable future. WHO policy had come full circle – from malaria control to malaria eradication, and back to control.

15. See R. Black, 'Economic and Health Justification for Implementing Malaria Control Programmes as Part of the Socio-economic and Health Development Plans', Mal/Exp.Com.16/73.3, 1973, pp. 1–5.
16. See OR 176, annex 13, 1969, pp. 117–18.
17. The coverage was not total, as in eradication programmes, but concentrated on those areas and populations which were in the greatest need of protection. See Brown *et al.*, *op. cit.*, p. 15.

27
HOW EFFECTIVE WAS THE MEP?

Our overview of the MEP has illustrated the problems that may arise in the international implementation of public health theory. The MEP represents an example of functional international cooperation supported by various actors on the international stage, including national governments, donor agencies and international organizations. These actors' divergent interpretations of their interests and priorities, as well as certain technical problems, contributed to the failure of the effort against malaria.

Whether the WHO should be held responsible for the failure of the MEP in view of the Organization's limited financial resources, the errors made by national Health Ministries and the discontinuation of financial assistance by donors is debatable. However, the role of the WHO in the implementation of the MEP has shown clearly that the influence of the WHO's Secretariat, its Executive Board and its Assembly far exceeds the limited financial power the Organization wields. Undoubtedly, the strength of the WHO lies not in its budget but rather in the virtual universality of its membership, the high regard in which it is held in scientific and public health circles and its position as the final health forum for international medical consensus. It is this high regard that led to the initial increase in funding for malaria eradication and to the faith that so many states placed in the eradicability of malaria.

The prevalence of malaria in many countries to this day attests to the failure of the MEP. However, it must be noted for the record that the degree of success of the MEPs varied from region to region. For instance, of all the developing countries with eradication programmes, those countries in the Americas Region of the WHO were the most successful. These states also received the largest amounts of funding. For instance, in the 1957–63 period 45 per cent of all funds available for malaria eradication were spent in this region. Malaria eradication was claimed in 42 per cent of the originally malarious areas of the Americas Region; 38 per cent of the Southeast Asia Region; 29 per cent of the Western Pacific Region; 3 per cent of the Eastern Mediterranean Region; 1.6 per cent of the African Region; and 83 per cent of the European Region.[1]

As indicated in the early chapters of this work, we propose to evaluate effectiveness under three main headings: (i) the general

1. See OR 135, 1964, p. 77; and TRS 357, 1967, p. 9.

aims, or 'mission', of the Organization; (ii) the targets hoped for, and results achieved, from its activity; and (iii) the totality of the measures and resources employed in pursuing these aims and targets.

In terms of the general aims, or 'mission', of the WHO, it is clear that some sort of control or eradication effort against malaria is mandated in the constitution of the WHO, which requires the Organization 'to stimulate and advance work to eradicate epidemic, endemic, and other diseases'. The general objective of the Organization to help in 'the attainment by all peoples of the highest possible level of health' can also be interpreted to include activities against a disease as pervasive and debilitating as malaria. There were ample precedents for a fight against malaria in the less ambitious international health organizations that preceded the WHO. The reversion to control, after the failure of the MEP, resulted from a change in ideas about the eradicability of malaria, and not from a new belief that the task did not lie within the mandate of the Organization.

Regarding the defining of targets hoped for, and results achieved, it may be said that the MEP was overly optimistic. The ultimate target of the programme was complete eradication of malaria from the planet within eight to ten years. The inadequacy of intermediate targets, together with a great initial momentum resulting from early successes, made the need for more thorough short-term plans, and contingency plans in case of failure, seem unnecessary.

Much long-term planning was retarded by the initial lack of short-term planning. For instance, the rush of developing countries to declare MEPs, due to the American decision to fund only malaria eradication (and not control), meant that little attention was paid first to establishing the national infrastructure needed to fight the long-term battle. This drive towards malaria eradication was to some extent encouraged, and certainly not discouraged, by the WHO itself.

After the reversion to malaria control, the WHO gave up on long-term planning for malaria and left such planning to the countries affected. During the eradication era, planning was frequently supplanted by financial exigencies in many countries. The fact that malaria was such a scourge at the time propelled countries towards MEPs without adequate consideration of the complications involved. For instance, the complexity of an international effort in which each national eradication programme was composed of many small programmes, each with its own features and its own rate of progress, was not fully appreciated or anticipated.

The new approach of an intensive time-limited eradication programme had received wide support as a direct consequence of promotional campaigns implying that lack of money was the sole constraint on global success in eradicating malaria. Many experts failed to appreciate that early successes, such as those of Venezuela, were the consequence of more than just the cook-book application of a new technique. A detailed knowledge of the epidemiology of the disease and of the methodology of malaria control and eradication was essential. It was not well understood that frequently the solution to one problem might expose previously unanticipated problems. The key to a successful campaign lay in the level of difficulty of these new problems and in the ability to anticipate them and to deal with them effectively through research and development. If this had been understood, the initial administrative response to the development of anophelines' resistance to residual insecticides would have stressed the need for a rapid expansion of basic research rather than the expansion of malaria eradication efforts that were attempted.

The method of fixing targets in the MEP led to misleading interpretations of the progress of the programme, and to unrealistic expectations. For instance, a fall in the number of cases of malaria reported was considered the greatest gauge of the MEP's success. Such a criterion did not take into consideration the fact that early efforts of the WHO were successful because of a very high degree of financial and manpower commitment to the MEP that could not be sustained for the whole duration of the programme. Moreover, early problems and set-backs were often overlooked, making the picture even more artificially optimistic.

As of 1969, evaluation of the MEP, in terms of the decrease in malaria cases, showed a failing programme. Many obstacles were evident by this stage, including inadequate planning, administrative and financial factors, operational difficulties and technical problems. As is clear from the earlier discussion of these obstacles, these were not just minor operational faults, such as spraying the wrong doses of DDT, but included major conceptual errors too. For example, as late as 1969 the WHO was claiming that 'rural health services are developing rapidly in the wake of the malaria eradication campaign.'[2] The truth was that jealousies and competition between the part of the public health services responsible for malaria programmes and the parts responsible for other health issues had in many cases made this impossible.[3]

At the inception of the worldwide eradication concept, several major premises were accepted. One was that a single weapon, the application of an insecticide to house walls, could interrupt the

2. TRS 357, 1967, p. 14; and OR 176, annex 13, 1969, p. 112.
3. Personal communication with M. A. Farid, Geneva, 6 Aug. 1987.

transmission of malaria wherever it existed. Another was that every country (with the exception of those in sub-Saharan Africa) possessed the necessary knowledge and resources to put this method to effective use. Not only was it felt that no new information was needed, it appeared that much which had been learned in the past could now be ignored and forgotten.

Knowledge of the etiology and treatment of malaria had expanded slowly since the beginning of the century, but by the middle of the century an impressive core of information was available to physicians and scientists. Yet, almost overnight, the sophisticated science of malaria control was transformed into a simple formula for malaria eradication: apply a given dose of insecticide to the interiors of all house walls, and watch the number of malaria cases wither into nothingness. With such faith in the technology of malaria eradication, it is hardly surprising that legislative bodies did not see the need to provide financial support for basic malaria research when they were at the same time led to believe that the disease was in retreat, and would be extinct within eight to ten years.[4]

The decision to throw the most support behind a programme of rapid eradication drew off funds which could have been used to support research on malaria. In the period 1957–63, approximately 1.4 per cent of the overall expenditure on WHO-supported malaria eradication programmes was spent on fundamental and applied research.[5] Moreover, with the major medical journals announcing the impending death of malaria, some of the better minds which might have entertained careers in malariology were lost to other fields. A whole generation of malariologists and malaria researchers has been lost. Indeed, since the failure of malaria eradication, anti-malaria programmes have faced a serious shortage of professional staff.[6]

Another reason for the failure of the MEP was the withdrawal of American funding. By 1969, USAID began to perceive malaria eradication as a lost cause. It now saw the eradication programme as another measure which, if successful, would further crowd the world. This realization led to the redirection of what were originally malaria funds towards family planning programmes. Accordingly, in 1966 the WHA confirmed 'that the role of WHO is to give

4. See general discussion in 'The Medical Research Programme of WHO, 1958–1963', *Report by the Director-General*, WHO, Geneva, Dec. 1963: also see 'Report on Development of Malaria Eradication Programmes', EB33/4, 18 Nov. 1963, pp. 33–41.

5. See OR 135, annex 6, 1964, p. 77; and 'Report on Development of Malaria Eradication Programmes', *op. cit.*, p. 42.

6. TRS 680, 1982, p. 42.

members technical advice, upon request, in the development of activities in family planning, as part of an organized health service, without impairing its normal preventive and curative functions'. This reversed the position the Assembly had taken in 1952, when it had refused to authorize a population programme.[7]

The totality of the measures employed in pursuing the targets of the MEP also contributed to its demise. For instance, although the budget of the MEP was either constant or increasing for the first few years, it dropped quite suddenly when the US government decided to withdraw its support for eradication efforts. The influence of this withdrawal was felt not only in the American-supported programmes but also in developing countries, which stepped down their national support for anti-malaria programmes, assuming that they could not confront the malaria Leviathan unassisted.

In the early years of the WHO, health was considered an exclusive preserve of medical experts. Even at the national level, WHO representatives only interacted with the Health Ministries; at the international level, the Organization jealously guarded its mandate, rarely allowing other agencies any input in its activities. This *modus operandi* was obvious in the early malaria work of the WHO: while other specialized agencies (such as UNICEF) were not consulted in the original planning for the MEP, by 1969 the Organization was hinting that other sectors were partly to blame for the failure of malaria eradication, because the WHO did 'not always receive the necessary expert advice on economic, sociological, and administrative aspects'.[8] Because of the pivotal, and exclusive, role of the WHO in planning malaria eradication, the Organization essentially became the key factor in the future of the programme – when it changed back to a policy of malaria control, the other organizations gave up their anti-malaria efforts too.

The funding of the MEP, the decline in which ultimately led to the death of the programme, was largely obtained from non-WHO sources. The largest source, as mentioned earlier, was the US government. Thus within the WHO there was little interest in raising funds from outside sources, as the US government had already pledged so much to the MEP. In fact, the problem with the funding of the MEP was that it was too dependent on one major backer – the US government. Its withdrawal of support effectively led to the demise of the whole programme.

For as long as the funding was available, it seems that the Organization was genuinely committed to the MEP in terms of providing

7. See OR 151, 1966, p. 21.
8. OR 176, annex 13, 1969, p. 114.

manpower and funding. The fact that the Director-General and many of the regional directors were malariologists made such commitment possible, if not desirable.

Finally, it seemed that at times inadequate provision had been made for continuous review and evaluation of the MEP so as to allow rapid modification when necessary. In addition, the almost total dependence on DDT meant a lack of diversification in the means of attack against the malaria vector, further limiting the choices available to the WHO in case of ineffectiveness. Essentially, the MEP was not flexible enough to accommodate set-backs and successes at short notice, save for an all-or-none response – when the early successes were evident, the WHO went ahead with the programme; when the failures appeared, the funding was withdrawn, the Organization abandoned the MEP and went back to malaria control.

As to functionalism, empirical evidence from malaria eradication points to certain problems with the theory. For instance, the functionalist faith in the technical was not borne out in the MEP. In fact, as we have shown, the exaggerated expectations of what technology could achieve in the eradication programme often stemmed from a lack of understanding of the technology involved and, even more so, of the political, social, administrative and financial arrangements required for the successful application of that technology. The fact that so many eradication programmes were in progress was a tribute more to widespread confidence in the effectiveness of the weapon (DDT) and the idea of participation in the international effort than to successes achieved as a result of good planning, careful execution and adequate evaluation. In this respect, the functionalists were too optimistic about the ability of technicians to understand all the factors involved in using technology.

Mitrany saw functional cooperation breaking down national loyalties in international affairs. Whatever the value of lessons learned and the functions performed by bodies such as the WHO, the net effect of much of their functioning, as in the case of the MEP, has been to highlight struggles and rivalries. As we have demonstrated, such struggles were not limited to those between states. Experts also exhibited the jealousies and rivalries that functionalists often attribute to political interactions, with different segments of the public health services of many countries competing for resources and attention; antagonisms led to non-cooperation between the two.

Functionalists also seem to have ignored the issue of finances. Mitrany, for instance, pays no attention to issues relating to financing in his works. As we have seen, financial considerations were not only crucial in stimulating the launch of the MEP, they were also one of the major reasons for its decline. The world of the functionalists may be one of unlimited resources; such is not generally the case over the long term in specific instances of functional cooperation, such as a malaria eradication programme.

Malaria eradication, like public health in general, is too large and dynamic a phenomenon to be encapsulated as a single static problem which functionalism and its assumptions may overcome. The role of functionalism is limited in a programme such as the MEP.

While functionalists predict that cooperation in one area will spill over to other areas, they shed little light on problems associated in creating cooperation between experts within one area. The assumption that experts within an area will cooperate seems to functionalists to be too obvious for discussion. In our case study, we find that this assumption was not always proved right. The assumption was not confirmed in the day-to-day running of the MEP; it was confirmed with regard to the donor agencies involved in malaria eradication. For example, once the malaria demonstration teams had been successful in eradicating or controlling malaria in a small area of given countries, the confidence that this engendered spilled over to change the attitude of agencies such as UNICEF and USAID in favour of the eradication programme. Trust and respect carried over from one set of functional relations to another.

At the same time, however, this spillover may be declared inappropriate or misleading because, as has been seen, it was not possible to extend by example the demonstration team successes to the rest of the country, despite the fact that the financial support for this was present. Functionalism does not offer a solution for such inappropriate or partial spillover.

There was also evidence of negative spillover: in some programmes it became necessary to suspend activities because of administrative deficiencies and it was only possible to resume work after a long and costly reorganization. These events had negative repercussions on other services.

The difficulties in the malaria eradication period of the WHO were crucial in that the programme's outcome affected the whole ideology of the Organization. After the failure of the programme, there were few who still supported the idea of a highly specialized 'vertical' approach, such as the programme had used, in which power was centralized and money and policy were distributed from the top down: 'In the zeal to get the massive military-like campaigns under way with a minimum of "red tape", a great deal of emphasis was given to the desirability of autonomy of the malaria service.'[9] The high priority and autonomy given to the vertical programme of malaria eradication produced many problems. For instance, in some countries it resulted in a loss of interest in the malaria campaign from parts of the public health service whose cooperation was necessary for its success.

We find that the functionalists' lack of discussion of potential competition for resources among specialists belies a lack of understanding of some aspects of human nature. We found that such competition was an inevitable part of an effort as massive as the MEP, and that it was fuelled by the vertical nature of the programme.

In fact, the WHO's present 'horizontal' approach to world health, with its multi-dimensional and multi-sectoral emphasis and its decentralization of power and money towards the rural populations, together with the consequent emphasis on preventive health measures, is one major result of the failure of malaria eradication. Thus, in leaving the control of malaria to the public health departments of the countries involved, contemporary WHO strategy against malaria reflects tactics that in the eradication programme were reserved for the maintenance phase, by which time malaria was to have been virtually eliminated. This new approach has essentially turned the original malaria eradication effort on its head.[10]

This 'primary health-care' approach now prevalent in developing countries is in many respects opposite to the vertical programmes of the eradication days. Not only does it lessen the importance of the advisory role of the WHO (relative to the eradication and 'demonstration team' days), it also radically decreases the significance of the role of the 'health specialist'. This new horizontal, basic health service approach is not compatible with the 'function determines form' mandate of functionalism. Taken to its extreme, every unique function for every unique national problem should require a unique institutional form. In contrast, present-day public health leaders are attempting to encompass all health-care in one generalized approach.

In summary, the MEP was a highly ineffective effort on the part

9. See 'Report on Development of Malaria Eradication Programmes', *op cit.*, p. 9.

10. For further discussion of the conversion of vertical MEPs into horizontal malaria control programmes, see TRS 712, 1984; 'Integration of Mass Campaigns against Specific Diseases into General Health Services', WHO unpublished document MHO/PA/116.64, June 1964; and C. L. Gonzalez, *Mass Campaigns and General Health Services*, WHO, Geneva, 1965.

of the WHO, judged on the basis of two out of the three sets of criteria established in Part I – namely the targets hoped for and goals achieved, and the totality of measures used to achieve the goals. Effectiveness was only achieved in terms of the establishment of the programme's aims.

Part IV
SUMMARY AND CONCLUSIONS

28

EVOLUTION OF INTERNATIONAL PUBLIC HEALTH PHILOSOPHY

From the earliest instances of international health cooperation, the International Sanitary Conferences of 1851 to 1903, we can discern threads of the later public health fabric of the OIHP, the League of Nations Health Organization and the World Health Organization. Not unlike the WHO's attack on malaria, the Sanitary Conferences concentrated only on cholera, plague and yellow fever, in what was essentially an early form of the 'vertical' or directed approach to public health-care. Little heed was paid to public health as a whole, as attention was focused on the given disease(s) which wreaked the most social, political and economic havoc in nineteenth-century Europe and its colonies. Thus the vertical approach to international health-care was not new to the WHO, having entrenched itself over a hundred years before the malaria eradication programme was launched. In fact, this was the only form of large-scale international public health action to which both political and health leaders had ever been exposed.

The persistence of the vertical approach to international public health well into the 1960s does not detract from the general evolution in public health measures which took place during the League of Nations days and later. Among the positive changes that the WHO inherited from its predecessors were the emphasis on international epidemiological reporting, the tradition of promulgating International Sanitary Conferences, the offering of expert medical advice to countries that sought it, biological standardization, and the convoking of meetings and distributing of literature on issues of international public health relevance.

The international disputes which often characterized the International Sanitary Conferences of the nineteenth century did not disappear with the discovery of the etiology of the three diseases that preoccupied those Conferences; however, the turn of the century did mark the first time in the history of international public health when scientific discovery was to be translated into practical public health measures. The scientific advances did not alter the emphasis on the vertical approach, because they were intimately linked with the three diseases that had interested European powers most.

Much of the early work of the League of Nations Health Organization was done in a frantic rush, frequently as a reaction to the latest epidemic devastating war-ravaged countries. Although the major epidemics in Europe receded by 1922, Asia continued to suffer from many of the same diseases, inspiring the establishment of the Eastern Bureau of the League of Nations Health Organization in 1925. The Eastern Bureau added to existing precedents for decentralization and later influenced the form that the WHO was to take. The establishment two years earlier of the League's Malaria Commission marked a shift in international public health philosophy that persists to this day. Previously, seventy years of international health cooperation had been devoted to the establishment of barriers against the importation of communicable diseases, but now the mandate of the Malaria Commission included studying and advising on the most suitable means to control malaria worldwide. International public health cooperation had taken the irrevocable leap from reaction to action.

In the years immediately preceding the Second World War, the League's Health Organization took a greater interest in public health issues not directly related to communicable diseases. At a time when the vertical approach to public health-care was prevalent, this broad outlook betrayed a shift towards what is now referred to as the 'horizontal' philosophy of public health-care. At this time, outstanding work was done in what contemporary WHO leadership sees as crucial components of horizontal 'primary health-care': nutrition, housing, hygiene and physical fitness. Indeed, as the war forced an end to the work of the League's Health Organization, the efforts that endured (even past the existence of the Organization itself) reflected the newly discovered horizontal philosophy.

Interestingly, the League's turn towards the horizontal approach in its final days had a significant influence on the founders of the WHO as they proceeded to define health, and thus the mandate of their Organization, more broadly than ever before; however, despite a new conceptualization of health as being far greater than the mere freedom from disease, the truly visionary WHO constitution did not strongly influence the Organization's early priorities. There were various reasons for this. First, even before the WHO was established, its Interim Commission was confronted with the 1947 cholera epidemic in Egypt, an emergency that could only be dealt with in a vertical manner. The prevalence of malaria, tuberculosis and venereal diseases also resulted in these being given top priority by the Interim Commission, and later by the WHO, with an assumption that the vertical approach which had been attempted before would continue. Secondly, the Second World War spawned scientific discoveries, most importantly penicillin and DDT, which enhanced the desirability of the vertical approach, with a one-problem-one-solution paradigm. Finally, the establishment of the WHO was coterminous with the international community's newly found faith in science as the most rational basis for world health and world peace. As science was more amenable to dealing with specifics than with generalities, it is not surprising that the vertical approach to public health-care prevailed over the horizontal as the World Health Organization started work.

As already demonstrated in Part II, the World Health Organization felt that its first priority lay in establishing an international infrastructure for health-care, starting with itself. Accordingly, it pursued decentralization and universality of membership actively and sincerely. Later, even though armed with a horizontal mandate to deal with all aspects of health, the temptation of available funding and disease-specific weapons such as DDT seduced it from that path. The newborn WHO embraced the vertical philosophy. The MEP was the earliest and most dramatic application of this vertical philosophy. The smallpox eradication programme was another example of the same thinking.

By the early 1970s, when the international infrastructure of the WHO was well entrenched,[1] and by which time attempts to eradicate malaria had been abandoned, there emerged a new health philosophy in the Organization. Former ideas about the use of an international health infrastructure for the eradication of diseases by medical experts using vertical programmes had lost their appeal. In addition, the inability of medical experts alone to eradicate malaria suggested a role for previously unwelcome non-medical experts, such as economists, sociologists, anthropologists and geographers.

The WHO's new health philosophy was dramatically different from that of the malaria eradication days. The WHO now believed that the health problems of developing countries could best be handled through the use of its international infrastructure to aid states in establishing national health-care infrastructures. It was

1. By now the membership of the WHO was virtually universal and included the PRC. Also, the regional structure was well established, even though there were attempts to move the regional office out of Egypt after the Camp David Accords.

envisaged that states would use these national infrastructures to address all their public health problems horizontally (that is, as a whole), rather than on a disease-by-disease (that is, vertical) basis. The new approach, or primary health-care, was enunciated in a speech by Halfdan Mahler in 1978, when he criticized the vertical approach, referring to world health as 'indivisible'.[2] The failure of malaria eradication resulted in the WHO's health philosophy veering towards the horizontal approach, the same direction that the League's Health Organization had taken prior to its demise.

While the failure of malaria eradication was the major impetus for the abandonment of the vertical approach, there were other compelling reasons for this too. The entry of the newly independent states into the UN system generally, and the WHO specifically, generated an organizational nightmare: as increasingly evident in the MEP, the effective coordination and cooperation of so large a number of states in any vertical programme became unimaginable. The vast disparities between the health infrastructures of these new states also rendered the vertical approach (which presumes the ability to follow similar steps in disease eradication at the same pace) increasingly unrealistic. Students of the UN system have also suggested that another explanation for the WHO's change of philosophical direction lies in the politically contentious nature of some issues, such as family planning, which are more easily engaged in by the Organization under the rubric of primary health-care than as individual vertical programmes.[3]

By 1993, the horizontal approach can safely be said to be the dominant philosophy of the World Health Organization. It is an integral part of the contemporary WHO concept of primary health-care, which emphasizes the establishment of efficient general health services that meet at least the basic minimum health requirements of a country's inhabitants. Virtually every programme of the WHO has been altered to fit the overall goals of primary health-care.

The goals of primary health-care are encapsulated in the WHO slogan 'health for all by the year 2000'. The primary health-care agenda includes programmes to provide essential drugs to developing countries, to prevent childhood diseases and to ensure a supply of clean water. All of these programmes are too new to allow for a proper analysis of their effectiveness. However, suffice it to say that the horizontal programmes of primary health-care are not immune

2. See Halfdan Mahler, 'World Health is Indivisible', Address to the 31st World Health Assembly, WHO, Geneva, 1978.
3. Discussed in Richard Symonds and Michael Carder, *The United Nations and the Population Question, 1945–1970*, McGraw-Hill, New York, 1973, pp. 156–7.

to international controversy and political intrigue. The discussion in the WHO's essential drugs programme (one component of primary health-care) of a code of conduct for the multinational pharmaceutical industry is but one example of a controversial issue that has stimulated some of the contemporary Western charges of politicization and ineffectiveness against the Organization.

29
CONCLUSIONS: THE ESSENCE OF POLITICIZATION AND EFFECTIVENESS

We have evaluated the influence of political and other factors on the WHO's effectiveness in its efforts to achieve universal membership, a workable decentralized structure and the eradication of malaria. This study has been largely inspired by contemporary Western charges against the UN system in general, and the WHO in particular, of 'politicization' and ineffectiveness. We have offered a summary of these charges and have used them as the starting point of our analysis of effectiveness, as well as of the factors that the contemporary detractors suggest are intimately linked with ineffectiveness: politicization, lack of consensus and breakdown of the functionalist model.

We set out to investigate whether the current charges of 'politicization' and ineffectiveness against the UN system generally accurately reflect the reality within the WHO. We sought to show that effectiveness is a much broader concept than envisaged by present Western critics. We sought to study the influence of politics on effectiveness: in practice, by way of a case study, and in theory, by examining the relevance of the two most controversial tenets of the functionalist theory – spillover and the separability-priority hypothesis – to the work of the WHO.

We have defined effectiveness in a manner identical to that of the WHO, as the 'extent or degree to which WHO has fulfilled its own explicitly stated mission, goal or objective in a specific area of interest'. Three sets of criteria were established to allow closer scrutiny of effectiveness. The areas of interest focused on involve the structural aspirations of universal membership and decentralization; and the Malaria Eradication Programme, the largest field effort ever implemented by the WHO.

In Part I, we argued that the two areas of interest selected for study have formed a continuum in the evolution of different approaches to international health-care within the WHO. The initial interest of the WHO's founders in universal membership and decentralization reflected their wish to establish an international infrastructure for health that could be utilized to address health problems with a technical and political legitimacy that was lacking in previous international health organizations such as the Health Organization of the League of Nations. Moreover, the added legitimacy of universal membership was essential for the vast task that the WHO faced. The MEP represented the first massive application of the international infrastructure vertically - that is, in a highly focused manner, independent of other aspects of public health. Following the failure of the MEP, the vertical approach in general fell into disrepute and a new approach to international health problems gained prominence. This new approach involved the use of the international infrastructure to establish or strengthen national health infrastructures to deal with all health problems horizontally - that is, as a whole. The contemporary primary health-care programmes of the WHO represent the horizontal approach.

Perceptions of effectiveness have changed over time within the WHO, as have the methods of quantifying it. The conversion from specific to broader, and more general, criteria for effectiveness has paralleled the Organization's evolution from the vertical to the present horizontal approach. It is virtually impossible to gauge the effectiveness of the WHO as a whole because of the vastness of the Organization's mandate. The scope of this book only allows a qualitative approach for the evaluation of effectiveness in areas examined, in the period 1948–85.

For measuring effectiveness, we have restricted ourselves to criteria that offer a method of assessing the Organization against its own standards and expectations - we call these internal criteria. For our purposes, external criteria - that is, the standards and expectations which individual member states, private groups and organizations demand of the WHO - have been avoided as far as possible.

We defined internal criteria as those that are promulgated by the Organization as standards and expectations expressed in current interpretations of its constitution, and/or those expressed at the start of a given programme or initiative. The three headings, or sets of criteria, under which we have evaluated effectiveness are: (1) the general aims, or 'mission' of the Organization; (2) the specific programmatic goals or targets hoped for, and results achieved; and (3) the totality of the measures and resources employed in pursuing these aims and targets. Under each heading, we have established certain criteria for effectiveness.

In Part II, we traced the evolution within the WHO of the strong consensus for a universal membership and for decentralization. We discussed some of the problems associated with realizing these aspirations. We distinguished two kinds of controversy concerning structural problems which have been evident in the WHO: those controversies that have faded away and the problems which have persisted to this day. The first category includes problems associated with the integration of regional organizations, the delineation of regional boundaries, and the Arab–Israeli conflict. The second includes problems with political and regional blocs.

In Part III, we examined the malaria eradication programme of the 1950s and 1960s. We showed how overwhelming consensus was developed in what turned out to be the largest international public health venture ever. Despite its massive expense, the worldwide eradication programme did not fulfil the promises made at its outset. The over-optimistic official reports on malaria as a disappearing disease later became a great source of embarrassment. While early successes provided legitimacy for the MEP, a major reason for the early 'takeoff' of malaria eradication programmes in the 1950s was the realization that some species of anopheles mosquitoes were becoming resistant to DDT; it was hoped that a concerted and relatively short universal campaign might eliminate the disease from very large areas before the insecticide resistance spread all over the globe. This hope was not justified. Finally, we outlined the original justification for the vertical approach to health-care which characterized the MEP, and traced the demise of this approach with the failure of the MEP itself.

We find the WHO to have been relatively effective in formulating and achieving its structural aspirations. We also find that the effectiveness of the WHO has been low in the Malaria Eradication Programme. Ineffectiveness is rarely attributable to weakness across all three sets of headings under which effectiveness was evaluated. In fact, the WHO's ineffectiveness in the MEP, and the problems it encountered in meeting its structural aspirations, were attributable to different factors. The structural aspirations have suffered mainly due to weaknesses in the specific programmatic goals or targets hoped for and in the results achieved. The malaria eradication programme showed weakness in the specific programmatic goals or targets hoped for and in the results achieved, and in the totality of the measures and resources employed in pursuing these aims and targets. These findings are now discussed in greater detail.

Structure

The WHO faced little difficulty in defining its aims with regard to its structure. Member states have generally been agreed on the idea (reflected in the WHO's constitution) that universal membership and a decentralized structure would best serve the needs of international public health. These structural goals can be said to be met in the contemporary WHO, which is a decentralized organization with virtually universal membership. Indeed, the fact that the WHO's membership has usually been greater than that of the United

Nations proper attests to the significance which states attach to joining the Organization. Clearly then, the Organization has had no difficulty in effectively enunciating its general aims, or 'mission', as far as universal membership and decentralization are concerned.

The present structure and membership of the WHO are the end product of much conflict and controversy over the four decades of the Organization's history: disputes over membership and over the integration of existing regional health organizations, such as the Pan American Sanitary Organization, have been consistent features. Moreover, the division of the WHO's membership, both now and historically, into political and regional blocs has at times detracted from the internationalist sentiment that considered universal membership so crucial for the WHO at the time of its formation: universality and unity have not gone hand in hand. The difficulties in the Eastern Mediterranean Region of the WHO, as well as the politics of exclusion, discussed in Part II, represent the most strikingly obvious examples of both politicization and ineffectiveness. These difficulties present a recurrent theme of negative political challenges to the Organization's structural aspirations. The danger that challenges pose to the future of international organization is rarely due to an individual incident, but rather to the impression they create collectively of an enduring pattern of worsening politicization which over time has become habitual.

While the Organization has dealt with individual instances of negative politics in membership and decentralization issues as well as it can be expected to do, the overall pattern of these instances continues to haunt it and contribute to the contemporary sense of crisis. The Organization has not been successful in influencing this pattern of continuing politicization. Nonetheless, it is noteworthy that the WHO has loyally adhered to its original target and principle of universal membership and decentralization. Thus in our study of the structural aspirations of the WHO we find both effectiveness and ineffectiveness with regard to our second set of criteria: or the specific programmatic goals or targets hoped for, and the results achieved.

Part II on the WHO structure illustrates the Organization's efforts to minimize negative politics and controversy in dealing with its problems of membership and decentralization. An example of such efforts is the Organization's refusal to let legal technicalities impede the membership of important states: by accepting the United States as a member despite the Americans' conditional ratification of the WHO constitution, while also refusing to formalize provisions for termination of membership, the Organization avoided losing its biggest contributor. Other instances of prudence on the part of the Organization in handling controversial political questions include the refusal by the Director-General to transfer Israel out of the Eastern Mediterranean Region, as demanded by the Arab states, and the refusal of the Organization to be hostile towards the socialist bloc countries which withdrew within a year of the formation of the Organization. Clearly, with regard to the totality of measures and resources employed in pursuing the aims of effective decentralization and universal membership, the Organization has an excellent record. Overall then, the WHO's aspirations of universal membership and decentralization are ineffective on the basis of one of the three sets of criteria we established in Part I.

Malaria Eradication Programme

We have shown that the aim of malaria eradication was clearly within the WHO's constitutional mandate and was consensually agreed upon by the Organization's membership in 1955. Even when the eradication programme was abandoned in 1969, it was agreed that this meant a change in ideas about the eradicability of malaria, and did not imply an end to the belief that the task lay within the mandate of the Organization. We concluded that, with regard to the Malaria Eradication Programme, the WHO defined its aims and mission clearly and effectively.

An evaluation of the hoped-for programmatic goals has shown considerable shortcomings. We have demonstrated how the Organization was overly optimistic about the prospects of malaria eradication; that much long-term planning was retarded by the initial lack of short-term planning; and that the availability of financial assistance, as much or more than the epidemiology of the disease, was crucial in propelling many countries towards declaring eradication programmes even though they lacked adequate control programmes to provide the support network necessary for an eradication effort. The contemporary prevalence of malaria may be considered a very stark sign of the ineffectiveness of the eradication programme.

We also find that the totality of measures used in pursuing the aims and targets of malaria eradication was highly ineffective. For instance, other specialized agencies were not consulted in the original WHO planning; there was too much dependence on one major source of funding (the United States); and the programme was not flexible enough to accommodate set-backs, leaving a complete U-turn as the only option when malaria eradication efforts were unsuccessful and American funding was withdrawn. Overall, the WHO's malaria eradication programme has failed to fulfil two of the three sets of criteria for effectiveness.

Consensus and Effectiveness

Contemporary Western critics of the WHO have linked consensus with effectiveness. Our findings about effectiveness suggest that there is certainly not as perfect a correlation between consensus and effectiveness as might be intuitively obvious to many observers of the UN system. From the selected issues and programmes examined in this study, we find that consensus in the WHO (however arrived at) has been associated with ineffectiveness, as much as with effectiveness. Furthermore, the belief that a lack of consensus in the establishment of internal criteria within the WHO is directly associated with the Organization's ineffectiveness, as the minority states have claimed, is not confirmed.

The non-controversial consensual establishment of internal criteria in the MEP did not protect it from ineffectiveness, which in turn did not result in overwhelming politicization. Not surprisingly, however, it seems that consensus, while it may not guarantee effectiveness, does make the implementation of the programme relatively smoother and less controversial. Consensus in this situation reflects 'common interests, a common understanding of those interests and of the fact that they are shared, and a common agreement on the means to advance them'.[1] This is the main reason that successive WHO Directors-General have preferred consensus to majority decisions. All this, however, is not sufficient to ensure effectiveness: indeed, consensus often entails unsatisfactory compromises on matters essential to effectiveness within a given programme.

The malaria case study serves to refute strict correlations between politicization and ineffectiveness, and between consensus and effectiveness. It demonstrates that politicization need not be the overriding reason for ineffectiveness in the WHO's initiatives, as the contemporary detractors seem to be claiming; moreover, it shows that consensus is not sufficient for effectiveness. This case study illustrates not just the early domination of Western states, especially the United States, in the setting of priorities within the WHO, but also the role of these states in defining the upper limit of what is considered by them acceptable action on the part of the Organization. For example, while playing a crucial role in the establishment of internal criteria for the malaria eradication programme, the USA also played a central role in its downfall. In this case, consensus on the aim of malaria eradication did not ensure full universal cooperation in eradication efforts; nor did it prevent the ultimate

1. Roger Scruton, *A Dictionary of Political Thought*, Macmillan, London, 1982, p. 88.

withdrawal of monies by funding sources and the subsequent complete failure of malaria eradication efforts.

An assessment of the structural aspirations of the WHO, and of the malaria case study, shows that the Organization has evolved from one in which the Western powers dominated the priority-setting and the establishment of internal criteria, and set the upper limit of the effort, to one in which the internal criteria are established by the developing country majority, while the original Western coalition still retains enough influence to limit the implementation of programmes established without its active support.

Part of the reason that our own findings do not coincide with the claims of the critics of the WHO is the differing meanings ascribed to effectiveness. The minority states' view of effectiveness has more often than not revolved around controversial issues or programmes; they perceive ineffectiveness in specific instances or programmes that they disapprove of, and extrapolate from this to the rest of the Organization's work.

Politicization and Effectiveness

The contemporary detractors of the WHO and other specialized agencies appear to conceptualize 'politics' in pejorative terms, while only recognizing any positive contributions of politics implicitly. The WHO Secretariat has made a more explicit acknowledgement of two types of politics, positive and negative. For our purposes, we have divided the political realm into four types of politics: (1) positive politics; (2) inevitable politics; (3) legitimate politics; and (4) negative politics.

We have defined the intrusion of negative politics into the work of the WHO as 'politicization', and have attempted to gauge the influence of politicization on effectiveness in our areas of interest. We find that the present critics of the WHO also have a similar conception of politicization, although our findings are not in agreement with some of their claims regarding the beginnings, incidence and effects of politicization on the WHO.

Some critics of the WHO have claimed that: (1) politicization is the major cause of ineffectiveness; (2) politicization (and the ineffectiveness it causes) is a recent – post-colonial – phenomenon; (3) the recent politicization is the result of actions of Eastern European and especially the Group 77 (G77) countries; (4) if unopposed, the developing countries have the most to gain politically, ideologically and financially from the recent politicization.

We find that in the areas of interest examined in this study in the period since 1945, politicization has been a recurrent, if not an ever-present, phenomenon. It is not a recent phenomenon. In Part II we made it clear that the desire of Arab member states of the Eastern Mediterranean Region to move the regional WHO headquarters out of Egypt was motivated by political concerns that were extraneous to health considerations; in the malaria case study, part of the motivation for the American financing of the eradication programme involved Cold War interests. In addition, with the exception of the Israeli case, the politics of exclusion from membership of the WHO has consistently been motivated by Western interests, and has almost exclusively worked against the socialist states involved.

With regard to the causes of ineffectiveness in the three areas studied, negative politics is not the exclusive detractor of effectiveness. The picture is much more complex. Several factors are responsible for ineffectiveness - politicization is one of these factors.

Only when politicization is present to an overwhelming degree can a causal relationship with ineffectiveness be established. The downfall of the malaria eradication programme, for instance, while indicative of ineffectiveness according to two of the three sets of our criteria, cannot be attributed to politicization, as defined by contemporary critics of the UN system. In the structural issues examined, however, politicization does seem to be the overwhelming factor causing ineffectiveness, judged by one of our sets of criteria. The two-year delay by the United States in ratifying the WHO constitution (a delay which was considered by many observers to be motivated by fears of Soviet domination of the Organization), and the insistence of the Arab states on denying Israel any say in the Eastern Mediterranean Region, are characteristic of such politicization. It is clear from the contemporary universality of membership of the WHO, and from its enduring decentralized structure, that even ineffectiveness caused largely by politicization need not be fatal to the Organization.

Our study also casts doubt on the claim that politicization is the result of the actions of Eastern bloc and G77 countries alone. We found that almost all blocs within the WHO, at one time or another, directly or indirectly, have introduced negative political issues within the Organization. Examples include the insistence of the American states on retaining the independence of the Pan American Sanitary Organization after agreeing to its future integration into the WHO at the International Health Conference; the withdrawal of the socialist bloc countries *en masse* from the WHO; and the denial of membership of the UN (and thus the WHO as well) to countries comprising a significant percentage of the earth's population (the PRC, East Germany, North Korea and North Vietnam), on purely ideological grounds.

Some contemporary Western critics of the WHO have suggested that politicization has adversely affected only Western interests, to the advantage of Eastern and Southern countries. This suggestion is disingenuous. Politicization has been present in the WHO since 1948 and has adversely, but not uniformly, affected the effectiveness of the Organization. It has been perpetuated by various political and regional blocs. Whether one bloc has been able consistently to reap benefits politically, ideologically or financially from politicization or ineffectiveness is not clear. Our finding is further strengthened by the fact that most member states of the WHO are unhappy with the *status quo*, either because they do not think their demands are being fulfilled, or because they feel that inappropriate priorities are being set. What is evident is that politicization is an undesirable phenomenon, and the term 'negative politics' is not an inappropriate description of it.

Despite the prevalence of politicization in the WHO in the period studied, the increasing membership and the associated change in focus of attention and in priorities has, in the post-colonial era, produced a very volatile atmosphere in which the charge of politicization is fairly commonly expressed.

The recent vocalization of such charges is an indication both of the fact that some member states believe they lack influence within the WHO, and of the new awareness of the phenomenon by the major contributors to the WHO, who traditionally dominated the Organization and who lost much of this influence after the entry of the developing countries. The present perception of ineffectiveness and politicization is most dangerous for the future of the Organization, because it alienates virtually all the member states of the WHO.

Functionalism and Effectiveness

Modern critics of the WHO have accused it of ineffectiveness and have attributed this to politicization, lack of consensus and the naked self-interest of some member states. Many of these criticisms are based on functionalist perceptions of the ideal role of international organizations, especially the separability-priority hypothesis – that is, the belief that political and technical considerations can be segregated from each other, with the former being totally removed from the work of the technical organizations: in our case, the WHO. Such functionalist logic is prevalent among the critics of the WHO, even though it is not, as we have seen, based on any mastery of the theory of functionalism. It was also prevalent in the discussions of the founders of the WHO in their deliberations at the Technical Preparatory Committee and the International Health Conference, just as it is now among WHO Secretariat members. Evidently, functionalist expectations are not novel in the context of the WHO.

Empirical evidence from our areas of investigation suggests that some of the tenets of functionalism do not hold for the World Health Organization. This is relevant in the light of criticisms of the Organization that appear to be based on functionalist assumptions. One such assumption is that (negative) politics can be excluded from the work of functional organizations like the WHO – this is essentially the separability-priority hypothesis of functionalism. The notion of medical experts that cooperation in one health area will lead to cooperation in others, which was one justification offered for the malaria eradication programme, reflects the spillover concept in functionalism. We find little evidence for either of these assumptions in our study.

The fact that technical and political spheres are found in close proximity within the WHO has offered an interesting chance to test both the separability-priority hypothesis and the spillover concept. From our earlier finding that politicization has been evident in the WHO throughout its history, we conclude that in the areas of interest to us it has not been possible for the Organization to segregate the technical sphere from the political one; moreover, in view of the inability of the WHO to prevent political issues arising in its supposedly technical fora, not only has cooperation not spilled over from technical areas to political ones, but it has not even spread within and between technical spheres.

The WHO has not succeeded in excluding politics from its functioning. As we have shown in the section on structural goals, politics has been present throughout the history of the Organization; moreover, when personal and national interests are at stake health professionals are often as negatively political as their professional diplomatic counterparts are paid to be – this is most evident in the problems faced by the WHO in the integration of the PAHO.

As we have shown, the MEP was a major failure for the WHO, and the eradication efforts had to be abandoned in 1969. Yet in many ways the programme represents the ideal form of functionalist cooperation: an international field project established by the consensus of technical experts. We found that the vertical nature of the programme made spillover into other health areas fairly difficult: specialists trained in one area cannot always be transferred to other projects without retraining. Also, cooperation could hardly spill over on a large scale to other efforts when malaria eradication itself was such a failure.

A large-scale failure of an enterprise in which the technical experts were initially agreed is not predicted by the functionalists. Functionalism places great faith in experts – it assumes that they can be gathered from around the world to address and resolve specific technical or welfare problems. It assumes that technical problems have technical solutions which can be agreed upon by objective, technical experts. In Mitrany's own words, 'functional arrangements have the patent virtue of technical self-determination.'[2] We have not found technical self-determination of experts in any of the areas scrutinized.

When speaking of technical self-determination, the functionalists have failed to pay attention to the fact that while technical experts may attack technical problems with seemingly technical tools, the ultimate control of their efforts is often in the hands of political bodies. An example of this is the funding of malaria eradication, which was summarily withdrawn when the political backers of the technical effort of eradication felt that the programme was ineffective and that other tasks were more pressing.

The functionalists tend not to discuss money. They assume that funding will materialize when the experts are agreed on how to tackle a technical problem. As one critic of functionalism has noted: 'Nowhere in the functionalist writings is any mention ever made of costs, of the unacceptability of solutions due to the necessity of forgoing something more desirable.'[3] In presuming unlimited resources, the functionalists have underestimated the importance of the political realm. In view of this underestimation, we lean towards McLaren's contention that 'technical self-determination is a fallacy'.[4]

The MEP has exposed another weakness of functionalism: the question of who is to establish priorities, given competing needs. By assuming that technical experts will all be able to agree on the same priorities, the functionalists have not been realistic. In the controversy that was generated by the MEP, not only was non-cooperation (and active opposition) by some states a fundamental restraint on the workings of the programme, but the political role of states was further strengthened. Thus, instead of breaking down political

2. See David Mitrany, 'The Prospect of Integration: Federal or Functional?', in A. J. R. Groom and P. Taylor (eds), *Functionalism*, University of London Press, 1975, p. 68.

3. See Robert McLaren, 'Mitranian Functionalism: Possible or Impossible?', *Review of International Studies*, vol. 11 (1985), p. 146.

4. *Ibid.*, p. 144.

barriers through functional cooperation, the barriers have at times been reinforced.

In the context of the contemporary crisis of multilateralism discussed in Part I, several questions arise. Is politicization any worse now than it was in the past history of the WHO? How real is the contemporary crisis in the WHO? Why was no similar sense of crisis felt during the early days of the Organization when so many socialist states withdrew, and when a significant proportion of the planet's population in the PRC and elsewhere were deprived of the opportunity to participate in the World Health Organization? Why was no similar sense of crisis felt when the malaria eradication programme failed?

It would be difficult to argue that the contemporary instances of politicization are any more serious than, say, the early problems with the integration of the PAHO into the WHO, or those associated with the exclusion of several socialist states from international health deliberations for over twenty years. One explanation for the absence of a sense of crisis in the earlier years of the WHO, despite significant politicization, is that the Western powers which dominated the priorities of the Organization at the time were also among those politicizing it. As the developing countries entered the WHO, the Western powers lost their majority. In the post-colonial age, politicization began to reflect the agenda of Second and Third World countries to some extent, even though the largest financial contributions continued to come from developed, Western countries. In her study of UNESCO, Clare Wells has proposed that 'it is not so much the number of states or the subject matter involved as the relative power of the contending interests which determines the extent to which a given issue becomes or is perceived as "politicised".'[5] Our study of the WHO corroborate Wells' proposition.

The fact that almost every group of states shares in the present sense of crisis testifies to its magnitude and reality, but not to its source. There is really very limited ground (except perhaps an ideologically partisan one) to assign culpability to one group of states or another for precipitating the current crisis. The fact that no international sense of crisis was palpable in the early days of the WHO does not deny its possible existence. It simply reflects the lack of influence of non-Western peoples on the communications media that are essential to shape public perceptions worldwide.

Ironically, the ineffectiveness of malaria eradication which prompted the Organization to make a philosophical change in

5. Clare Wells, *The UN, UNESCO and the Politics of Knowledge*, Macmillan, London, 1987, pp. 187–8.

of greater magnitude than ever before appears to have done far less damage to the professional integrity of the WHO than any administrative bungle or political machination before or since has done. Even at the MEP's worst hour, when culpability was being assigned in various directions, there was no great sense of crisis internationally, no premonitions of the end of multilateral cooperation of the type we have heard recently in connection with the politicization of the WHO and other specialized agencies. This may have been the most dramatic example of ineffectiveness, a genuine disaster in international public health of crisis proportions, but it was one in which the perception of (political) crisis was never cultivated by the same Western governments which are now eloquently fearful for the future of the WHO if politicization and ineffectiveness are not stemmed. One can only speculate on why genuine crises such as the failure of malaria eradication, something of great significance for international public health, have not aroused so strong a reaction from the Western powers as the decline of their symbolic authority has done. One suspects that the shift of the balance of influence, if not ultimate power, is a critical factor in determining what denotes political, if not organizational, crisis for the Western critics of the WHO.

Despite the absence of an international sense of crisis after the abandonment of malaria eradication, the experts in the WHO clearly understood the magnitude of their failure. There was an obvious sense of organizational crisis. The WHO dealt with its own mistakes of the malaria era quite decisively, totally reorganizing the Organization to focus on the new goals of primary health-care. Unsurprisingly, the change in direction for the WHO has not lessened the politicization that pre-dates the Organization. If ignored, contemporary politicization in the WHO may go the way of previous instances of the same and join the junk heap of history. However, this is not a likely outcome in the present climate.

In summary, our study of selected aspects of the WHO and its work has shown that the contemporary Western charges of its politicization and ineffectiveness are academically unsophisticated, historically incomplete (if not inaccurate) and at times frankly misleading. The charges have been painted with broad brushes; and they reflect more an erosion of Western influence in the UN system than any newly concocted conspiracy on the part of Second and Third World countries to abuse and distort the proper mandates of specialized agencies. Certainly, these countries have politicized the WHO for their own purposes; and we have documented many of these instances in this book. But that is hardly new. We have also given instances of similar politicization by Western powers at different times in the WHO's history. Having contributed to it themselves, Western governments should be no more shocked to find politicization in the WHO than to stumble across gambling in a casino.

Since the earliest examples of international health cooperation, world politics has been inseparable from world health. After 140 years of international public health, it is either disingenuous or ignorant to suggest that politicization is a post-colonial phenomenon, twenty-five years old, from which the developing or former socialist world has benefited. The same is true of ineffectiveness. The link between politicization and ineffectiveness is possible, but not automatic.

We find mixed results with regard to the effectiveness of specific areas examined, with relatively more ineffectiveness than effectiveness in malaria eradication efforts, and vice versa in organizational efforts towards decentralization and a universal membership. The observations that lead us to this conclusion are based on a different, perhaps more systematic, analysis of effectiveness than has been carried out by many detractors of the WHO. Our understanding of this ineffectiveness is also different from theirs.

One thing is clear. Neither a resounding condemnation of the WHO nor a striking exoneration is in order. A final judgement on the balance between achievements and failures can only be impressionistic and subjective, because of the impossibility of extrapolating from the specific areas studied to the Organization as a whole. However, the fact that major achievements (in the meeting of structural aspirations, and in areas not studied in this work, such as smallpox eradication) have been possible suggests that the Organization as a whole is certainly far from deficient or ineffective.

The general trends which one can identify from a survey of the structural aspirations and the MEP suggest that great efforts have been made within the WHO to evolve away from the Organization's earlier mistakes. The demise of the vertical approach, and the ascension of the contemporary horizontal approach, is one major instance of the WHO's desire to learn from, and improve upon, past mistakes. Other examples of the Organization's pragmatism are evident in its handling of numerous difficult situations with patience and diplomacy. Such pragmatism, if continued, will undoubtedly help in cushioning the Organization against life-threatening politicization and ineffectiveness.

30

AFTERWORD
THE FUTURE OF INTERNATIONAL HEALTH COOPERATION

Interestingly, the WHO has managed to recover from devastating organizational ineffectiveness in its malaria eradication programme only to find itself in a political crisis which the functionalists failed to predict, and over which the Organization has least control. Although politicization is the cause of its greatest dishonour, the contemporary sense of crisis in the WHO is as much a product of facts as of perceptions. While the facts remain the same, there is ample room for the perceptions to escalate the sense of crisis. The latter renders the perceptions more dangerous for the future health of the WHO than any individual instance of politicization has been. The greatest danger at the moment is that genuine problems of substance will be displaced by ones of perception, and a century and a half of international public health experience will wither away.

Not surprisingly, there is no easy answer to the current dilemma of the WHO and of international organizations in general. In what has been called the crisis of multilateralism, the disparity between population size and power is as critical as that between financial contribution and influence. These disparities will have to be addressed if international cooperation through the UN specialized agencies is to thrive. Certainly, in the case of the WHO, there is little choice but to address the issues promptly and frankly. It is self-evident that the WHO serves a purpose much greater than the sum of its individual health programmes: if it were to disintegrate tomorrow, it would have to be rejuvenated the day after. Accordingly, even the WHO's strongest critics have not called for its dismemberment.

Dozens of books have been written in the past decade on the need to reform the UN system. There is great emphasis on ways and means to improve organizational and structural functions, and to lessen the overlap between UN specialized agencies. Indeed, such initiatives may improve the effectiveness of specific programmes of individual organizations and make the system work better overall. However, few suggestions offer any enduring reprieve from the heart of the contemporary sense of crisis: politicization. The root causes of politicization remain the same as they were when the WHO was founded: sovereignty, national self-interest, the politics of exclusion. It is highly unlikely that these will magically vanish in the twenty-first century, displaced by a blanket of international goodwill.

The pervasiveness of contemporary disillusionment with the WHO, and with the UN system generally, renders reform inevitable. It is unclear what exact form this reform is to take. Disparate ideas have to be scrutinized thoroughly to produce something acceptable to all parties. The most important ingredient for change is political will. Of course, a common understanding of politicization and effectiveness would accelerate the acceptance of commonly conceived reforms. Such a unity of vision is not imminent.

The WHO has made valiant attempts to overcome politicization and ineffectiveness, with greater success in rooting out the latter than the former. Its recent changes in administrative practice to ensure consensus decisions on issues dear to the major donors have averted a budgetary and political crisis. Since the end of the Cold War and the subsequent disintegration of the Soviet Union, better relations between East and West have somewhat eased the tensions that the WHO and other specialized agencies lived and worked under. Certainly, the ideological tug of war between capitalist and socialist philosophies is now a rare phenomenon in the WHO.

In the past decade alone, the nature of future international relations has undergone dramatic change with the emergence of a single superpower, the United States. The Persian Gulf War reinforced American pre-eminence globally. The 'new world order' will inevitably affect the WHO, but it is yet to be seen exactly how. With the socialist influence in the UN system evaporated, the dominant clash remains that between North and South.

While the disenfranchised of the world comprise the majority in an ever-increasing number of member states of the UN system, the influence and power of major donors such as the United States appear proportionately greater. Both developed and developing countries have an interest in the survival of specialized agencies such as the WHO. However, unless we are to return to an increasingly disagreeable hegemonic relationship in the UN system, where the United States and its allies determine most if not all initiatives and priorities, dramatic changes in attitudes will be necessary for the Organization to endure. Both North and South blocs will need to acknowledge the politicization that each has contributed in the history of the WHO, and to accept the determining role they can play now if they adopt a new, more constructive mode of interaction. This is easier said than done.

In the next century, international public health cooperation will be no less critical than it was in its earliest beginnings. Diseases such as malaria, tuberculosis and AIDS will compel common action, as will over-population and malnutrition. Perhaps the answer to the effective operation of functional organizations in the future lies in abandoning the Mitranian distinction of 'technical' and 'political' altogether. An overt acceptance and understanding of positive, inevitable and legitimate politics might help mitigate the perceptions of crisis and allow important health work to continue.

The immediate prospects for the WHO are ones of frustration and uncertainty. With increasing membership and a limited budget, the Organization is about to face an administrative and budgetary challenge of immense proportions. The legitimate concerns of North and South will have to be accommodated in a sensitive manner without excluding the critical priorities of either. The World Health Organization is at a dynamic moment in history; by the turn of the century, it will either entrench itself as an indispensable component of multilateral health diplomacy or become marginalized as another instrument of superpower foreign policy. In either scenario, world health and world politics will likely remain inseparable but aloof bedfellows.

APPENDIXES

A

W.H.O. MEMBER STATES: DATES OF ENTRY AND SHARE OF THE BUDGET

	Date of entry	*1992/3 contribution*[1] %	*net*
Afghanistan	19 Apr. 1948	0.01	75,270
Albania	26 May 1947	0.01	75,270
Algeria	8 Nov. 1962	0.15	1,129,110
Angola	15 May 1976	0.01	75,270
Antigua and Barbuda	12 Mar. 1984	0.01	75,270
Argentina	22 Oct. 1948	0.65	4,892,810
Armenia	4 May 1992	*a*	*a*
Australia	2 Feb. 1948	1.54	11,592,190
Austria	30 June 1947	0.73	5,495,000
Azerbaijan	2 Oct. 1992	*a*	*a*
Bahamas	1 Apr. 1974	0.02	150,550
Bahrain	2 Nov. 1971	0.02	150,550
Bangladesh	19 May 1972	0.01	75,270
Barbados	25 Apr. 1967	0.01	75,270
Belarus (Byelorussia)	7 Apr. 1948	*a*	*a*
Belgium	25 June 1948	1.15	8,656,510
Belize	23 Aug. 1990	0.01	75,270
Benin	20 Sept. 1960	0.01	75,270
Bhutan	8 Mar. 1982	0.01	75,270
Bolivia	23 Dec. 1949	0.01	75,270
Bosnia Herzegovina	10 Sept. 1992	*b*	*b*
Botswana	26 Feb. 1975	0.01	75,270
Brazil	2 June 1948	1.42	10,688,910
Brunei	25 Mar. 1985	0.04	301,100
Bulgaria	9 June 1948	0.15	1,129,110
Burkina Faso	4 Oct. 1960	0.01	75,270
Burundi	22 Oct. 1962	0.01	75,270
Cambodia	17 May 1950	0.01	75,270
Cameroon	6 May 1960	0.01	75,270
Canada	29 Aug. 1946	3.03	22,875,000
Cape Verde	5 Jan. 1976	0.01	75,270

	Date of entry	1992/3 contribution[1] %	net
Central African Republic	20 Sept. 1960	0.01	75,270
Chad	1 Jan. 1961	0.01	75,270
Chile	15 Oct. 1948	0.08	602,200
China	22 July 1946	0.77	5,796,100
Colombia	14 May 1959	0.14	1,053,840
Comoros	9 Dec. 1975	0.01	75,270
Congo	26 Oct. 1960	0.01	75,270
Cook Islands	9 May 1984	0.01	75,270
Costa Rica	17 Mar. 1949	0.02	150,550
Côte d'Ivoire	28 Oct. 1960	0.02	150,550
Croatia	11 June 1992	*b*	*b*
Cuba	9 May 1950	0.09	677,470
Cyprus	16 Jan. 1961	0.02	150,550
Czech Republic	22 Jan. 1993	*c*	*c*
Denmark	19 Apr. 1948	0.68	5,118,630
Djibouti	10 Mar. 1978	0.01	75,270
Dominica	13 Aug. 1981	0.01	75,270
Dominican Republic	21 June 1948	0.03	225,830
Ecuador	1 Mar. 1949	0.03	225,830
Egypt	16 Dec. 1947	0.07	526,920
El Salvador	22 June 1948	0.01	75,270
Equatorial Guinea	5 May 1980	0.01	75,270
Ethiopia	11 Apr. 1947	0.01	75,270
Fiji	1 Jan. 1972	0.01	75,270
Finland	7 Oct. 1947	0.50	3,763,700
France	16 June 1948	6.13	48,142,930
Gabon	21 Nov. 1960	0.03	225,830
Gambia	26 Apr. 1971	0.01	75,270
Georgia	26 May 1992	*a*	*a*
Germany	29 May 1951	9.18	69,101,490
Ghana	8 Apr. 1957	0.01	75,270
Greece	12 Mar. 1948	0.39	2,935,690
Grenada	4 Dec. 1974	0.01	75,270
Guatemala	26 Aug. 1949	0.02	150,550
Guinea	19 May 1959	0.01	75,270
Guinea-Bissau	29 July 1974	0.01	75,270
Guyana	27 Sept. 1966	0.01	75,270
Haiti	12 Aug. 1947	0.01	75,270
Honduras	8 Apr. 1949	0.01	75,270
Hungary	17 June 1948	0.20	1,505,480
Iceland	17 June 1948	0.03	225,830
India	12 Jan. 1948	0.36	2,709,870
Indonesia	23 May 1950	0.15	1,129,110
Iran	23 Nov. 1946	0.68	5,118,630
Iraq	23 Sept. 1947	0.12	903,290

	Date of entry	1992/3 contribution[1] %	net
Ireland	20 Oct. 1947	0.18	1,354,940
Israel	21 June 1949	0.20	1,505,480
Italy	11 Apr. 1947	3.91	29,432,110
Jamaica	21 Mar. 1963	0.01	75,270
Japan	16 May 1951	11.17	84,081,010
Jordan	7 Apr. 1947	0.01	75,270
Kazakhstan	19 Aug. 1992	*a*	*a*
Kenya	27 Jan. 1964	0.01	75,270
Kiribati	26 July 1984	0.01	75,270
Korea (Democratic People's Republic of)	19 May 1973	0.05	376,370
Korea (Republic of)	17 Aug. 1949	0.21	1,580,760
Kuwait	9 May 1960	0.28	2,107,680
Kyrgyzstan	29 Apr. 1992	*a*	*a*
Laos	17 May 1950	0.01	75,270
Latvia	4 Dec. 1991	*a*	*a*
Lebanon	19 Jan. 1949	0.01	75,270
Lesotho	7 July 1967	0.01	75,270
Liberia	14 Mar. 1947	0.01	75,270
Libya	16 May 1952	0.27	2,032,400
Lithuania	25 Nov. 1991	*a*	*a*
Luxembourg	3 June 1949	0.06	451,650
Madagascar	16 Jan. 1961	0.01	75,270
Malawi	9 Apr. 1965	0.01	75,270
Malaysia	24 Apr. 1958	0.11	828,020
Maldives	5 Nov. 1965	0.01	75,270
Mali	17 Oct. 1960	0.01	75,270
Malta	1 Feb. 1965	0.01	75,270
Marshall Islands	5 June 1991	*d*	*d*
Mauritania	7 Mar. 1961	0.01	75,270
Mauritius	9 Dec. 1968	0.01	75,270
Mexico	7 Apr. 1948	0.92	6,925,210
Micronesia	14 Aug. 1991	*e*	*e*
Moldova	4 May 1992	*a*	*a*
Monaco	8 July 1948	0.01	75,270
Mongolia	18 Apr. 1962	0.01	75,270
Morocco	14 May 1956	0.04	301,100
Mozambique	11 Sept. 1975	0.01	75,270
Myanmar	1 July 1948	0.01	75,270
Namibia	23 Apr. 1990	0.01	75,270
Nepal	2 Sept. 1953	0.01	75,270
Netherlands	25 Apr. 1947	1.62	12,194,390
New Zealand	10 Dec. 1946	0.23	1,731,310
Nicaragua	24 Apr. 1950	0.01	75,270
Niger	5 Oct. 1960	0.01	75,270

	Date of entry	1992/3 contribution[1] %	net
Nigeria	25 Nov. 1960	0.20	1,505,480
Norway	18 Aug. 1947	0.54	4,064,800
Oman	28 May 1971	0.02	150,550
Pakistan	23 June 1948	0.06	451,650
Panama	20 Feb. 1951	0.02	150,550
Papua New Guinea	29 Apr. 1976	0.01	75,270
Paraguay	4 Jan. 1949	0.03	225,830
Peru	11 Nov. 1949	0.06	451,650
Philippines	9 July 1948	0.09	677,470
Poland	6 May 1948	0.55	4,140,070
Portugal	13 Feb. 1948	0.18	1,354,940
Qatar	11 May 1972	0.05	376,370
Romania	8 June 1948	0.19	1,430,210
Russian Federation	24 Mar. 1948	*a*	*a*
Rwanda	7 Nov. 1962	0.01	75,270
Saint Kitts and Nevis	3 Dec. 1984	0.01	75,270
Saint Lucia	11 Nov. 1980	0.01	75,270
Saint Vincent and the Grenadines	2 Sept. 1983	0.01	75,270
Samoa	16 May 1962	0.01	75,270
San Marino	12 May 1980	0.01	75,270
São Tome and Principé	23 Mar. 1976	0.01	75,270
Saudi Arabia	26 May 1947	1.00	7,527,400
Senegal	31 Oct. 1960	0.01	75,270
Seychelles	11 Sept. 1979	0.01	75,270
Sierra Leone	20 Oct. 1961	0.01	75,270
Singapore	25 Feb. 1966	0.11	828,020
Slovak Republic	4 Feb. 1993	*c*	*c*
Slovenia	7 May 1992	*b*	*b*
Solomon Islands	4 Apr. 1983	0.01	75,270
Somalia	26 Jan. 1961	0.01	75,270
South Africa	7 Aug. 1947	0.44	3,312,080
Spain	28 May 1951	1.91	14,377,330
Sri Lanka	7 July 1948	0.01	75,270
Sudan	14 May 1956	0.01	75,270
Suriname	25 Mar. 1976	0.01	75,270
Swaziland	16 Apr. 1973	0.01	75,270
Sweden	28 Aug. 1947	1.19	8,957,610
Switzerland	26 Mar. 1947	1.06	7,979,040
Syria	18 Dec. 1946	0.04	301,100
Tajikistan	4 May 1992	*a*	*a*
Tanzania (United Republic of)	15 Mar. 1962	0.01	74,270
Thailand	26 Sept. 1947	0.10	752,740
Togo	13 May 1960	0.01	75,270

	Date of entry	1992/3 contribution[1] %	net
Tonga	14 Aug. 1975	0.01	75,270
Trinidad and Tobago	3 Jan. 1963	0.05	376,370
Tunisia	14 May 1956	0.03	225,830
Turkey	2 Jan. 1948	0.31	2,339,500
Turkmenistan	2 July 1992	*a*	*a*
Uganda	7 Mar. 1963	0.01	76,070
Ukraine	3 Apr. 1948	1.23	9,258,720
United Arab Emirates	30 Mar. 1972	0.19	1,430,210
United Kingdom	22 July 1946	4.77	35,905,670
United States of America	21 June 1948	25.0	190,184,900
Uruguay	22 Apr. 1949	0.04	301,100
Uzbekistan	22 May 1992	*a*	*a*
Vanuatu	7 Mar. 1983	0.01	75,270
Venezuela	7 July 1948	0.56	4,215,350
Vietnam	17 May 1950	0.01	75,270
Yemen	20 Nov. 1953	0.02	194,550
Yugoslavia	19 Nov. 1947	*b*	*b*
Zaire	24 Feb. 1961	0.01	75,270
Zambia	2 Feb. 1965	0.01	75,270
Zimbabwe	16 May 1980	0.02	154,550
Associate Members			
Puerto Rico	7 May 1992	*f*	*f*
Tokelau	8 May 1991	*f*	*f*
	Total	100	757,318,400

Notes

1. Net contribution is calculated in US dollars from the gross assessment (based on a formula to determine the percentage of the budget to be assessed from each member state), minus the credit from the Tax Equalization Fund.

a. All the former republics of the Soviet Union have a total 1992/3 contribution of 9.8%, or $73,768,470 net. This whole sum remained unpaid as of March 1993. Estonia joined on 31 March 1993, and its contribution is set at 0.07%.

b. These are the states that formerly comprised the Socialist Federal Republic of Yugoslavia, and have a total 1992/3 contribution of 0.45%, or $3,387,330 net. This whole sum remained unpaid as of March 1993. Macedonia joined on 22 April 1993 (contribution 0.02%).

c. Czechoslovakia ceased to exist on 1 January 1993, at which time the Czech Republic and the Slovak Republic were formed, having a total 1992/3 contribution of 0.65%, or $4,892,810 net, which is fully paid.

d. Inactive member, thus no contribution assessed.

e. The Federated States of Micronesia joined the WHO in 1991, after the WHO assessments for 1992/3 were published. Their approximate contribution is 0.01%, or $75,270 for 1992/3.

f. Both these associate members joined after the 1992/3 assessments were published in 1990. Puerto Rico has paid fully its 1992 assessment of $12,430. Tokelau's assessment for 1992 was $37,290. The following joined subsequently: Tuvalu (7 May 1993), Eritrea (24 July 1993), Niue (4 May 1994) and Nauru (9 May 1994). The budget contributions of all four are set at 0.01%.

a, b, c. These had yet to be broken down in the Proposed Programme Budget of 1992/3 by (newly independent) state, as this budget was formulated in 1990, when many of these states had either not yet achieved independence or had not joined the WHO.

Sources: 'Proposed Programme Budget 1992–1993', PB/92–93, World Health Organization, Geneva, 1990; 'Interim Financial Report for the Year 1992', A46/16, World Health Organization, Geneva, Mar. 1993.

B

W.H.O. STAFF DISTRIBUTION BY EMPLOYMENT CATEGORY AND LOCATION, FEBRUARY 1993

Location	*Professional/general*	*No.*
Headquarters: Geneva (IARC[a] included)	662/938	1,600
The six regions	851/1,839	2,690
Africa	284/719	1,003
The Americas	103/221	324
Southeast Asia	106/335	441
Europe	79/167	246
Eastern Mediterranean	99/222	321
Western Pacific	113/242	355
Inter-regional	41/25	66
Seconded staff	11/0	11
Unassigned staff	21/70	91
Grand totals	1,586/2,872	4,458

a. International Agency for Research in Cancer.
Source: 'Staffing Report', WHO, Geneva, 28 Feb. 1993.

C

TERMINOLOGY OF MALARIA CONTROL AND ERADICATION

Malaria eradication refers to the ending of the transmission of malaria and the elimination of the reservoir of infective cases in a campaign limited in time and carried to such a degree of perfection that, when it comes to an end, there is no resumption of transmission.

Three concepts must be distinguished clearly from one another: malaria control, vector eradication and malaria eradication. *Malaria control* – until 1955 the sole aim of campaigns in most countries – implies the reduction of the disease to a point where its prevalence is no longer a major public health problem; the concept carries the implication that the programme is unending, with control having to be maintained by continuous active work.[1] *Vector eradication* involves the total elimination of all members of the species concerned so that they do not breed when the work is ended. It is therefore a project limited in time. It has been achieved in a number of places by attack both on the larva and on the adult mosquito. But experience shows that the chances of success turn very much on the nature and habits of the species concerned. Although it may be feasible in some places, there is no justification for advising vector eradication as a general or universal mechanism of malaria prevention.[2] *Malaria eradication* is the application of the same principle, not to the mosquito but to the malaria parasite. It has been shown to be applicable in many countries and is applicable to a very much wider range of conditions than is vector eradication. As generally used, the term does not normally imply that vector eradication has been achieved. When the campaign ends, vector anophelines may persist and the state in the area would then be one of anophelism without malaria. Malaria eradication was considered by the WHO to be a goal attainable in four stages or phases:[3]

1. *Preparatory phase*. This phase involves the initial survey of the malariogenic areas and the establishment of operation priorities, as well as staff recruitment and pilot operations. This phase was meant to be limited to one year.
2. *Attack phase*. This involves total coverage of the internal walls of all dwellings in the area with residual insecticide spray; the investigation of

1. See *Terminology of Malaria and Malaria Eradication*, WHO, Geneva, 1963.
2. The eradication of every vector, as implied by vector eradication, is virtually impossible in the case of malaria in tropical countries. Also, in light of the fact that only a small percentage of the anophelines are actually responsible for malaria transmission, an all-out vector eradication effort would seem a waste of time and effort.
3. For greater detail of these four stages, see E. J. Pampana, *A Textbook of Malaria Eradication*, 2nd edn, Oxford University Press, 1969.

results by house-to-house case-finding after the first year; and maintaining the attack on the vector until transmission has ceased and the parasite reservoir is emptied. This stage should last no longer than four years.

3. *Consolidation phase*. This involves attacking the residual pockets of transmission, located by case-finding, by means of drugs or respraying. This phase is maintained until no new indigenous cases have been discovered for a three-year period.

4. *Maintenance phase*. In this phase, the malaria eradication ultrastructure in the area or the country is disbanded or converted, any introduced cases being handled by the public health department. If the absence of detected indigenous cases can be proved to have been based on an adequate surveillance system, and if cases alleged to be imported can be proved to have been so, the country (or major area) may be entered on the WHO's Register as malaria-free.

D
BRIEF NOTES ON SMALLPOX ERADICATION

In any discussion of the failure of the MEP, one must inevitably confront the issue of the success of the smallpox eradication programme. Why did malaria eradication fail and smallpox eradication succeed? While a discussion of the smallpox eradication programme is not within the scope of this book, it is worth noting that there were various factors unique to the disease of smallpox, and to the battle against it, which undoubtedly played a part in rendering smallpox eradication more practicable than malaria eradication. Some of these factors are listed here:[1]

1. Clinical recognition of smallpox is fairly simple. Sub-clinical infections are not a source of worry, because the individuals so infected have not been shown to transmit infection.
2. There are no known animal vectors or reservoirs in smallpox, which is transmitted solely from person to person.
3. Smallpox epidemics develop slowly because the transmissibility of infection is low. Between each generation of infected cases there is an interval of two to three weeks. When transmission does occur, the infected individual usually only infects between one and five others.
4. Infected individuals can be easily identified because transmission requires close contact between infected and susceptible persons, most commonly in the home, hospital or school.
5. Chains of transmission are required for an epidemic to occur. The number of chains of transmission at any one time is usually relatively small.
6. If all outbreaks are investigated promptly, small but rapid and thorough containment actions can break the transmission chains and thus smallpox can be eradicated within a relatively short time.
7. Rather than being a disease that simultaneously and randomly affects many parts of an area or country, smallpox is usually found to be a slowly spreading disease that at any one time affects only a small proportion of population centres.
8. The prevalence of smallpox internationally, at the start of the WHO's eradication programme in 1966, was fairly limited compared to the prevalence of malaria at the start of the MEP in 1955. In 1966, there were 92,799 reported cases of smallpox worldwide. In 1955, there were between 200 million and 250 million cases of malaria.
9. The limited extent of smallpox worldwide meant that it could be eradicated for a relatively small cost. For instance, while expenditure on smallpox eradication in the period 1967–79 amounted to US$313 million (of

1. For general reviews on the smallpox eradication programme, consult F. Fenner, D.A. Henderson, I. Arita, Z. Jezek and I.D. Ladnyi, *Smallpox and Its Eradication*, WHO, Geneva, 1988, and *The Global Eradication of Smallpox*, WHO, Geneva, 1980, pp. 31–3.

which $200 million came from national governments; $43 million from the WHO's Voluntary Fund for Health Promotion; $38 million from the regular budget of the WHO; and $32 million from bilateral aid), the MEP cost approximately $1,500 million in the period 1955–69.

10. Certain technical advances, such as the development of the freeze-dried vaccine and the bifurcated needle, made the eradication of smallpox practicable without presenting any sort of real or imagined danger to the environment (as was the case with the use of DDT).

E

CONSTITUTION OF THE WORLD HEALTH ORGANIZATION

The States Parties to this Constitution declare, in conformity with the Charter of the United Nations, that the following principles are basic to the happiness, harmonious relations and security of all peoples:

Health is a state of complete physical, mental and social well-being and not merely the absence of disease or infirmity.

The enjoyment of the highest attainable standard of health is one of the fundamental rights of every human being without distinction of race, religion, political belief, economic or social condition.

The health of all peoples is fundamental to the attainment of peace and security and is dependent upon the fullest co-operation of individuals and States.

The achievement of any State in the promotion and protection of health is of value to all.

Unequal development in different countries in the promotion of health and control of disease, especially communicable disease, is a common danger.

Healthy development of the child is of basic importance; the ability to live harmoniously in a changing total environment is essential to such development.

The extension to all peoples of the benefits of medical, psychological and related knowledge is essential to the fullest attainment of health.

Informed opinion and active co-operation on the part of the public are of the utmost importance in the improvement of the health of the people.

Governments have a responsibility for the health of their peoples which can be fulfilled only by the provision of adequate health and social measures.

Accepting these principles, and for the purpose of co-operation among themselves and with others to promote and protect the health of all peoples, the Contracting Parties agree to the present Constitution and hereby establish the World Health Organization as a specialized agency within the terms of Article 57 of the Charter of the United Nations.

CHAPTER I - OBJECTIVE

Article 1

The objective of the World Health Organization (hereinafter called the Organization) shall be the attainment by all peoples of the highest possible level of health.

CHAPTER II – FUNCTIONS

Article 2

In order to achieve its objective, the functions of the Organization shall be:

(*a*) to act as the directing and co-ordinating authority on international health work;

(*b*) to establish and maintain effective collaboration with the United Nations, specialized agencies, governmental health administrations, professional groups and such other organizations as may be deemed appropriate;

(*c*) to assist Governments, upon request, in strengthening health services;

(*d*) to furnish appropriate technical assistance and, in emergencies, necessary aid upon the request or acceptance of Governments;

(*e*) to provide or assist in providing, upon the request of the United Nations, health services and facilities to special groups, such as the peoples of trust territories;

(*f*) to establish and maintain such administrative and technical services as may be required, including epidemiological and statistical services;

(*g*) to stimulate and advance work to eradicate epidemic, endemic and other diseases;

(*h*) to promote, in co-operation with other specialized agencies where necessary, the prevention of accidental injuries;

(*i*) to promote, in co-operation with other specialized agencies where necessary, the improvement of nutrition, housing, sanitation, recreation, economic or working conditions and other aspects of environmental hygiene;

(*j*) to promote co-operation among scientific and professional groups which contribute to the advancement of health;

(*k*) to propose conventions, agreements and regulations, and make recommendations with respect to international health matters and to perform such duties as may be assigned thereby to the Organization and are consistent with its objective;

(*l*) to promote maternal and child health and welfare and to foster the ability to live harmoniously in a changing total environment;

(*m*) to foster activities in the field of mental health, especially those affecting the harmony of human relations;

(*n*) to promote and conduct research in the field of health;

(*o*) to promote improved standards of teaching and training in the health, medical and related professions;

(*p*) to study and report on, in co-operation with other specialized agencies where necessary, administrative and social techniques affecting public health and medical care from preventive and curative points of view, including hospital services and social security;

(*q*) to provide information, counsel and assistance in the field of health;

(*r*) to assist in developing an informed public opinion among all peoples on matters of health;

(*s*) to establish and revise as necessary international nomenclatures of diseases, of causes of death and of public health practices;

(*t*) to standardize diagnostic procedures as necessary;

(*u*) to develop, establish and promote international standards with respect to food, biological, pharmaceutical and similar products;

(*v*) generally to take all necessary action to attain the objective of the Organization.

CHAPTER III – MEMBERSHIP AND ASSOCIATE MEMBERSHIP

Article 3

Membership in the Organization shall be open to all States.

Article 4

Members of the United Nations may become Members of the Organization by signing or otherwise accepting this Constitution in accordance with the provisions of Chapter XIX and in accordance with their constitutional processes.

Article 5

The States whose Governments have been invited to send observers to the International Health Conference held in New York, 1946, may become Members by signing or otherwise accepting this Constitution in accordance with the provisions of Chapter XIX and in accordance with their constitutional processes provided that such signature or acceptance shall be completed before the first session of the Health Assembly.

Article 6

Subject to the conditions of any agreement between the United Nations and the Organization, approved pursuant to Chapter XVI, States which do not become Members in accordance with Articles 4 and 5 may apply to become Members and shall be admitted as Members when their application has been approved by a simple majority vote of the Health Assembly.

Article 7[1]

If a Member fails to meet its financial obligations to the Organization or in other exceptional circumstances, the Health Assembly may, on such conditions as it thinks proper, suspend the voting privileges and services to which a Member is entitled. The Health Assembly shall have the authority to restore such voting privileges and services.

Article 8

Territories or groups of territories which are not responsible for the conduct of their international relations may be admitted as Associate Members by the Health Assembly upon application made on behalf of such territory or

1. The amendment to this Article adopted by the 18th World Health Assembly (Resolution WHA18.48) has not yet come into force.

group of territories by the Member or other authority having responsibility for their international relations. Representatives of Associate Members to the Health Assembly should be qualified by their technical competence in the field of health and should be chosen from the native population. The nature and extent of the rights and obligations of Associate Members shall be determined by the Health Assembly.

CHAPTER IV – ORGANS

Article 9

The work of the Organization shall be carried out by:

(*a*) The World Health Assembly (herein after called the Health Assembly);

(*b*) The Executive Board (hereinafter called the Board);

(*c*) The Secretariat.

CHAPTER V – THE WORLD HEALTH ASSEMBLY

Article 10

The Health Assembly shall be composed of delegates representing Members.

Article 11

Each Member shall be represented by not more than three delegates, one of whom shall be designated by the Member as chief delegate. These delegates should be chosen from among persons most qualified by their technical competence in the field of health, preferably representing the national health administration of the Member.

Article 12

Alternates and advisers may accompany delegates.

Article 13

The Health Assembly shall meet in regular annual session and in such special sessions as may be necessary. Special sessions shall be convened at the request of the Board or of a majority of the Members.

Article 14

The Health Assembly, at each annual session, shall select the country or region in which the next annual session shall be held, the Board subsequently fixing the place. The Board shall determine the place where a special session shall be held.

Article 15

The Board, after consultation with the Secretary-General of the United Nations, shall determine the date of each annual and special session.

Article 16

The Health Assembly shall elect its President and other officers at the beginning of each annual session. They shall hold office until their successors are elected.

Article 17

The Health Assembly shall adopt its own rules of procedure.

Article 18

The functions of the Health Assembly shall be:

(*a*) to determine the policies of the Organization;

(*b*) to name the Members entitled to designate a person to serve on the Board;

(*c*) to appoint the Director-General;

(*d*) to review and approve reports and activities of the Board and of the Director-General and to instruct the Board in regard to matters upon which action, study, investigation or report may be considered desirable;

(*e*) to establish such committees as may be considered necessary for the work of the Organization;

(*f*) to supervise the financial policies of the Organization and to review and approve the budget;

(*g*) to instruct the Board and the Director-General to bring to the attention of Members and of international organizations, governmental or non-governmental, any matter with regard to health which the Health Assembly may consider appropriate;

(*h*) to invite any organization, international or national, governmental or non-governmental, which has responsibilities related to those of the Organization, to appoint representatives to participate, without right of vote, in its meetings or in those of the committees and conferences convened under its authority, on conditions prescribed by the Health Assembly; but in the case of national organizations, invitations shall be issued only with the consent of the Government concerned;

(*i*) to consider recommendations bearing on health made by the General Assembly, the Economic and Social Council, the Security Council or Trusteeship Council of the United Nations, and to report to them on the steps taken by the Organization to give effect to such recommendations;

(*j*) to report to the Economic and Social Council in accordance with any agreement between the Organization and the United Nations;

(*k*) to promote and conduct research in the field of health by the personnel of the Organization, by the establishment of its own institutions or by co-operation with official or non-official institutions of any Member with the consent of its Government;

(*l*) to establish such other institutions as it may consider desirable;

(*m*) to take any other appropriate action to further the objective of the Organization.

Article 19

The Health Assembly shall have authority to adopt conventions or agreements with respect to any matter within the competence of the Organization. A two-thirds vote of the Health Assembly shall be required for the adoption of such conventions or agreements, which shall come into force for each Member when accepted by it in accordance with its constitutional processes.

Article 20

Each Member undertakes that it will, within eighteen months after the adoption by the Health Assembly of a convention or agreement, take action relative to the acceptance of such convention or agreement. Each Member shall notify the Director-General of the action taken, and if it does not accept such convention or agreement within the time limit, it will furnish a statement of the reasons for non-acceptance. In case of acceptance, each Member agrees to make an annual report to the Director-General in accordance with Chapter XIV.

Article 21

The Health Assembly shall have authority to adopt regulations concerning:

(*a*) sanitary and quarantine requirements and other procedures designed to prevent the international spread of disease;

(*b*) nomenclatures with respect to diseases, causes of death and public health practices;

(*c*) standards with respect to diagnostic procedures for international use;

(*d*) standards with respect to the safety, purity and potency of biological, pharmaceutical and similar products moving in international commerce;

(*e*) advertising and labelling of biological, pharmaceutical and similar products moving in international commerce.

Article 22

Regulations adopted pursuant to Article 21 shall come into force for all Members after due notice has been given of their adoption by the Health Assembly except for such Members as may notify the Director-General of rejection or reservations within the period stated in the notice.

Article 23

The Health Assembly shall have authority to make recommendations to Members with respect to any matter within the competence of the Organization.

CHAPTER VI – THE EXECUTIVE BOARD

Article 24

The Board shall consist of thirty-one persons designated by as many Members. The Health Assembly, taking into account an equitable geographical distribution, shall elect the Members entitled to designate a person to serve on the Board, provided that, of such Members, not less than three shall be elected from each of the regional organizations established pursuant to Article 44. Each of these Members should appoint to the Board a person technically qualified in the field of health, who may be accompanied by alternates and advisers.

Article 25

These Members shall be elected for three years and may be reelected, provided that of the eleven Members elected at the first session of the Health Assembly held after the coming into force of the amendment to this Constitution increasing the membership of the Board from thirty to thirty-one the term of office of the additional Member elected shall, insofar as may be necessary, be of such lesser duration as shall facilitate the election of at least one Member from each regional organization in each year.

Article 26

The Board shall meet at least twice a year and shall determine the place of each meeting.

Article 27

The Board shall elect its Chairman from among its members and shall adopt its own rules of procedure.

Article 28

The functions of the Board shall be:

(*a*) to give effect to the decisions and policies of the Health Assembly;

(*b*) to act as the executive organ of the Health Assembly;

(*c*) to perform any other functions entrusted to it by the Health Assembly;

(*d*) to advise the Health Assembly on questions referred to it by that body and on matters assigned to the Organization by conventions, agreements and regulations;

(*e*) to submit advice or proposals to the Health Assembly on its own initiative;

(*f*) to prepare the agenda of meetings of the Health Assembly;

(*g*) to submit to the Health Assembly for consideration and approval a general programme of work covering a specific period;

(*h*) to study all questions within its competence;

(*i*) to take emergency measures within the functions and financial resources of the Organization to deal with events requiring immediate action. In particular it may authorize the Director-General to take the necessary steps to combat epidemics, to participate in the organization of health relief to victims of a calamity and to undertake studies and research the urgency of which has been drawn to the attention of the Board by any Member or by the Director-General.

Article 29

The Board shall exercise on behalf of the whole Health Assembly the powers delegated to it by that body.

CHAPTER VII – THE SECRETARIAT

Article 30

The Secretariat shall comprise the Director-General and such technical and administrative staff as the Organization may require.

Article 31

The Director-General shall be appointed by the Health Assembly on the nomination of the Board on such terms as the Health Assembly may determine. The Director-General, subject to the authority of the Board, shall be the chief technical and administrative officer of the Organization.

Article 32

The Director-General shall be *ex-officio* Secretary of the Health Assembly, of the Board, of all commissions and committees of the Organization and of conferences convened by it. He may delegate these functions.

Article 33

The Director-General or his representative may establish a procedure by agreement with Members, permitting him, for the purpose of discharging his duties, to have direct access to their various departments, especially to their health administrations and to national health organizations, governmental or non-governmental. He may also establish direct relations with international organisations whose activities come within the competence of the Organization. He shall keep regional offices informed on all matters involving their respective areas.

Article 34

The Director-General shall prepare and submit to the Board the financial statements and budget estimates of the Organization.

Article 35

The Director-General shall appoint the staff of the Secretariat in accordance with staff regulations established by the Health Assembly. The paramount consideration in the employment of the staff shall be to assure that the efficiency, integrity and internationally representative character of the Secretariat shall be maintained at the highest level. Due regard shall be paid also to the importance of recruiting the staff on as wide a geographical basis as possible.

Article 36

The conditions of service of the staff of the Organization shall conform as far as possible with those of other United Nations organizations.

Article 37

In the performance of their duties the Director-General and the staff shall not seek or receive instructions from any government or from any authority external to the Organization. They shall refrain from any action which might reflect on their position as international officers. Each Member of the Organization on its part undertakes to respect the exclusively international character of the Director-General and the staff and not to seek to influence them.

CHAPTER VIII - COMMITTEES

Article 38

The Board shall establish such committees as the Health Assembly may direct and, on its own initiative or on the proposal of the Director-General, may establish any other committees considered desirable to serve any purpose within the competence of the Organization.

Article 39

The Board, from time to time and in any event annually, shall review the necessity for continuing each committee.

Article 40

The Board may provide for the creation of or the participation by the Organization in joint or mixed committees with other organizations and for the representation of the Organization in committees established by such other organizations.

CHAPTER IX – CONFERENCES

Article 41

The Health Assembly or the Board may convene local, general, technical or other special conferences to consider any matter within the competence of the Organization and may provide for the representation at such conferences of international organizations and, with the consent of the Government concerned, of national organizations, governmental or non-governmental. The manner of such representation shall be determined by the Health Assembly or the Board.

Article 42

The Board may provide for representation of the Organization at conferences in which the Board considers that the Organization has an interest.

CHAPTER X – HEADQUARTERS

Article 43

The location of the headquarters of the Organization shall be determined by the Health Assembly after consultation with the United Nations.

CHAPTER XI – REGIONAL ARRANGEMENTS

Article 44

(*a*) The Health Assembly shall from time to time define the geographical areas in which it is desirable to establish a regional organization.

(*b*) The Health Assembly may, with the consent of a majority of the Members situated within each area so defined, establish a regional organization to meet the special needs of such area. There shall not be more than one regional organization in each area.

Article 45

Each regional organization shall be an integral part of the Organization in accordance with this Constitution.

Article 46

Each regional organization shall consist of a regional committee and a regional office.

Article 47

Regional committees shall be composed of representatives of the Member States and Associate Members in the region concerned. Territories or groups of territories within the region, which are not responsible for the conduct of their international relations and which are not Associate

Members, shall have the right to be represented and to participate in regional committees. The nature and extent of the rights and obligations of these territories or groups of territories in regional committees shall be determined by the Health Assembly in consultation with the Member or other authority having responsibility for the international relations of these territories and with the Member States in the region.

Article 48

Regional committees shall meet as often as necessary and shall determine the place of each meeting.

Article 49

Regional committees shall adopt their own rules of procedure.

Article 50

The functions of the regional committee shall be:

(*a*) to formulate policies governing matters of an exclusively regional character;

(*b*) to supervise the activities of the regional office;

(*c*) to suggest to the regional office the calling of technical conferences and such additional work or investigation in health matters as in the opinion of the regional committee would promote the objective of the Organization within the region;

(*d*) to co-operate with the respective regional committees of the United Nations and with those of other specialized agencies and with other regional international organizations having interests in common with the Organization;

(*e*) to tender advice, through the Director-General, to the Organization on international health matters which have wider than regional significance;

(*f*) to recommend additional regional appropriations by the Governments of the respective regions if the proportion of the central budget of the Organization allotted to that region is insufficient for the carrying-out of the regional functions;

(*g*) such other functions as may be delegated to the regional committee by the Health Assembly, the Board or the Director-General.

Article 51

Subject to the general authority of the Director-General of the Organization, the regional office shall be the administrative organ of the regional committee. It shall, in addition, carry out within the region the decisions of the Health Assembly and of the Board.

Article 52

The head of the regional office shall be the Regional Director appointed by the Board in agreement with the regional committee.

Article 53

The staff of the regional office shall be appointed in a manner to be determined by agreement between the Director-General and the Regional Director.

Article 54

The Pan American Sanitary Organization[2] represented by the Pan American Sanitary Bureau and the Pan American Sanitary Conferences, and all other inter-governmental regional health organizations in existence prior to the date of signature of this Constitution, shall in due course be integrated with the Organization. This integration shall be effected as soon as practicable through common action based on mutual consent of the competent authorities expressed through the organizations concerned.

CHAPTER XII – BUDGET AND EXPENSES

Article 55

The Director-General shall prepare and submit to the Board the budget estimates of the Organization. The Board shall consider and submit to the Health Assembly such budget estimates, together with any recommendations the Board may deem advisable.

Article 56

Subject to any agreement between the Organization and the United Nations, the Health Assembly shall review and approve the budget estimates and shall apportion the expenses among the Members in accordance with a scale to be fixed by the Health Assembly.

Article 57

The Health Assembly or the Board acting on behalf of the Health Assembly may accept and administer gifts and bequests made to the Organization provided that the conditions attached to such gifts or bequests are acceptable to the Health Assembly or the Board and are consistent with the objective and policies of the Organization.

Article 58

A special fund to be used at the discretion of the Board shall be established to meet emergencies and unforeseen contingencies.

2. Renamed 'Pan American Health Organization' by decision of the XV Pan American Sanitary Conference, Sept.–Oct. 1958.

CHAPTER XIII - VOTING

Article 59

Each Member shall have one vote in the Health Assembly.

Article 60

(*a*) Decisions of the Health Assembly on important questions shall be made by a two-thirds majority of the Members present and voting. These questions shall include: the adoption of conventions or agreements; the approval of agreements bringing the Organization into relation with the United Nations and inter-governmental organizations and agencies in accordance with Articles 69, 70 and 72; amendments to this Constitution.

(*b*) Decision on other questions, including the determination of additional categories of questions to be decided by a two-thirds majority, shall be made by a majority of the Members present and voting.

(*c*) Voting on analogous matters in the Board and in committees of the Organization shall be made in accordance with paragraphs (a) and (b) of this Article.

CHAPTER XIV - REPORTS SUBMITTED BY STATES

Article 61

Each Member shall report annually to the Organization on the action taken and progress achieved in improving the health of its people.

Article 62

Each Member shall report annually on the action taken with respect to recommendations made to it by the Organization and with respect to conventions, agreements and regulations.

Article 63

Each Member shall communicate promptly to the Organization important laws, regulations, official reports and statistics pertaining to health which have been published in the State concerned.

Article 64

Each Member shall provide statistical and epidemiological reports in a manner to be determined by the Health Assembly.

Article 65

Each Member shall transmit upon the request of the Board such additional information pertaining to health as may be practicable.

CHAPTER XV – LEGAL CAPACITY, PRIVILEGES AND IMMUNITIES

Article 66

The Organization shall enjoy in the territory of each Member such legal capacity as may be necessary for the fulfilment of its objective and for the exercise of its functions.

Article 67

(*a*) The Organization shall enjoy in the territory of each Member such privileges and immunities as may be necessary for the fulfilment of its objective and for the exercise of its functions.

(*b*) Representatives of Members, persons designated to serve on the Board and technical and administrative personnel of the Organization shall similarly enjoy such privileges and immunities as are necessary for the independent exercise of their functions in connexion with the Organization.

Article 68

Such legal capacity, privileges and immunities shall be defined in a separate agreement to be prepared by the Organization in consultation with the Secretary-General of the United Nations and concluded between the Members.

CHAPTER XVI – RELATIONS WITH OTHER ORGANIZATIONS

Article 69

The Organization shall be brought into relation with the United Nations as one of the specialized agencies referred to in Article 57 of the Charter of the United Nations. The agreement or agreements bringing the Organization into relation with the United Nations shall be subject to approval by a two-thirds vote of the Health Assembly.

Article 70

The Organization shall establish effective relations and co-operate closely with such other inter-governmental organizations as may be desirable. Any formal agreement entered into with such organizations shall be subject to approval by a two-thirds vote of the Health Assembly.

Article 71

The Organization may, on matters within its competence, make suitable arrangements for consultation and co-operation with non-governmental international organizations and, with the consent of the Government concerned, with national organizations, governmental or non-governmental.

Article 72

Subject to the approval by a two-thirds vote of the Health Assembly, the Organization may take over from any other international organization or agency whose purpose and activities lie within the field of competence of the Organization such functions, resources and obligations as may be conferred upon the Organization by international agreement or by mutually acceptable arrangements entered into between the competent authorities of the respective organizations.

CHAPTER XVII – AMENDMENTS

Article 73

Texts of proposed amendments to this Constitution shall be communicated by the Director-General to Members at least six months in advance of their consideration by the Health Assembly. Amendments shall come into force for all Members when adopted by a two-thirds vote of the Health Assembly and accepted by two-thirds of the Members in accordance with their respective constitutional processes.

CHAPTER XVIII – INTERPRETATION

Article 74[3]

The Chinese, English, French, Russian and Spanish texts of this Constitution shall be regarded as equally authentic.

Article 75

Any question or dispute concerning the interpretation or application of this Constitution which is not settled by negotiation or by the Health Assembly shall be referred to the International Court of Justice in conformity with the Statute of the Court, unless the parties concerned agree on another mode of settlement.

Article 76

Upon authorization by the General Assembly of the United Nations or upon authorization in accordance with any agreement between the Organization and the United Nations, the Organization may request the International Court of Justice for an advisory opinion on any legal question arising within the competence of the Organization.

Article 77

The Director-General may appear before the Court on behalf of the Organization in connexion with any proceedings arising out of any such request

3. The amendment to this Article adopted by the 31st World Health Assembly (Resolution WHA31.18) has not yet come into force.

for an advisory opinion. He shall make arrangements for the presentation of the case before the Court, including arrangements for the argument of different views on the question.

CHAPTER XIX - ENTRY-INTO-FORCE

Article 78

Subject to the provisions of Chapter III, this Constitution shall remain open to all States for signature or acceptance.

Article 79

(*a*) States may become parties to this Constitution by
(i) signature without reservation as to approval;
(ii) signature subject to approval followed by acceptance; or
(iii) acceptance.

(*b*) Acceptance shall be effected by the deposit of a formal instrument with the Secretary-General of the United Nations.

Article 80

This Constitution shall come into force when twenty-six Members of the United Nations have become parties to it in accordance with the provisions of Article 79.

Article 81

In accordance with Article 102 of the Charter of the United Nations, the Secretary-General of the United Nations will register this Constitution when it has been signed without reservation as to approval on behalf of one State or upon deposit of the first instrument of acceptance.

Article 82

The Secretary-General of the United Nations will inform States Parties to this Constitution of the date when it has come into force. He will also inform them of the dates when other States have become parties to this Constitution.

IN FAITH WHEREOF the undersigned representatives, having been duly authorized for that purpose, sign this Constitution.

DONE in the City of New York this twenty-second day of July 1946, in a single copy in the Chinese, English, French, Russian and Spanish languages, each text being equally authentic. The original texts shall be deposited in the archives of the United Nations. The Secretary-General of the United Nations will send certified copies to each of the Governments represented at the Conference.

F

SUMMARY OF AREAS OF INTEREST OF OTHER U.N. BODIES INVOLVED IN HEALTH

African Development Bank
- Strengthening of health services
- Health manpower development
- Disease prevention and control
- Promotion of environmental health

Asian Development Bank
- Promotion of environmental health

Food and Agriculture Organization
- Strengthening of health services
- Disease prevention and control
- Promotion of environmental health

Inter-American Development Bank
- Strengthening of health services
- Health manpower development
- Disease prevention and control
- Promotion of environmental health

International Atomic Energy Agency
- Disease prevention and control
- Promotion of environmental health

International Bank for Reconstruction and Development (World Bank Group)
- Strengthening of health services
- Health manpower development
- Disease prevention and control
- Promotion of environmental health
- Health statistics

International Labour Organization
- Strengthening of health services
- Disease prevention and control
- Promotion of environmental health

UN Capital Development Fund
- Strengthening of health services
- Disease prevention and control
- Promotion of environmental health

UN Children's Fund
Strengthening of health services
Health manpower development
Disease prevention and control
Promotion of environmental health

UN Development Programme
Strengthening of health services
Health manpower development
Disease prevention and control
Promotion of environmental health

UN Educational, Scientific and Cultural Organization
Strengthening of health services
Promotion of environmental health

UN Emergency Operation
Emergencies

UN Environmental Programme
Health manpower development
Disease prevention and control
Promotion of environmental health

UN Fund for Drug Abuse Control
Disease prevention and control

UN Fund for Population Activities
Strengthening of health services

UN High Commissioner for Refugees
Strengthening of health services

UN Industrial Development Organization
Disease prevention and control
Promotion of environmental health

UN Office for Technical Cooperation
Strengthening of health services
Promotion of environmental health

UN Regional Economic Commissions
Strengthening of health services
Promotion of environmental health

World Food Programme
Strengthening of health services

BIBLIOGRAPHY

Explanatory note

Because of the large number of WHO documents, meeting records and secondary sources used in this work, this bibliography has been subdivided into several categories, as listed below. Newspaper and magazine articles are only referred to in footnotes and do not appear here.

Interviews

Primary Sources

Official Records of the WHO

- Technical Preparatory Committee Minutes
- International Health Conference Proceedings and Final Acts
- Interim Commission Proceedings
- World Health Assembly Proceedings
- Executive Board Reports
- Annual/Biannual Reports of the Director-General
- Proposed Programme and Budget Estimates
- Reports on World Health Situation

Technical Report Series on Malaria

Unpublished WHO Documents on Malaria

Documents from other Organizations

Secondary Sources

General WHO Publications

Journal Articles

Books and Theses

Interviews

Acheson, M., Chief, Community Water Supply and Sanitation, WHO, Geneva, 27 Mar. 1986.

Akram, Z., Second Secretary, Pakistan Permanent Mission, Geneva, 25 July 1985.

Arnold, R., Executive Vice-President, IFPMA, Geneva, 3 Apr. 1986.

Barmes, D., Chief, Division of Oral Health, WHO, Geneva, 16 Jan. 1986.

Bartley, W.C., International Health Attaché, United States Permanent Mission to the UN Office and other International Organizations at Geneva, Geneva, 24 July 1986.

Beigbeder, Y., Personnel Officer, WHO, Geneva, 25 Mar. 1986, 10 Aug. 1987, 3 Aug. 1988 and 27 July 1989.

Boyer, N., Director, Health and Narcotics Programs, Bureau of International Organization Affairs, Department of State, Washington DC, 4 Oct. 1985.

Cohen, J., Special Advisor to the Director-General, WHO, Geneva, 2 Apr. 1986 and 2 Aug. 1986.

Cook, R., medical officer, Division of Family Health, WHO, Geneva, 15 Jan. 1986.

Davis, A., Director, Parasitic Diseases Programme, WHO, Geneva, 17 Jan. 1986.

Dodu, S., Chief, Cardiovascular Diseases, WHO, Geneva, 16 Jan. 1986.

Donald, J., Director, Internal Audit, WHO, Geneva, 18 Jan. 1986.

Eggleston, R., Assistant Chief, Personnel, WHO, Geneva, 15 Jan. 1986 and 29 July 1986.

Farid, M.A., Regional Advisor on Malaria Eradication, WHO, Geneva, 6 Aug. 1987, 11 Aug. 1987 and 3 Aug. 1989.

Gibson, H., seconded from IBM, Division of Community Water Supply and Sanitation, WHO, Geneva, 18 Jan. 1986.

Hamon, J., Assistant Director-General, and Chairman of Headquarters Programming Committee, WHO, Geneva, 26 Mar. 1986.

Hashmi, J., responsible officer, Research Capability Strengthening, Tropical Diseases Research, WHO, Geneva, 2 Aug. 1988.

Hellberg, H., Director, Health for All Strategy Coordination, WHO, Geneva, 2 Feb. 1988.

Henderson, D.A., Dean, Johns Hopkins University School of Public Health, Baltimore, Maryland, 2 Oct. 1985.

Henderson, R., Director, Expanded Programme on Immunization, WHO, Geneva, 16 Jan. 1986.

Herzog, F., briefing officer, WHO, Geneva, 14 Jan. 1986 and 10 Aug. 1988.

Jayasuriya, D., consultant, Division of Mental Health, WHO, Geneva, 7 Oct. 1985, 8 Apr. 1986 and 3 July 1988.

Khan, I., medical officer, UN Treaties Concerning Psychotropic and Narcotic Drugs, Division of Mental Health, WHO, Geneva, 27 Mar. 1986.

Khanna, M., Director, Health for All Strategy Coordination, WHO, Geneva, 2 Apr. 1986.

Kingma, S., Chief, Health Resources Mobilization, WHO, Geneva, 17 Jan. 1986.

Lauridsen, E., Director, Drugs Action Programme, WHO, Geneva, 17 Jan. 1986 and 29 July 1986.

Ling, J., Director, Division of Public Information and Education for Health, WHO, Geneva, 18 Jan. 1986.

Lucas, O., Director, Tropical Diseases Research, WHO, Geneva, 18 Jan. 1986.

Martinez, L., scientist, Malaria Action Programme, WHO, Geneva, 18 Jan. 1986.

Mirza, T.H., Head of Treasury, WHO, Geneva, 27 July 1989.

Pawlowski, Z., medical officer, Parasitic Diseases Programme, WHO, Geneva, 16 Jan. 1986.

Piel, A., Advisor to the Director-General, Headquarters Programming Committee, WHO, Geneva, 17 Jan. 1986 and 10 July 1987.

Pigott, W., programme manager, Staff Development and Training, WHO, Geneva, 10 July 1988.

Quamina, E., member of the Executive Board, WHO, Geneva, 16 Jan. 1986.

Robertson, A., programme manager, Staff Development and Training, WHO, Geneva, 14 Jan., 1 Apr. and 29 July 1986.

Rochon, R., Consul-General, Canadian Permanent Mission, Geneva, (Chairman, Committee B of 1985 WHA), 18 July 1985.

Rosenfield, P., scientist, Tropical Diseases Research, WHO, Geneva, 18 Jan. 1986.

Smith, A., scientist/entomologist, Vector Biology and Control, WHO, Geneva, 16 Jan. 1986.

Vignes, C., legal counsel, Director-General's Office, WHO, Geneva, 26 Mar. 1986.

Primary Sources

Official Records of the WHO

		OR/Doc. no.
Technical Preparatory Committee Minutes	1946	1
International Health Conference Proceedings and Final Acts	1946	2
Interim Commission Proceedings		
First session	1946	3
Second	1946	4
Third	1947	5
Fourth	1947	6
Fifth	1948	7
Report to First WHA, I	1948	9
Report to First WHA, II	1948	10
Supplementary Report	1948	12
World Health Assembly Proceedings		
First session	1948	13
Second	1949	21
Third	1950	28
Fourth	1951	35
Fifth	1952	42
Sixth	1953	48

World Health Assembly Proceedings (*contd*)

		OR/Doc. no.
Seventh	1954	55
Eighth	1955	63
Ninth	1956	71
Tenth	1957	79
Tenth anniversary session	1958	86
Eleventh	1958	87
Twelfth	1959	95
Thirteenth	1960	102–3
Fourteenth	1961	110–11
Fifteenth	1962	118–19
Sixteenth	1963	127–8
Seventeenth	1964	135–6
Eighteenth	1965	143–4
Nineteenth	1966	151–2
Twentieth	1967	160–1
Twenty-first	1968	168–9
Twenty-second	1969	176–7
Twenty-third	1970	184–5
Twenty-fourth	1971	193–4
Twenty-fifth	1972	201–2
Twenty-sixth	1973	209–10
Twenty-seventh	1974	217–18
Twenty-eighth	1975	226–7
Twenty-ninth	1976	233–4
Thirtieth	1977	240–1
Thirty-first	1978	247–8
Thirty-second	1979	WHA32/1979/REC/1–3
Thirty-third	1980	WHA33/1980/REC/1–3
Thirty-fourth	1981	WHA34/1981/REC/1–3
Thirty-fifth	1982	WHA35/1982/REC/1–3
Thirty-sixth	1983	WHA36/1983/REC/1–3
Thirty-seventh	1984	WHA37/1984/REC/1–3
Thirty-eighth	1985	WHA38/1985/REC/1–3
Thirty-ninth	1986	WHA39/1986/REC/1–3
Fortieth	1987	WHA40/1987/REC/1–3
Forty-first	1988	WHA41/1988/REC/1–3
Forty-second	1989	WHA42/1989/REC/1–3

Executive Board Reports

First and Second sessions	1948	14
Third	1949	17
Fourth	1949	22
Fifth	1950	25–6
Sixth	1950	29
Seventh	1951	32–3

Executive Board Reports (*contd*)

		OR/Doc. no.
Eighth	1951	36
Ninth	1952	40
Tenth	1952	43
Eleventh	1953	46
Twelfth	1953	49
Thirteenth	1954	52–3
Fourteenth	1954	57
Fifteenth	1955	60–1
Sixteenth	1955	65
Seventeenth	1956	68–9
Eighteenth	1956	73
Nineteenth	1957	76–7
Twentieth	1957	80
Twenty-first	1958	83–4
Twenty-second	1958	88
Twenty-third	1959	91–2
Twenty-fourth	1959	96
Twenty-fifth	1960	99–100
Twenty-sixth	1960	106–7
Twenty-seventh	1961	108
Twenty-eighth	1961	112
Twenty-ninth	1962	115–16
Thirtieth	1962	120
Thirty-first	1963	124–5
Thirty-second	1963	129
Thirty-third	1964	132–3
Thirty-fourth	1964	137
Thirty-fifth	1965	140–1
Thirty-sixth	1965	145
Thirty-seventh	1966	148–9
Thirty-eighth	1966	153
Thirty-ninth	1967	157–8
Fortieth	1967	162
Forty-first	1968	165–6
Forty-second	1968	170
Forty-third	1969	173–4
Forty-fourth	1969	178
Forty-fifth	1970	181–2
Forty-sixth	1970	186
Forty-seventh	1971	189–90
Forty-eighth	1971	195
Forty-ninth	1972	198–9
Fiftieth	1972	203
Fifty-first	1973	206–7
Fifty-second	1973	211
Fifty-third	1974	215–16

Executive Board Report (*contd*)

		OR/Doc. no.
Fifty-fourth	1974	219
Fifty-fifth	1975	223–4
Fifty-sixth	1975	228
Fifty-seventh	1976	231–2
Fifty-eighth	1976	235
Fifty-ninth	1977	238–9
Sixtieth	1977	242
Sixty-first	1978	244
Sixty-second	1978	249
Sixty-third	1979	EB63/48
Sixty-fourth	1979	EB64/1979/REC/1–2
Sixty-fifth	1980	EB65/1980/REC/1–2
Sixty-sixth	1980	EB66/1980/REC/1–2
Sixty-seventh	1981	EB67/1981/REC/1–2
Sixty-eighth	1981	EB68/1981/REC/1–2
Sixty-ninth	1982	EB69/1982/REC/1–2
Seventieth	1982	EB70/1982/REC/1–2
Seventy-first	1983	EB71/1983/REC/1–2
Seventy-second	1983	EB72/1983/REC/1–2
Seventy-third	1984	EB73/1984/REC/1–2
Seventy-fourth	1984	EB74/1984/REC/1–2
Seventy-fifth	1985	EB75/1985/REC/1–2
Seventy-sixth	1985	EB76/1986/REC/1–2
Seventy-seventh	1986	EB77/1986/REC/1–2
Seventy-eighth	1986	EB78/1986/REC/1–2
Seventy-ninth	1987	EB79/1987/REC/1–2
Eightieth	1987	EB80/1987/REC/1–2
Eighty-first	1988	EB81/1988/REC/1–2
Eighty-second	1988	EB82/1988/REC/1–2
Eighty-third	1989	EB83/1989/REC/1–2
Eighty-fourth	1989	EB84/1989/REC/1–2

Annual/Biannual Reports of the Director-General

1948	16
1949	24
1950	30
1951	38
1952	45
1953	51
1954	59
1955	67
1956	75
1957	82
1958	90
1959	98

Annual/Biannual Report of Director-General (*contd*)

	OR/Doc. no.
1960	105
1961	114
1962	123
1963	131
1964	139
1965	147
1966	156
1967	164
1968	172
1969	180
1970	188
1971	197
1972	205
1973	213
1974	221
1975	229
1976–7	243

The Work of WHO: 1978–79, WHO, Geneva, 1980
The Work of WHO: 1980–81, WHO, Geneva, 1982
The Work of WHO: 1982–83, WHO, Geneva, 1984
The Work of WHO: 1984–85, WHO, Geneva, 1986
The Work of WHO: 1986–87, WHO, Geneva, 1988.

Proposed Programme and Budget Estimates

1950	18
1951	23
1952	31
1953	39
1954	44
1955	50
1956	58
1957	66
1958	74
1959	81
1960	89
1961	97
1962	104
1963	113
1964	121
1965	130
1966	138
1967	146
1968	154
1969	163
1970	171

Programme and Budget Estimates (*contd*)

		OR/Doc. no.
	1971	179
	1972	187
	1973	196
	1974	204
	1975	212
	1976–7	220
	1978–9	236
	1980–1	250
	1982–3	PB/82–3
	1984–5	PB/84–5
	1986–7	PB/86–7
	1988–9	PB/88–9

Reports on the World Health Situation

First Report	1954–6	94
Second Report	1957–60	122
Third Report	1961–4	155
Fourth Report	1965–8	192
Fifth Report	1969–72	225
Sixth Report	1973–77	Parts I and II, WHO, Geneva, 1980
Seventh Report ('Evaluation of the Strategy of Health for All by the Year 2000')	1978–84	Vols 1–7, WHO, Geneva, 1987

Technical Report Series on Malaria

No.

8 'Report on the Third Session of the Expert Committee', 1950.
38 'Malaria Conference in Equatorial Africa (Kampala, Uganda, 1950), Report', 1951.
39 'Report on the Fourth Session of the Expert Committee', 1951.
80 'Fifth Report of the Expert Committee', 1954.
103 'Malaria Conference for the Western Pacific and South-East Asia Regions (Second Asian Malaria Conference)', 1956.
123 'Sixth Report of the Expert Committee', 1957.
132 'Malaria Conference for the Eastern Mediterranean and European Regions', 1957.
162 'Seventh Report of the Expert Committee', 1959.
191 'Tenth Report of the Expert Committee on Insecticides', 1960.
205 'Eighth Report of the Expert Committee', 1961.
243 'Ninth Report of the Expert Committee', 1962.
272 'Tenth Report of the WHO Expert Committee', 1964.

291 'WHO Expert Committee on Malaria: Eleventh Report', 1964.
296 'Resistance of Malaria Parasite to Drugs, Report of a WHO Scientific Group', 1965.
324 'WHO Expert Committee on Malaria: Twelfth Report', 1966.
357 'WHO Expert Committee on Malaria: Thirteenth Report', 1967.
374 'Prevention of the Re-introduction of Malaria, Report of a WHO Meeting', 1967.
382 'WHO Expert Committee on Malaria: Fourteenth Report', 1968.
467 'WHO Expert Committee on Malaria: Fifteenth Report', 1971.
537 'Malaria Control in Countries Where Time-Limited Eradication is Impracticable at Present, Report of a WHO Inter-Regional Conference', 1974.
549 'WHO Expert Committee on Malaria: Sixteenth Report', 1974.
640 'WHO Expert Committee on Malaria: Seventeenth Report', 1979.
712 'Malaria Control as Part of Primary Health Care, Report of a WHO Study Group', 1984.

Unpublished WHO Documents on Malaria

'Appraisal of Typical Malaria Eradication Programmes in the Eastern Mediterranean Region: Iran', Expert Committee, Geneva, Mal/Exp. Com.8/WP/20, 15 June 1960.

'Approach to Malaria Eradication in the African Region', Expert Committee, Geneva, Mal/Exp.Com.13/66.2, 13 Sept. 1966.

'Assessment of Present Status of Malaria Eradication Programmes', Geneva, Mal/Exp.Com.13/66.3, 13 Sept. 1966.

'Integration of Mass Campaigns against Specific Diseases into General Health Services', Report of a Study Group, Geneva, MHO/PA/116.64, 9 June 1964.

'The Medical Research Programme of WHO: 1958–1963', Report of the Director-General, Geneva, MHO/AD/86a.63, Dec. 1963.

'New Insecticides to be Used in Malaria Eradication – Definition of Criteria and Standards', Expert Committee, Geneva, Mal/Exp. Com.11/WP/19, 16 June 1964.

'Registration of Areas in which Malaria has been Eradicated', Expert Committee, Geneva, Mal/Exp.Com.8/WP/23, 15 June 1960.

'Report on Development of Malaria Eradication Programmes', Geneva, EB33/4, 1963.

'Report of the Second Scientific Working Group on Social and Economic Research: Guidelines to Assess the Social and Economic Consequences of the Tropical Diseases', Geneva, TDR/SER-SWG(2)/80.3, 22 Oct. 1980.

'Report on the Second Regional Conference on Malaria Eradication', Addis Ababa, WHO/Mal/265, 20 May 1959.

'Review of the Major Factors Affecting the Progress of Malaria Eradication Programmes: Administration and Finance', Geneva, Mal/Exp.Com.13/ 66.5, 13 Sept. 1966.

'Review of the Major Factors Affecting the Progress of Malaria

Eradication Programmes: Operations', Geneva, Mal/Exp.Com.13/66 Sept. 1966.

'Review of the Major Factors Affecting the Progress of Malaria Eradication Programmes: Personnel and Training', Geneva, Mal/Exp.Com.13/66.7, 13 Sept. 1966.

'Review of the Major Factors Affecting the Progress of Malaria Eradication Programmes: Planning', Geneva, Mal/Exp.Com.13/66 Sept. 1966.

'Review of the Major Factors Affecting the Progress of Malaria Eradication Programmes: Technical', Geneva, Mal/Exp.Com.13/66 Sept. 1966.

Andary, M., 'Progress of the Malaria Control Programme: Administrative Patterns, Advisability and Practicability of Eradication', Inter-regional Conference on Malaria, Working Paper 22, 27 Apr. 1956.

Annecke, S., 'Report on Malaria Control in Transvaal', Geneva, WHO/Mal/48, 3 Oct. 1950.

——, 'Economic Importance of Malaria', Geneva, WHO/Mal/57, 24 Oct. 1950.

——, 'Malaria Control in the Transvaal', Geneva, WHO/Mal/90, 19 June 1953.

Bertagna, P., 'New Insecticides in Malaria Eradication Programmes', Geneva, Mal/Exp.Com.9/WP/18, 23 Mar. 1962.

Black, R., 'Economic and Health Justification for Implementing Malaria Control Programmes as Part of the Socioeconomic and Health Development Plans', Geneva, Mal/EC16/73.3, 14 Nov. 1973.

da Silva, T., 'Criteria for Assessing the Prospects of Success of Malaria Eradication Programmes', Geneva, Mal/Exp.Com.9/WP/4, 21 Mar. 1962.

Farid, M., 'Problem Areas in Malaria Eradication Programmes', Rio de Janeiro, Mal/Exp.Com.10/WP/15, 14 June 1963.

Farinaud, M., 'Thoughts on Problems of Malaria Eradication and Their Solution', Rio de Janeiro, Mal/Exp.Com.10/WP/27, 9 July 1963.

Fritz, R. and Johnson, R., 'Dosages and Frequency of Application of Insecticides for Malaria Eradication', Geneva, Mal/Exp.Com.8/ WP/9, 31 May 1960.

Gabaldon, A., 'Malaria Eradication: Definitions, Criteria, and Terminology', Expert Committee on Malaria, Working Paper E.8, 25 May 1956.

Gramiccia, G., 'The Organization of Malaria Eradication within the Framework of General Public Health Administration', Expert Committee on Malaria, Lisbon, Working Paper 29, 26 Aug. 1958.

Keeny, S., 'Organizing for the Last Battle against Malaria', Inter-regional Conference on Malaria, Working Paper 25, 11 May 1956.

Kerr, A., 'Problem Areas in Malaria Eradication Programmes', Rio de Janeiro, Mal/Exp.Com.10/WP/20, 24 June 1963.

Livadas, G., 'The Present Position of the Malaria Control Demonstration Project in Terai', WHO/Mal/76, 5 Feb. 1952.

Meillon, B., 'Species and Sub-species of Vectors and Their Bionomics', Geneva, WHO/Mal/54, 10 Oct. 1950.

——, 'Malaria Survey of South West Africa', Geneva, WHO/Mal/61, 24 Nov. 1950.

Mofidi, C., Mohtadi, A., Moradpour, K. and Djalali, G., 'Present Aspect of Malaria Problem and its Control among Nomadic Tribes in Iran', Expert Committee on Malaria, Lisbon, Working Paper 34, 28 Aug. 1958.

Pampana, E., 'The Control of Malaria Vectors in Regions where the Vector Has Become Resistant to DDT and Other Chlorinated Hydrocarbon Insecticides', Inter-Regional Conference on Malaria, Working Paper 26, 21 May 1956.

——, 'Unexpected Cost Increases of Malaria Eradication Programmes', WHO/Mal/208, 26 Aug. 1958.

——, 'Problem Areas', Geneva, Mal/Exp.Com.14/67.10, 12 Sept. 1967.

Ray, A., 'Review of the Present Status of Malaria Eradication and Prospects for the Future', Geneva, Mal/Exp.Com.8/WP/15, 15 June 1960.

Ray, A., 'Maintenance of Achieved Eradication', Geneva, Mal/Exp. Com.12/WP/2.65, 21 Sept. 1965.

Russell, P., 'Advisability and Practicability of Eradication', Working Paper No. 13, Inter-regional Conference on Malaria, 16 Apr. 1956.

Russell, P., 'Surveillance in Malaria Eradication Projects', Geneva, WHO/ Mal/Inform, 28 Nov. 1957.

Russell, P., 'Malaria Eradication Defined', Geneva, Mal/Exp.Com. 8/WP/35, 11 July 1960.

Singh, J., 'Administrative Pattern of Malaria Programmes', Inter-regional Conference on Malaria for the Eastern Mediterranean and European Regions, Working Paper 6, 9 Apr. 1956.

Smith, E. A., 'Present Status of the Global Malaria Eradication Programme and Prospects for the Future', Geneva, Mal/Exp.Com.14/67.4, 12 Sept. 1967.

Trapido, H., 'Recent Experiments on Possible Resistance to DDT by Anopheles Albimanus in Panama', Geneva, WHO/Mal/85, 15 May 1953.

Vincke, I., 'Practical Methods for the Study of Factors Causing Difficulties in Malaria Eradication', Rio de Janeiro, Mal/Exp.Com.10/WP/36, 9 Aug. 1963.

Weeks, E., 'Minimum Conditions to be Met before Initiating a Malaria Eradication Programme', Geneva, Mal/Exp.Com.14/67.2, 12 Sept. 1967.

Yekutiel, P., 'Notes on Basic Problems of Eradication and Surveillance in Malaria Eradication', Expert Committee on Malaria, Working Paper No. 9, Geneva, 5 Aug. 1958.

Zaphiropoulos, M., 'Final Report of Malaria Pilot Project: 1956–1959', Alexandria, Em/Mal/42, Sept. 1959.

Documents from Other Organizations

Basic Documents, Pan American Sanitary Bureau, Publication no. 188, Washington, DC, 1983.

Halverston, W., 'Suggestions Regarding Malaria Eradication and Sanitation', International Development Advisory Board, Washington, DC, 20 Dec. 1955.

League of Nations, *Official Journal*, vol. 4, London, 1923, p. 250.

'Malaria Eradication: 'Report to the UNICEF Executive Board by the Director-General of WHO', ECOSOC document E/ICEF/417, 3 May 1961.

Masters, R., 'International Organizations in the Field of Public Health', Carnegie Endowment for International Peace, Washington, DC, 1947.

National Council for International Health, Selected Papers from International Health Conference, Washington, DC, 25 Apr. 1973.

Organization of American States, *Charter*, Washington, DC, 1948.

Summary Minutes, *International Development Advisory Board*, Washington, DC, 13 Apr. 1956.

United Nations, *Charter*, New York, 1945.

United Nations, *Repertory of Practice of UN Organs*, vol. I, New York, 1982.

United Nations, *Yearbook of the United Nations*, New York, 1948/9.

United Nations, *Yearbook of the United Nations*, New York, 1950.

United States Congress, Committee on Foreign Affairs, Subcommittee on National and International Movements, Hearings, 'United States Membership in the World Health Organization', *Congressional Records*, 80th Congress, 1st session, Washington DC, 1947.

United States Government, 'US Gives Seven Million Dollars to Malaria Eradication Campaign', *Bulletin*, US Department of State, Washington, DC, 23 Dec. 1957.

United States Senate, 'Providing for Membership and Participation by the US in the World Health Organization and Authorizing Appropriations Therefor', 80th Congress, 1st session, *Senate Report 421*, Washington, DC, 1947.

Secondary Sources

General WHO Publications

Mahler, H., 'World Health is Indivisible', speech, WHO, Geneva, 9 May 1978.

The First Ten Years of the World Health Organization, Geneva, 1958.

Malaria Eradication: a Plea for Health, Geneva, 1958.

Terminology of Malaria and Malaria Eradication, Geneva, 1963.

The Second Ten Years of the World Health Organization, Geneva, 1968.

Health Aspects of Chemical and Biological Weapons, Geneva, 1970.

Handbook of Resolutions and Decisions, 1948–1972, vol. I, Geneva, 1973.

Development of Indicators for Monitoring Progress towards Health for All by the Year 2000, Geneva, 1981.
Health Programme Evaluation, Geneva, 1981.
Effects of Nuclear War on Health and Health Services, Geneva, 1984.
Handbook of Resolutions and Decisions, 1973–1984, vol. II, Geneva, 1985.
Status of Collection of Assessed Contributions and Status Advances to the Working Capital Fund, Geneva, 1985.
World Health Statistics, Geneva, 1985.
Basic Documents, 36th edn., Geneva, 1986.
Global Strategy for Health for All by the Year 2000: Political Dimensions, Geneva, 1986.
Handbook of Resolutions and Decisions, 1985–1986, vol. III, Geneva, 1987.

Journal Articles

Allen, C., 'World Health and World Politics', *International Organization*, vol. 14, no. 1 (1950), p. 33.
Binka, J. Y. and Wieniawski, W., 'Quality Control – Think Small', *World Health*, Dec. 1985, p. 12.
Brown, A. W., J. Haworth and A. Zahar, 'Malaria Eradication and Control from a Global Standpoint', *J. Med. Ent.*, vol. 13, no. 1 (1976), p. 1.
Bruce-Chwatt, L. J., 'Problems of Malaria Control in Tropical Africa', *British Medical J.*, 23 Jan. 1954, p. 169.
——, 'Global Review of Malaria Control and Eradication by Attack on the Vector', *Misc. Publ. of the Entomol. Soc. of America*, vol. 7, no. 1 (1970), p. 7.
——, 'Resurgence of Malaria and Its Control', *Am. J. Trop. Med. and Hyg.*, vol. 77, no. 4, suppl. (1974), p. 62.
Calderwood, H., 'The WHO and Its Regional Organizations', *Temple Law Quarterly*, vol. 37, no. 1 (Fall 1963), p. 15.
——, 'The Founding of a Single International Health Organization', *WHO Chronicle*, vol. 29 (1975), p. 435.
Caldwell, M. E., 'The UN and Science: Past and Future Implications for World Health', *Am. Soc. of International Law Proceedings*, vol. 64, no. 4 (1970), p. 172.
Cleaver, H., 'Malaria and the Political Economy of Public Health', *International J. of Health Services*, vol. 7, no. 4 (1977), p. 559.
Colbourne, M. J., 'A Review of Malaria Eradication Campaigns in the Western Pacific', *Annals of Trop. Med. Parasitol.*, vol. 56 (1962), p. 33.
Cone, E. N., 'International Regulation of Pharmaceuticals: the Role of the World Health Organization', *Virginia J. of International Law*, vol. 23 (1982/3), p. 337.
Davidson, G., 'Experiments on the Effect of Residual Insecticides in

Houses against *Anopheles gambiae* and *Anopheles funestus*', *Bulletin Ent. Res.*, vol. 44 (1953), p. 231.

Donini, A., 'Resilience and Reform: Some Thoughts on the Process of Change in the United Nations', *International Relations*, vol. IX, no. 4 (Nov. 1988), p. 289.

Doyal, L., 'The Drug Industry and the Underdevelopment of Health', *Danish Medical Bulletin*, vol. 31, suppl. 1 (Nov. 1984), p. 10.

Farid, M.A., 'The Malaria Programme – from Euphoria to Anarchy', *World Health Forum*, vol. I, nos 1 and 2, World Health Organization, Geneva, 1980, p. 8.

Fatouros, A., 'On the Hegemonic Role of International Functional Organizations', *German Yearbook of Int'l Law*, vol. 23 (1980), p. 15.

——, 'On the Implementation of International Codes of Conduct: an Analysis of Future Experience', *Am. U. Law Review*, vol. 30 (1981), p. 941.

Fikentscher, W., 'United Nations Codes of Conduct: New Paths in International Law', *Am. J. of Comparative Law*, vol. 30 (1982), p. 577.

Gabaldon, A., 'The Time Required to Reach Eradication in Relation to Malaria Constitution', *Am. J. Trop. Med. and Hyg.*, vol. 5 (1956), p. 966.

——, 'Difficulties Confronting Malaria Eradication', *Am. J. Trop. Med. and Hyg.*, vol. 21, no. 5 (1972), p. 634.

Garcia-Martin, G., 'Status of Malaria Eradication in the Americas', *Am. J. Trop. Med. and Hyg.*, vol. 21 (1972), p. 617.

Georghiou, G.P., 'Studies on Resistance to Carbamate and Organophosphorus Insecticides in *Anopheles albimanus*', *Am. J. Trop. Med. and Hyg.*, vol. 77, supp. (1974), p. 797.

Ghebali, V., 'The Politicization of UN Specialized Agencies: a Preliminary Analysis', *Millennium: J. of International Studies*, vol. 14, no. 3 (Winter 1985), p. 317.

Giglioli, G., 'Eradication of *Anopheles darlingi* from the Inhabited Areas of British Guiana by DDT Residual Spraying', *J. Nati. Malar. Soc.*, vol. 10 (1951), p. 142.

Gramiccia, G. and Hempel, 'Mortality and Morbidity from Malaria in Countries where Malaria Eradication is Not Making Satisfactory Progress', *Am. J. Trop. Med. and Hyg.*, vol. 75, no. 10 (1972), p. 187.

Grosse, R., 'Codes of Conduct for Multinational Enterprises', *J. of World Trade Law*, vol. 16 (1982), p. 414.

Haas, E., 'International Integration: the European and the Universal Process', *International Political Communities*, 1966, p. 95.

Hamon, J., J. Mouchet, G. Chauvet and R. Lumaret, 'Bilan de quatorze années de lutte controle de paludisme dans les pays francophone d'Afrique tropicale', *Bull. Soc. Path. Exot.*, vol. 56 (1963), p. 933.

Hamon, J., J. Brengues and G. Chauvet, 'Problems Facing Anopheline Vector Control', *Misc. Publ. of the Entomol. Soc. of America*, vol. 7, no. 1 (1970), p. 28.

Holst, E., 'Conclusions', *Danish Medical Bulletin*, vol. 31, suppl. 1 (Nov. 1984), p. 25.

Huff, C., 'Unfinished Business', *Am. J. Trop. Med. and Hyg.*, vol. 13 (1964), p. 243.
Hyde, V. Z., 'The International Health Conference', *Bulletin*, US Department of State, 8 Sept. 1946, p. 453.
Imber, M., 'Re-reading Mitrany: a Pragmatic Assessment of Sovereignty', *Review of International Studies*, vol. 10 (1984), p. 112.
Jacobson, H. K., 'The USSR and ILO', *International Organization*, vol. XIV, no. 3 (Summer 1960), p. 404.
Jeffery, G. M., 'Malaria Control in the 20th Century', *Am. J. Trop. Med. and Hyg.*, vol. 25, no. 3 (1976), p. 361.
Jenks, C., 'Coordination in International Organization: an Introductory Survey', *British Yearbook of International Law*, vol. 27 (1951), p. 29.
Johnson, D. R., 'Development of the Worldwide Malaria Eradication Programme', *Mosquito News*, June 1966, p. 113.
Leonard, L., 'UNRRA and the Concept of Regional International Organization', *Iowa Law Review*, vol. 30, no. 4 (1945), p. 489.
Lepes, T. 'Present Status of the Global Malaria Eradication Programme and Prospects for the Future', *Am. J. Trop. Med. and Hyg.*, vol. 77, supp. 4 (1974), p. 47.
——, 'Review of Research on Malaria', *Bulletin of the World Health Organization*, vol. 50 (1974), p. 173.
Mackenzie, M., 'Potentialities of International Collaboration in the Field of Public Health', *Am. J. of Public Health and the Nation's Health*, vol. 35, no. 2 (1945), p. 100.
Mahler, H., 'Health for All by the Year 2000', *WHO Chronicle*, vol. 29 (1975), p. 458.
——, 'The Meaning of "Health for All by the Year 2000" ', *World Health Forum*, vol. 2, no. 1 (1981), p. 5.
McLaren, R., 'Mitranian Functionalism: Possible or Impossible?', *Review of International Studies*, vol. 11 (1985), p. 146.
Mitrany, D., 'The Functional Approach in Historical Perspective', *International Affairs*, vol. 47, no. 3 (1971), p. 532.
——, 'The End of Morality in War', *International Relations*, vol. 14, no. 4 (Nov. 1973), p. 231.
Morawiecki, W., 'Some Problems Connected with the Organs of International Organizations', *International Organization*, vol. 19, no. 4 (Autumn 1965), p. 913.
——, 'Institutional and Political Conditions of Participation of Socialist States in International Organizations: a Polish View', *International Organization*, vol. 22, no. 2 (Spring 1968), p. 494.
Mustafa, G., 'The Nettle Grasped', *World Health*, July 1984, p. 6.
Myers, D. P., 'Liquidation of the League of Nations', *Am. J. of International Law*, vol. 42 (1948), p. 320.
Nerfin, M., 'Is a Democratic United Nations Possible?', *Development Dialogue*, vol. 2 (1976), p. 79.
Pampana, E. J. and Russell, P. F., 'Malaria – a World Problem', *WHO Chronicle*, vol. 9 (1955), p. 31.

Parran, T., 'Charter for World Health', *Public Health Reports*, vol. 61 (1946), p. 1265.

—— and F. G. Boudreau, 'The World Health Organization: Cornerstone of Peace', *Am. J. of Public Health*, vol. 36 (1946), p. 1267.

Patel, M., 'An Economic Evaluation of "Health for All" ', *Health Policy and Planning*, vol. 1, no. 1 (1986), p. 37.

Phelps, J. R., 'The New International Economic Order and the Pharmaceutical Industry', *Food, Drug, and Cosmetic Law J.*, vol. 37 (1982), p. 200.

Pilon, J., 'For the WHO, the Moment of Truth', *Backgrounder*, Heritage Foundation, Washington, DC, 1986.

Prince, C., *Am. J. of International Law*, vol. 36, no. 3 (July 1942).

Sharp, W., 'The New WHO', *Am. J. of International Law*, vol. 41, no. 3 (1947), p. 509.

Sikkink, K., 'Codes of Conduct for Transnational Corporations: the Case of the WHO/UNICEF Code', *International Organization*, vol. 40, no. 4 (Aug. 1986), p. 837.

Sinton, A. J., 'What Malaria Costs India', *Record of the Malaria Survey, India*, no. 6, Delhi, 1936.

Smith, E. A., 'AID Policy on Malaria', *Proc. Calif. Mosq. Contr. Assoc.*, vol. 42 (1974), p. 19.

Soper, F. L., 'General Principles of the Eradication Programmes in the Western Hemisphere', *J. of the National Malaria Soc.*, vol. 10 (1951), p. 183.

Sweetser, A., 'The Non-Political Achievements of the League', *Foreign Affairs*, vol. 19, no. 1 (Oct. 1940).

Taylor, J., 'First Steps', *World Health*, WHO, Geneva, Mar. 1968.

Taylor, P., 'Prescribing for the Reform of International Organizations: the Logic of Arguments for Change', *Review of International Studies*, vol. 13 (1987), p. 19.

Turshen, M. and A. Thebaud, 'International Medical Aid', *Monthly Review*, New York, Dec. 1981, p. 39.

Urquhart, B., 'The United Nations System and the Future', *International Affairs*, vol. 65, no. 2 (Spring 1989), p. 225.

Venkat Rao, V., 'A Critical Review of Malaria Control Measures in India', *Indian J. of Malariology*, vol. 3 (Dec. 1949), p. 313.

Weller, T. H., 'World Health in a Changing World', *Am. J. Trop. Med. and Hyg.*, vol. 77, suppl. (1974), p. 54.

Wessen, A., 'Human Ecology and Malaria', *Am. J. Trop. Med. and Hyg.*, vol. 21, no. 5 (1972), p. 658.

World Health Organization, 'Malaria Control Measures in Africa', *Chronicle of WHO*, vol. II, no. 5 (1957), p. 133.

——, 'Malaria Eradication throughout the World', *Chronicle of WHO*, vol. 13, nos 9–10 (1959), p. 359.

——, 'World Malaria Situation: 1982', *Weekly Epidemiological Record*, vol. 59 (1984).

Wright, J., Fritz, R. and Haworth, J., 'Changing Concepts of Vector

Control in Malaria Eradication', *Annual Review of Entomology*, vol. 17 (1972), p. 75.

Yudkin, J.S., 'Provision of Medicines in a Developing Country', *Lancet*, vol. I (1978), p. 810.

Books and Theses

Abi-Saab, G. (ed.), *The Concept of International Organization*, UNESCO, Paris, 1981.

Ameri, H., *Politics and Process in the Specialized Agencies of the United Nations*, Gower, Aldershot, 1982.

Angell, N., *The Great Illusion*, Heinemann, London, 1911.

Archer, C., *International Organizations*, Allen and Unwin, London, 1983.

Baker, E., *The Politics of Aristotle*, Oxford University Press, 1948.

Beigbeder, Y., *Management Problems in United Nations Organizations*, Pinter, London, 1987.

——, *Threats to the International Civil Service*, Pinter, London, 1988.

Beker, A., *The United Nations and Israel*, Lexington Books, Lexington, Mass., 1988.

Bennett, A.L., *International Organizations*, Prentice-Hall, Englefield Cliffs, NJ, 1991.

Berkov, R., 'The World Health Organization: a Study in Decentralized International Administration', PhD thesis, University of Geneva, 1957.

Bertrand, M., *Some Reflections on Reform of the United Nations*, United Nations, Geneva, 1985.

——, *The Third Generation World Organization*, Martinus Nijhoff, The Hague, 1989.

Bingham, J.B., *Shirt-Sleeve Diplomacy: Point 4 in Action*, Freeport Books, New York, 1953.

Brockington, F., *World Health*, Churchill Livingstone, London, 1975.

Bruce, R., *The Development of International Cooperation in Economic and Social Affairs*, League of Nations, Geneva, 1939.

Bruce-Chwatt, L.J., *Essential Malariology*, John Wiley, New York, 1985.

Bryant, J., *Health and the Developing World*, Cornell University Press, Ithaca, NY, for Rockefeller Foundation, 1969.

Bustamente, M., *The Pan American Sanitary Bureau: Half a Century of Health Activities, 1902–1954*, Pan American Sanitary Bureau, Washington, DC, 1955.

Cassen, R. and Associates, *Does Aid Work?*, Clarendon Press, Oxford, 1986.

Chen, S.S., *The Theory and Practice of International Organization*, Kendal/Hunt Publishing Co., Dubuque, Iowa, 1979.

Claude, I., *Swords into Plowshares*, 4th edn, Random House, New York, 1971.

Conly, G., *The Impact of Malaria on Economic Development*, Pan American Health Organization, Washington, DC, 1975.

Cox, R. (ed), *International Organization: World Politics*, Praeger, New York, 1969.
—— and H. Jacobson (eds), *The Anatomy of Influence*, Yale University Press, New Haven, Conn., 1973.
Dallin, A., *The Soviet Union at the United Nations*, Methuen, London, 1962, p. 64.
de Cooker, C. (ed.), *International Administration – Law and Management Practices in International Organizations*, UNITAR/Martinus Nijhoff, London, 1990.
Deutsch, K.W., *The Analysis of International Relations*, Prentice-Hall, Englewood Cliffs, NJ, 1968.
Eisenhower, D., 'Annual Message to Congress on the State of the Union', *Public Papers of the Presidents: D. Eisenhower*, National Archives and Record Service, Washington, DC, 9 Jan. 1958.
Elmandjra, M., *The UN System: an Analysis*, Faber and Faber, London, 1973.
Evang, K., *Health of Mankind*, Ciba Foundation Symposium, Boston, Mass., 1967.
Fenner, F., D.A. Henderson, I. Arita, Z. Jezek and I.D. Ladnyi, *Smallpox and its Eradication*, WHO, Geneva, 1988.
Finer, H., *The United Nations Economic and Social Council*, World Peace Foundation, Boston, Mass., 1946.
——, *The T.V.A.: Lessons for International Application*, Da Capo Press, New York, 1972.
Finger, S.M. and J.R. Harbert (eds), *U.S. Policy in International Institutions*, Westview Press, Boulder, Colo., 1982.
Finkelstein, L. (ed.), *Politics in the United Nations System*, Duke University Press, Durham, NC, 1988.
Franck, T., *Nation against Nation*, Oxford University Press, 1985.
Gati, T.T. (ed.), *The US, the UN, and the Management of Global Change*, New York University Press, 1983.
Ghebali, V.-Y., *The International Labour Organization: a Case Study in the Evolution of United Nations Specialized Agencies*, Martinus Nijhoff, Dordrecht, 1989.
Gish, O., *Planning the Health Sector*, Croom Helm, London, 1975.
Gonzalez, C.L., *Mass Campaigns and General Health Services*, WHO, Geneva, 1965.
Goodman, N., *International Health Organizations and Their Work*, Churchill Livingstone, Edinburgh, 1971.
Groom, A.J.R., and P. Taylor (eds), *Functionalism*, University of London Press, 1975.
Haas, E., *Beyond the Nation State*, Oxford University Press, 1964.
Harrod, J. and N. Schrijver (eds), *The United Nations under Attack*, Gower, Aldershot, 1988.
Hoggart, R., *An Idea and its Servants: UNESCO from Within*, Chatto and Windus, London, 1978.

Hoole, F., *Politics and Budgeting in the World Health Organization*, Indiana University Press, 1976.

Howard-Jones, N., *The Scientific Background of the International Sanitary Conferences*, WHO, Geneva, 1975.

——, *International Public Health between the Two World Wars – the Organizational Problems*, WHO, Geneva, 1978.

——, *The Pan American Health Organization: Origins and Evolution*, WHO, Geneva, 1981.

Jackson, J.H., and W.J. Davey (eds), *Legal Problems in International Economic Relations*, West Publishing Co., St Paul, Minn., 1986.

Jacobson, H.K., *The USSR and the UN's Economic and Social Activities*, University of Notre Dame Press, Notre Dame, Ind., 1963.

Jenks, B.F.E., 'The Concept of International Organization: the Case of UNESCO', unpubl. DPhil thesis, University of Oxford, 1982.

Jordan, R. (ed.), *International Administration*, Oxford University Press, New York, 1971.

Kapur, H. (ed.), *China and the Specialized Agencies*, Graduate Institute of International Studies, Geneva, 1986.

Kay, D., *The UN Political System*, Wiley, New York, 1967.

——, ed., *The Changing United Nations: Options for the United States*, Academy of Political Science, New York, 1977.

——, *The Functioning and Effectiveness of Selected United Nations System Programs*, American Society of International Law, Washington, DC, 1980.

Kelsen, H., *Peace through Law*, University of North Carolina Press, Chapel Hill, NC, 1944.

Leonard, L., *International Organization*, McGraw-Hill, New York, 1951.

Lie, T., *In the Cause of Peace*, Macmillan, New York, 1954.

Lissner, J., *The Politics of Altruism*, Lutheran World Federation, Geneva, 1977.

Luard, E. (ed.), *The Evolution of International Organizations*, Thames and Hudson, London, 1966.

——, *History of the United Nations*, vol. I, St Martin's Press, New York, 1982.

Masset, J.-P., 'Une Non-Institution. Le Groupe de Genève', *Les Organizations Internationales Contemporaines*, Perdonne, Paris, 1988.

Melrose, D., *Bitter Pills*, Oxfam, Oxford, 1982.

Mitrany, D., *The Progress of International Government*, Yale University Press, New Haven, Conn., 1933.

——, *A Working Peace System*, Oxford University Press, Oxford, 1943.

——, *The Road to Security*, National Peace Council, pamphlet 29, London, 1944.

Molineaux, L. and G. Gramiccia, *The Garki Project*, WHO, Geneva, 1980.

Moll, A., *The Pan American Sanitary Bureau: 1902–1944*, PASB publication 240, Washington, DC, 1948.

Morgenthau, H., *Politics among Nations*, Alfred Knopf, New York, 1978.

Moynihan, D.P., *A Dangerous Place*, Atlantic/Little, Brown, Boston, Mass., 1978.

Nicholas, H.G., *The United Nations as a Political Institution*, 3rd edn, Oxford University Press, 1967.

Northedge, F.S., *The League of Nations: Its Life and Times, 1920–1946*, Leicester University Press, 1986.

Osakwe, C., *The Participation of the Soviet Union in Universal International Organizations*, A.W. Sijthoff, Leiden, 1972.

Pampana, E.J., *A Textbook of Malaria Eradication*, 2nd edn, Oxford University Press, London, 1969.

Peterson, M.J., *The General Assembly in World Politics*, Allen and Unwin, Boston, Mass., 1986.

Pines, B.Y. (ed.), *A World without the UN – What Would Happen if the United Nations Shut Down*, Heritage Foundation, Washington, DC, 1984.

Pitt, D., and T. Weiss (eds), *The Nature of United Nations Bureaucracies*, Croom Helm, London, 1986.

Pletsch, D.J., F.E. Gartrell and E.H. Hinman, *A Critical Review of the National Malaria Eradication Programme of India*, US Technical Cooperation Mission to India, New Delhi, 1960.

Quenum, A.A., *Twenty Years of Political Struggle for Health*, WHO, Brazzaville, 1985.

Quimby, F., *Science, Technology and the American Government*, Congressional Record Service, Washington, DC, 1971.

Reinsch, P.S., *Public International Unions*, Ginn and Co., Boston, Mass., 1911.

Roberts, A., and B. Kingsbury (eds), *United Nations: Divided World*, Oxford University Press, 1988.

Roche, D., *United Nations Divided World*, NC Press, Toronto, 1984.

Ross, R., *The Prevention of Malaria*, John Murray, London, 1911.

Rubinstein, A.Z., *The Soviets in International Organization*, Princeton University Press, 1964.

Russell, P., *Man's Mastery of Malaria*, Oxford University Press, 1955.

Scruton, R., *A Dictionary of Political Thought*, Macmillan, London, 1982.

Sewell, J.P., *Functionalism in World Politics*, Princeton University Press, 1966.

Snow, J., *On the Mode of Communication of Cholera*, 2nd edn (unknown publisher), London, 1855.

Stampar, A., *Serving the Cause of Public Health, Selected Papers*, ed. M.D. Grmek, Zagreb, 1966.

Starells, J.M., *The World Health Organization: Resisting Third World Ideological Pressures*, Heritage Foundation, Washington, DC, 1985.

Steele, D., *The Reform of the United Nations*, Croom Helm, London, 1987.

Symonds, R. and M. Carder, *The United Nations and the Population Question, 1945–1970*, McGraw-Hill, New York, 1973.

Templeton, K.S. Jr., *The Politicization of Society*, Liberty Press, Indianapolis, 1979.

United Nations, *Is Universality in Jeopardy?*, UN Dept of Public Information, New York, 1987.

United Nations Association of the United States of America, *A Successor Vision: the United Nations of Tomorrow*, New York, 1987.

United States Government, *Health in the Americas and the Pan American Health Organization*, Committee on Government Operations of the United States Senate, Washington, DC, 1960.

Walsh, J.A., and K. Warren (eds), *Strategies for Primary Health Care*, Chicago University Press, 1986.

Walters, F.P., *A History of the League of Nations*, Oxford University Press, 1952.

Wang, Kuo-Chang, *United Nations Voting on Chinese Representation*, Institute of American Culture, Taipei, 1984.

Weiss, T., *International Bureaucracy*, Lexington Books, Lexington, Mass., 1975.

Wells, C., 'The UN, UNESCO and the Politics of Knowledge', unpubl. DPhil thesis, Oxford University, 1984.

——, *The UN, UNESCO and the Politics of Knowledge*, Macmillan, London, 1987.

Williams, D., *The Specialized Agencies of the United Nations*, Hurst, London, 1987.

Wood, C. (ed.), *Tropical Medicine: from Romance to Reality*, Academic Press, London, 1978.

Woodbridge, G. (ed.), *UNRRA, the History of the United Nations Relief and Rehabilitation Administration*, Columbia University Press, New York, 1950.

Woolf, L.S., *International Government*, Brentano's, New York, 1916.

INDEX